LEADING CREATORS OF TWENTIETH-CENTURY CZECH THEATRE

ROUTLEDGE HARWOOD POLISH AND EAST EUROPEAN THEATRE ARCHIVE

A series of books edited by Daniel Gerould, Graduate School, City University of New York, USA

This book is part of a series. The publisher will accept continuation orders which may be cancelled at any time and which provide for automatic billing and shipping of each title in the series upon publication. Please write for details.

LEADING CREATORS OF TWENTIETH-CENTURY CZECH THEATRE

Jarka M. Burian

London and New York

First published 2002
by Routledge
2 Park Square, Milton Park, Abingdon, Oxon, OX14 4RN

Routledge is an imprint of the Taylor & Francis Group

Transferred to Digital Printing 2005

Typeset in Times by RefineCatch Limited, Bungay, Suffolk

British Library Cataloguing in Publication Data
A catalogue record for this book is available from the British Library

Library of Congress Cataloguing in Publication Data
Burian, Jarka, 1927–
Leading creators of twentieth-century Czech theatre / Jarka M. Burian.
p. cm.—(Polish and East European theatre archive; v. 7)
Includes bibliographical references and index.
1. Theater—Czech Republic—History—20th century. 2. Czech
drama—20th century—History and criticism. I. Title. II. Series.

PN2859.C9 B835 20012
792′.094371—dc21   2001048108

ISBN 0–415–27030–8

Printed and bound by Antony Rowe Ltd, Eastbourne

This book is dedicated to the countless unsung Czech theatre people whose art and craft, on stage and off stage, created the living environment that helped draw the world's attention to the work of their celebrated colleagues.

CONTENTS

CONTENTS

INTRODUCTION TO THE SERIES

The Routledge Harwood *Polish and East European Theatre Archive* makes available in English translation works of dramatic literature as well as monographs and informative studies on playwrights, theatre artists, theatres and stage history. Although emphasis is placed on the contemporary period, the Routledge Harwood *Polish and East European Theatre Archive* also encompasses the nineteenth-century roots of modern theatre practice in Romanticism and Symbolism. The individual plays will contain authoritative introductions that place the works in their historical and theatrical contexts.

Daniel Gerould

PLATES

ACKNOWLEDGMENTS

It is a pleasure to acknowledge my indebtedness and thanks to a variety of organizations and individuals.

For granting me permission to reprint parts of articles originally appearing in their journals and periodicals, I am grateful to the editors of *American Theatre*, *The Drama Review*, *Drama Survey*, *Educational Theatre Journal*, *Modern Drama*, *Slavic and East European Performance*, *Theatre Design and Technology*, *Theatre History Studies*, *Theatre Journal*, and *Theatre Survey*.

I am equally indebted to numerous photographic artists whose work enhances this book. Above all I wish to acknowledge the contribution made by the photographs of the late Jaromír Svoboda, and to thank his widow, Zdena Svobodová, for her authorization to use a selection of his photos here. Others whose photographic artistry is to be found in the following pages are Ludvik Dittrich, M. Hák, Alexandr Paul, Martin Poš, Lubomír Rohan, Otto Skall, Hana Smejkalová, Josef Svoboda, and Vladimír Svoboda.

My research and subsequent publications relating to Czech theatre were encouraged and facilitated by the generous support of others. I am deeply grateful to the administrations, committees, and councils of the following institutions: The U.S. State Department specialist's grant supported my stay in Czechoslovakia in the fall of 1965, when I lectured at several universities and became seriously involved in Czech theatre. The Inter-University Committee on Travel Grants supported my research in Czechoslovakia in 1968–69; the International Research Exchanges Board (IREX) underwrote two of my extended research visits to Prague (1974–75, 1993–94); the Council for International Exchange of Scholars (Fulbright Program) funded my research visit to Prague in the spring of 1988. My gratitude extends to several offices and ministries of the Czechoslovak Socialist Republic and its successor the Czech Republic for sharing in the support of these international cooperative grants. The National Endowment for the Humanities awarded me a valuable summer research grant in the 1970s; and from 1965 onward the State University of New York (SUNY) and the Administration of University at

Albany provided me with a variety of grants and leaves of absence for my research and publications in Czech theatre.

Several specific institutions and archives in Prague provided me with cordial and sustained assistance in my studies: since 1965, the Prague Theatre Institute (Divadelní ústav) has been instrumental in my liaison with Czech theatres and their artists and has also granted me access to its own library and archives. I am especially grateful to its directors and other personnel, in particular the following: Eva Soukupová, director from the 1960s until the late 1980s, and subsequent directors Helena Albertová and Ondřej Černý. Jarmila Gabrielová, head of the Institute's international liaison section, has for four decades continued to be a friendly counselor and guide. Others who provided generous help over the years include Blanka Calábková, Alena Kulhanková, Jaroslav Máchek, Květoslava Marková, Ladislava Petišková, Miroslava Potučková, Věra Ptáčková, and the personnel of the Institute's archives.

The Theatre Section of the National Museum was a rich source of materials, especially those concerning Czech theatre from its beginnings to the mid-twentieth century. Some of its key personnel who provided me with valuable guidance were Jiří Hilmera, Jaroslav Janů, and Vilemína Pecharová. The National Theatre Archive, headed by Zdena Benešová, was equally generous in providing access to its special resources.

The Cabinet for the Study of Czech Theatre, of the Czech Academy of Science, comprises specialist scholars dedicated to ongoing projects and publications in the history of Czech theatre. My work in Czech theatre owes a great deal to their scholarship and friendly counsel. Those with whom I had the most communication included: František Černý (for long its guiding spirit), Milan Obst, Adolf Scherl, Eva Šormová, and Evžen Turnovský.

The Department of Theatre and Film Studies of Charles University often was a source of supplemental information from its store of graduate dissertations and its audio library, and also provided valuable assistance from its faculty and staff, among whom I would particularly mention Josef Herman, Jan Hyvnar, and Eva Kolárová, in addition to the already cited František Černý, dean of Czech theatre scholars.

Czech theatre artists were not only a constant source of pleasure when I observed their work as a member of the audience, but also a unique fountain of information and insight when I met with them to converse about their work and associations in the past as well as the present. They belonged to several generations, and several were creative in more than one area of theatre. Here, I should like to mention them with regard to their primary activity. Actors included Bohumil Bezouška, Ladislav Boháč, Pavel Landovský, Martin Liška, Radovan Lukavský, Marie Málková, Miloš Nedbal, Ladislav Pešek, Luba Skořepová, Vladimír Šmeral, Jiřina Stránská, Jiří Voskovec, and Jan Werich.

Directors or choreographers generous with their time were Hana

Burešová, Lída Engelová, Jan Grossman, Miloš Hynšt, Nina Jirsíková, Jan Kačer, Zdeněk Kaloč, Petr Kracik, Otomar Krejča, František Laurin, Petr Lébl, Miroslav Macháček, Ota Ornest, Karel Palouš, Luboš Pistorius, Jaromír Pleskot, Alfred Radok, Ivan Rajmont, Jan Schmid, Evald Schorm, Ladislav Smoček, Vladimír Strnisko, and Jaroslav Vostrý.

Designers who shared insights concerning not only their distinctive art but their broader awareness of Czech theatre were Jan Dušek, Jaroslav Malina, Miroslav Melena, Marta Roszkopfová, Josef Svoboda, Ladislav Vychodil, Jana Zbořilová, and Ivo Žídek.

Many others had still other roles or functions relating to modern Czech theatre (pedagogues, playwrights, dramaturges, critics, theorists, editors, administrators), but all provided me with the benefit of their experience and knowledge: Milan Calábek, Antonín Dvořák, Anna Freimanová, Aleš Fuchs, Vlasta Gallerová, Arnošt Goldflam, Václav Havel, Milena Honzíková, Ondřej Hrab, Dana Kalvodová, Jan Kopecký, Miroslav Kouřil, Karel Kraus, Milan Lukeš, Petr Oslzlý, Karel Steigerwald, and Ivan Vyskočil.

The preparation of the manuscript of this book was greatly aided by the secretarial staff and facilities of the Department of Theatre of the University at Albany (Chair, W. Langdon Brown). The subsequent evaluation and processing of the manuscript by Harwood Academic Publishers involved people to whom I am particularly beholden for their expertise and good judgment in the critical stages from initial submission, through revisions, to final form: Daniel Gerould, Michael Heim, Robert Robertson, and Oona Campbell.

My wife, Grayce Susan Burian, has been closely involved not only with all stages in the evolution of this work, but also with all my prior research and resultant publications. Her unflagging assistance has ranged from sustained personal support during the travels and residencies underlying this study, to proofreading and secretarial activities, to valuable critical responses as this work evolved from initial notes to final manuscript. To her my gratitude lies beyond words.

INTRODUCTION

My recent book, *Modern Czech Theatre: Reflector and Conscience of a Nation*, is an historical survey of Czech theatre from the late eighteenth through the twentieth century, with emphasis on the past hundred years. Having scanned the terrain of this remarkable theatre as a whole, I felt that more must be said about some of the twentieth-century Czech theatre artists whose significance transcended the generally high level of the theatre of their time. Without attempting full-scale analytic studies of these creative figures and their times, I nevertheless wanted to probe more deeply into each one's background, temperament, and creative output. That was the genesis of this book.

At the heart of this work are studies of people who cannot be ignored in any consideration of twentieth-century Czech theatre: Karel Hugo Hilar, Jiří Voskovec and Jan Werich, Emil František Burian, Alfred Radok, Otomar Krejča, Josef Svoboda, and Václav Havel. These artists not only made an indelible impression on Czech audiences but also shaped the profile by which Czech theatre became known abroad. Producers, directors, designers, and actors, several of them had multiple talents. I have even included a playwright. I say 'even' a playwright because this book is meant to be a study of theatre – i.e., an activity primarily of production and performance – not of dramatic literature. Nevertheless, to omit playwrights entirely seemed extreme; therefore, I added the chapter on Václav Havel. Of course, it is also true that Voskovec and Werich wrote their own plays. But why not include Karel Čapek, perhaps the single best known Czech playwright? I shall address that issue in Chapter 11 on Havel.

Any such selection of 'stars' is always hazardous and subject to strong disagreement. Choosing the people just mentioned was not difficult for me, but I was aware that *other* Czech theatre artists also had strong claims for inclusion. Therefore, in an attempt to forestall at least some cries of pain at my choices, yet wanting to keep this work short of encyclopedic proportions, I have included briefer studies of several other directors and designers, as well as a chapter on various Czech productions of *Hamlet* involving not only the people already mentioned but still other artists of merit, particularly actors.

Like its predecessors, this book had its roots in my Czech family background, which gave me a grounding in the Czech language and Czech culture even though I was born and raised in New Jersey. The prime igniter of my attraction to Czech theatre, however, was my direct, on-site observation of it during many longer and shorter residencies and visits dating back to the late 1930s and the late 1940s, and on a more systematic basis since 1965. Such direct observation vivified the more traditional scholarly research I pursued in libraries and archives.

When Czechs refer to someone as an *osobnost* they mean not only someone who possesses a distinctive personality and character, but also someone who has made a mark on his or her world, whether it be the world of art, politics, or sport; in other words, someone with a degree of fame. Each of the people found in the chapters that follow warrants the designation *osobnost*, and in the course of more than thirty years, it has been my pleasure and good fortune to make the acquaintance of many of them. I interviewed them and corresponded with them, I saw their work, sat in on their rehearsals, and even worked with one of them (Josef Svoboda) on productions. During those years, I also wrote and published accounts of their work as well as that of other Czech theatre artists. This book draws on that material and adds to it.

* * *

An awareness of some aspects of Czech history and culture provides a background against which the individual artists and their works may be more fully appreciated. Sheer geography has played a key role in the history of the Czechs, including their culture and arts. Precariously situated at the political and military crossroads of Europe, the Czechs have had their destiny repeatedly influenced and often determined by the ambitions and aggressions of more powerful neighbors. Nevertheless, being at the heart of Europe facilitated the Czech theatre's contacts with the theatre traditions and practices of the French, German, and Russian theatres, which often became inspirational models for the Czechs.

Underlying all questions of the Czech theatre's identity is the special bond between the Czechs and their theatre, which had its roots in the role theatre played in the Czechs' nineteenth-century National Revival movement. Beginning in the 1780s, theatre joined in the broader efforts of the Czechs to reassert their language, culture, and autonomy after centuries of suppression within the Habsburg empire. These efforts took a giant step forward with the opening of the Czech National Theatre in Prague in the 1880s. The project, which took over thirty years from conception to opening night, was substantially funded by voluntary contributions from the people, a fact memorialized in the motto above the theatre's proscenium arch: 'Narod Sobě' (The Nation to Itself). The sense of patriotic pride and ethical responsibility implicit in such ideals persisted in twentieth-century Czech theatre.

Several other considerations are germane to a study of Czech theatre. The sheer compactness of the country and its underlying ethnic unity have contributed to the relative coherence of its theatre world; playwrights, directors, designers, and actors tend to know each other and each other's work, partly because most of them are graduates of one of two theatre academies, in Prague and Brno, and partly because it is easy to travel to any given theatre.

Another important factor in Czech theatre (indeed, in most continental European theatres) is a government-supported repertory system. Personnel are engaged on a long-term basis with relatively little turnover, and – with few exceptions – theatres are usually subsidized for at least half their budgets by local, regional, or national government. Such companies are organized to produce a body of plays to be performed in alternating sequence – a different play performed each day from an ever-freshened stock of five to fifteen plays available at any given time. Some plays remain in the repertory for several seasons. Others, not well received, may be withdrawn after a few performances, their places taken by newly prepared productions. In complete contrast, the commercial Broadway or West End theatre concentrates all efforts and monies on a single production with artists individually chosen for the event, in order to achieve maximum audience impact and box office appeal, with little regard for any broader considerations.

The repertory system also implies the presence of a dramaturge, a crucial figure only vaguely understood in most non-repertory theatre cultures. The usual English translation is 'literary adviser,' which conveys only part of a dramaturge's traditional function. The dramaturge is a virtually indispensable collaborator of repertory directors, under the overall supervision of a theatre's administrative and artistic heads. A dramaturge not only supplies in-depth information about plays and their authors, but also may function as a translator, reviser, or adapter of plays or other text sources, usually in collaboration with a director. Equally important, a dramaturge may strongly influence or even determine the profile of a theatre by his or her long-range planning of a repertoire with plays related to a company's abilities and goals, as well as to the climate of the times.

* * *

In the twentieth century, Czech theatre evolved in the context of decisive political changes. In 1900, while still within the Habsburg Empire, Czech theatre was a youthful and earnest emulator of its older, grander counterparts on the continent. By 1920, two years after the creation of an independent Czechoslovakia at the end of World War I, Czech theatre was in the mainstream of modern European theatre, and within the next twenty years it was arguably at the forefront of its contemporaries before being traumatized by political crises of the late 1930s culminating in World War II, which began less than a year after the loss of Czech independence at Munich.

Hard upon the stresses of World War II and a few brief years of liberation came the political transformation of Czechoslovakia from independent republic to Communist satellite in 1948, and years of rigidly imposed constraints. After a period of thawing, a high tide of Czech theatre returned in the 1960s, when its artists and ensembles drew international attention to their theatres in Prague as well as their performances abroad. But this breakthrough of talents was aborted by the Warsaw Pact invasion of 1968. Then, following an ebb tide of some ten years, Czech theatre people began to rally and finally spearhead the forces that contributed to the eventual overthrow of a moribund but still domineering Communist regime. The Velvet Revolution of 1989 was a cathartic experience involving the direct participation of theatres and theatre artists and culminating in the installation of a dissident playwright as president.

At the start of the twenty-first century, Czech theatre, like Czech society itself, is still in the process of reacting to the economic, political, and social changes following the abrupt freedoms gained at the end of 1989 and the split of Czechoslovakia into sovereign Czech and Slovak republics in 1993. It is difficult to make many secure generalizations about the present identity of Czech theatre other than to say it is surviving within new, more austere economic realities while sustaining its tradition of artistic quality and social awareness. New freedoms have prompted some commercial, non-repertory productions, mainly musicals and farces produced by private entrepreneurs, but the core of Czech theatre remains in the network of repertory theatres. Although they now must operate with reduced subventions, place a greater premium on building audiences, and seek supplementary financing from sponsors while cutting expenses, the repertory theatres continue to be the standard-bearers of Czech theatre as it enters the twenty-first century.

The variety of personalities and careers in this survey of leading creators of Czech theatre is as striking as the variety of times and pressures they experienced in the twentieth century. The personal destinies and professional paths of the individuals on view here form a microcosm of the broader Czech experience during the past hundred years. Noting how these artists and citizens responded to the sociopolitical conditions of their time can be as interesting as becoming aware of each one's special talents and artistic achievements. Indeed, it has been the interplay of stage and society that has so often distinguished Czech theatre in the twentieth century, providing its creators with a motivation beyond the commercial or even the aesthetic: to produce works that reflect the world they live in and resonate with the concerns of their public.

*　*　*

Before proceeding, I should clarify my use of 'Czech' theatre as distinct from 'Czechoslovakian' theatre. The Czechs and Slovaks were united politically in the new state of Czechoslovakia at the end of World War I. From 1919 to 1939, with the assistance of more experienced Czech theatre artists, the

Slovaks established their own theatre culture after centuries of political and cultural domination by the Hungarians, during which time the creation of an organized Slovak theatre culture was not possible. Thereafter, despite various joint committees and councils, and guest appearances in each other's theatres, Czech and Slovak theatre developed independently of each other. I have known and admired many Slovak theatre artists – the major scenographer Ladislav Vychodil, for example – but in this book I am dealing with artists who are identified primarily with the Czech theatre.

1

K. H. HILAR

Let us honor and praise Hilar's great work, without which I
absolutely cannot imagine progress in Czech theatre.

E. F. Burian[1]

Karel Hugo Hilar was the single strongest Czech director during the last
twenty years of his life.[2] Along with Karel Čapek he brought Czech theatre
to world attention as Czechoslovakia itself began to experience national
independence after World War I. Unlike many modern directors, Hilar never
worked in small theatres or studio facilities; his more than seventy productions were equally divided between Prague's two largest Czech theatres, in
which he was not only chief director but also chief of all drama activity,
which is to say that he had final word concerning which plays would be
performed and who would direct them. From 1910 through 1920 he established an outstanding reputation at the Municipal Theatre, a large, modern
theatre in the Vinohrady section of Prague. Then, leaving Vinohrady, he
assumed the leadership of drama production at Prague's National Theatre, a
position he held until his death in 1935.

Born in 1885 and coming of age at the turn of the century, Hilar was part
of the far-flung movement that rejected realism as a meaningful artistic
mode. Obviously influenced by the symbolists, yet inherently eclectic and too
vigorous a man of the tangible world to reside in a passive aestheticism,
Hilar may most nearly be related to the expressionists. To be more precise,
his artistic evolution reflected various characteristics of expressionism,
modified by his own distinctive temperament and talents. In the broadest
sense, his creativity – without losing its urge toward striking expressiveness –
developed from a primary concern with provocative theatrical effects to a
more thoughtful, probing exploration of the complexities of human
experience.

From the perspective of the more than sixty years since his death, his work
overshadows that of his predecessors and contemporaries, and it anticipates
in many ways the work of his most notable successors. The directorial
excitement of men like Alfred Radok and Otomar Krejča owes much to
Hilar, and even the earlier, avant-garde directors like E. F. Burian, Jindřich
Honzl, and Jiří Frejka acknowledged and drew from Hilar's pioneering
effects. Hilar and his work are like a massif, in relation to which the work of

Jaroslav Kvapil, his most important predecessor, forms the foothills, and the work of later major directors forms lesser though striking individual peaks.

Hilar was born in southern Bohemia but grew up in Prague, where he had a traditional education that centered in literature and pointed to a career as a writer or critic. Although a student of classical philology, he most closely affiliated himself with the symbolist and decadent movements of the early 1900s, finding particular attraction in the works of Barrès (on whom he wrote his Ph.D. dissertation), Huysmans, Laforgue, Wilde, and Strindberg of *The Inferno* period. Before he began work in the theatre he had already served as editor of a series of volumes of contemporary literature and he had seen his own poetry, fiction, literary criticism, translations, and theatre reviews published in periodicals and books. His theatre exposure was not restricted to Prague but included Berlin (where Brahm and Reinhardt were producing), Munich, and Paris; in Prague itself he had the opportunity to see many important visiting companies, such as the Moscow Art Theatre under Stanislavsky in 1906.

It was, therefore, as a literary person with a sophisticated acquaintance with theatre from the audience side of the footlights that Hilar came to the theatre at Vinohrady as a secretary and reader in 1910. Although he claimed that he never wanted to be a director – if anything, a playwright – he directed his first play there in 1911. Two years later, Hilar assumed the post of dramaturge. In 1914 he capped his swift rise by becoming chief of drama at what was Prague's second most prestigious theatre. During the next six years – which witnessed World War I and its attendant social and political upheavals – he consolidated his power at Vinohrady by ridding the theatre of its operetta ensemble and by staging a series of productions that took Prague by storm and brought the Czech theatre into the mainstream of contemporary European theatre. His achievements at Vinohrady made him the obvious choice to head drama at the National Theatre when that most esteemed, representative national stage needed a strong successor to Jaroslav Kvapil, who had resigned in 1918.

* * *

When Hilar took over leadership of drama production at the National Theatre in 1921, he was at the peak of his powers. He had made the Vinohrady theatre Prague's most vigorous and successful theatre, one that overshadowed the aimless, erratic work of the National Theatre following Kvapil's departure in 1918. Much later, in retrospect, after a seemingly unending series of erosive conflicts with actors, staff members, and politicians and government bureaus related to the National Theatre, he expressed bitter regret at having made the change. At Vinohrady he had virtually complete control of every phase of operations and worked with a corps of loyal, enthusiastic actors and other personnel. At the National Theatre he experienced chronic frustration, which had its most dramatic (and perhaps psychogenetic) embodiment in 1924 when he suffered the first of his two strokes. He was disabled for a year and a half, after which he returned a nearly broken man. Nevertheless, he went on to a final phase of creativity during which he staged some of his most deeply moving productions before suffering the second and fatal stroke in 1935.

Hilar embodied the Craig ideal of autonomous, absolute directors (or 'Theatre Artists'), like Reinhardt or Meyerhold, who use all production elements, including the script, as raw material for a unifying, creative vision embodied in a production marked by theatrically striking, imaginative exploitation of stage space, lighting, and dynamically expressive acting, all of which are closely controlled and sensitively orchestrated by the director. Like most significant, innovative directors of the early twentieth century, with the possible exception of Stanislavsky, Hilar rejected the theatre of naturalistic or Meiningen-like illusion. By temperament and instinct he also had little interest in a theatre of psychological complexity or nuance, witty or philo-sophic conversation, nor (despite his early flirtation with the decadents) in a theatre of symbolistic atmosphere. Instead, Hilar saw theatre as a Dionysian or perhaps Baroque rite, a full-blooded, provocative, vibrant celebration. His instinctive histrionic, hyperexpressive sense evolved and manifested itself in various forms, sometimes in grotesque distortions, sometimes tamed and camouflaged in his more restrained 'civilism' period after his stroke, but it never really left him and it distinguished his personal style of expressionism from those of others. Some indication of his vision is evident in an essay entitled 'Direction as an Expression of World Outlook':

> What do we actually mean by the style of a production? . . . [Is it] even in the best sense a mechanically refined blend of taste and truth, form and convention? or is it . . . something different, higher, spon-taneous, and, in the poetic sense, passionate, which, like ecstasy, creates the higher truth of a performance, which invests it with suggestive power . . . which adds to theatre that force as a result of which an actor ceases to be an actor, a flat a flat, a spectator a spectator, but all fuse in one feeling, a feeling of dramatic ecstasy in which the participants forget their everyday existence and essay a higher, that is, artistic, experience?[3]

In the same piece Hilar speaks of liberating theatre from the rigid forms of the past century and 'returning theatre to its Dionysian origins, making it once again a pulsating cosmos . . . an image not only of a world already finished but one that is only now emerging.'[4]

For Hilar, theatre was essentially self-justifying, certainly not a servant of any ideology or other extrinsic cause, yet it achieved its highest purpose when it reflected or, better, resonated with its time and public. Theatre needs to sense the inner atmosphere of its time, to feel its pulse. The director must transform his art in the spirit of his age, to join 'the mentality of the poet with that of the public.'[5] The ideal was

> a community in which poet fuses with spectator, director with poet, designer with actor, and the theatre aesthetician with this entire circle that burns with dramatic enthusiasm. [Then theatre may become] the highest expression of the world view of its time and nation.[6]

Such sentiments, partly inspired by patriotic enthusiasm for the newly independent state of Czechoslovakia, reached their peak in the early postwar years. Perhaps the least politicized of all Czech directors, he was primarily an enthusiast. When he spoke of helping change the world, Hilar was speaking of inexplicit, ecstatic, aesthetic values rather than sociopolitical, much less Marxist ones. It is in that sense that the following must be interpreted:

> It is necessary to stage Hamlet's 'To be or not to be' so that the spectator ... would flee the theatre in horror and only he would remain who understands that this scene deals with a question concerning his whole life. He either dies or decides to live. If he decides to stay alive after our scene, he must work with us to better the world, and we with him. That is the point of our acting and staging concentration, our design and entire program. To create a world and its evolution together.[7]

Hilar's personality was as striking as his productions, and he was less noted for a systematic, organized grasp of his multiple responsibilities than for obeying the impulse of the moment. A large man, well over 6 feet tall, he was afflicted with a slight speech impediment that often produced an inadvertently comic lisp. There were other inconsistencies or paradoxes: 'life fatigue and steel nerves ... an aesthete with peasant robustness ... a dandy [in attire] whose features resemble those of an antique mask, in which the deep melancholy of velvet black eyes conflicted with the crooked smile of a satyr.'[8]

One of his favorite actors, Ladislav Pešek, recalled his early impressions of Hilar, before his first stroke:

> Hilar: a locomotive! ... An overheated steam boiler, with steam under extraordinary pressure escaping through the cracks. Or perhaps a strange, huge clown. There is strength in his expression, perhaps barbaric, but powerful.[9]

Other contradictions were evident. He was not of the people, but a loner, yet one who needed the approval and applause of the public. His affinity for the Dionysian and elemental was balanced by his equally genuine gift of rational, literary control, just as his most extreme expressionistic productions had their anchor in recognizable, tangible realities rather than mystical or surreal abstractions. Jiří Frejka, an avant-garde director who later became a young associate and eventual successor of Hilar at the National Theatre, neatly defined his cultural orientation: 'His school is Shakespeare, not Goethe, not Marx. That is, a stormily individual faith, not an objectified, harmonized, sweetened bourgeoisism, nor faith in social justice and revolution. He is always alone.'[10]

* * *

When Hilar began his directorial career the Czech theatre was in a period of stagnation. It had passed through successive phases of naturalism, genre historicism, psychological realism, and lyrical impressionism, the last two brought to a considerable distinction by Jaroslav Kvapil (1868–1950), Hilar's most illustrious predecessor and amicable rival as leading Czech director. Kvapil had done much to bring Czech theatre into the twentieth century. In staging, he rid the stage of operatic settings and the dead conventions of naturalism and Saxe-Meiningen, and in dramaturgy he championed Ibsen and Chekhov over Sardou. He was perhaps most celebrated for his Shakespeare productions; in fact, his most impressive achievement was the staging of a cycle of sixteen Shakespeare plays in the spring of 1916 at the National Theatre, as confirmation of the international stature of the Czech theatre and a thinly veiled sign of the Czech pro-Allied feeling in the middle of the war.

Kvapil's theatre, unlike Hilar's, was one of suggestive moods and lyrical harmony, of intimate, poetic realism. Clearly influenced by Stanislavsky, he encouraged acting that sought inner realism over external declamation, that explored critical states of soul but in doing so achieved a degree of subjectivity that often threatened the clarity of overall form. It was, moreover, a theatre that had its greatest interest in the work of a few great actors, above all Eduard Vojan, whose Hamlet in 1905 attracted interest from the rest of Europe. A production would key on Vojan or a few other actors, while Kvapil devoted most of his attention to the atmosphere, which was usually understated, tasteful, lightly stylized, harmoniously blended, and slightly academic. The staging carried signs of Appia's influence in its simplification of forms and poetic lighting, but, as later critics pointed out, it didn't have the essence of Appia's reforms in the interaction and mutual transformation of space, time, light, and movement.

Miroslav Rutte commented on the difference between Kvapil and Hilar: 'For Kvapil, the stage was always a picture . . . for Hilar, severe architecture. . . . Kvapil feels the scene as flat surface, Hilar spatially. The basis of dialogue for Kvapil is melody and nuance, for Hilar rhythm and counterpoint.'[11] Hilar himself revealed an appreciation of Kvapil's contributions and limitations:

Kvapil's work seemed to have valuable decorative refinement but without true dramatic rhythm and tension, since the improvisation of the actors' ensemble and the license of individual acting manner-isms scattered the rich and cultivated taste of the director. Kvapil's direction seemed to me a cluster of lucky accidents, not the work of a powerfully cast, unifying artistic program. I always saw excellent individuals, but rarely a fine whole. Kvapil simply never grasped direction as an ensemble operation. He created moods rather than drama. The impressionistic taste of the time seemed reflected in this vacillating stage work, which took impressionistic theatre ad absur-dum. . . . [On the other hand,] in an era of dilettantism, Kvapil's work meant . . . the first conscious Czech direction as a synthesis of stage crafts according to creative and poetic aesthetic principles.[12]

* * *

An overview of Hilar's productions reveals that several of his recurrent characteristics as a director appeared in his earliest work: restricting actors' habitual mannerisms to the immediate demands of the play at hand, tightly controlling their intonation, expression, and rate of speech, drawing on the theatrical stylization of *commedia dell'arte* even for modern works, and introducing elements of the grotesque in characterization, movement, and delivery, especially in such works as Molière's *Georges Dandin* (1913) and Carl Sternheim's *Merchant Schippel* (1914). It was a sharper, more con-centrated, heightened form of theatre compared to that of Kvapil, more aggressive and hard edged, and with a distinct inclination toward irony and satire.

Hilar's work during the next ten years at both the Vinohrady and National theatres, prior to his crippling stroke in 1924, took several forms as it evolved to maturity. His penchant for satire with grotesque, commedia over-tones found expression in productions like Sternheim's *The Snob* (1915) and Sheridan's *The School for Scandal* (1916), as well as Molière's *Don Juan* (1917) and *Malade Imaginaire* (1921), while darker, more spastic variations of this basic tendency were quite evident in his staging of Strindberg's *The Dance of Death* (1917). He did not abandon the grotesque but heightened and expanded it in another series of works that strove for a certain heroic, monumental pathos: Heinrich von Kleist's *Penthesilea* (1914), Shakespeare's *Antony and Cleopatra* (1917), Corneille's *The Cid* (1919), and Euripides' *Medea* (1921). Psychological realism was subordinated if not suppressed in favor of markedly stylized, rhythmically orchestrated voices, sculpturesque blocking, and artificially imposed movement as Hilar, the master shaper of the total stage work, found vent for his will toward form.

As the war drew to a close and was followed by revolutionary movements and the birth of new states throughout Europe, Hilar was attracted to plays dealing with the masses, their turbulence and aspiration, their ecstasy and pathos. In productions like Zygmunt Krasiński's *The Undivine Comedy* (1918), C. Van Lerberghe's *Pan* (1919), Arnošt Dvořák's *The Hussites* (1919), Émile Verhaeren's *The Dawns* (1920) (Plate 1), and Shakespeare's *Coriolanus* (1921), Hilar reflected the postwar spirit of feverish social turmoil and class conflict not literally but metaphorically. These were not, as one critic pointed out, 'Reinhardt spectacles of mass movements but dramatic battles of individuals and collectives for truth and justice.'[13] The same critic also noted: 'No one else on the Czech stage showed a collective hero, presented by a collective, with a comparable sense for its powerful moving drama and suggestive force.'[14]

In all these works, from *Penthesilea* (1914) onward, Hilar was evolving his own brand of expressionism, which for him was far less a matter of theory or philosophy than of performance style and spirit as a reflection of the age. The specific manifestations of Hilar's expressionism were a constant stylization if not distortion of vocal and bodily expression that produced a highly dynamic, rhythmicized total presentation. Characterization was sacrificed to artificial constructs of essential forces and ideas; physical staging and lighting were deliberately and drastically manipulated to achieve striking contrasts and confrontations; the grotesque was a constant though variable

Plate 1 Vlastislav Hofman's drawing of the set for Karel Hugo Hilar's production of Émile Verhaeren's *The Dawns* (1921), in the Vinohrady Theatre. Photo: J. Burian.

7

element, and a middle range of emotional display was rejected in favor of extreme pathos or ecstasy. What distinguished Hilar's form of expressionism from that of others was a balance and resultant enrichment provided by his inherent common sense and wit, his freedom from didacticism, his respect for literary values, and his affinity for the sensual and physiological. Moreover, the presence of the grotesque was less a matter of arbitrary 'effect' or self-indulgence than an appropriate reflection of wartime stress and horror.

In one special production, the world premiere of Karel and Josef Čapek's *The Insect Comedy* (1922), the subject matter (contemporary humanity in the form of insects) lent itself completely to Hilar's most radical methods. It was among the last surges of his expressionist period and his greatest public success at the National Theatre. (William Brady invited Hilar to stage the work on Broadway, and although Hilar was not able to obtain sufficient leave of absence to do it, his *Regiebuch* formed the basis of the New York production in October 1922.)

Nevertheless, several other productions made it clear that Hilar was overreaching himself, and that his extreme approach had become reduced to certain schematic formulas. The world had changed and the spastic distortions no longer had much relation to social reality. These extreme tendencies were most evident in Marlowe's *Edward II* (1922) and Strindberg's *Queen Christina* (1922), and reached the ultimate in grotesque schematics at the expense of the human element in Juliusz Słowacki's *Balladyna* (1932), a curious mixture of tragedy, farce, and fairy tale which, it must be admitted, offered scope for artistic distortion in performance. According to the actor Eduard Kohout, it was 'Hilar's greatest failure at the National Theatre.' Nevertheless, Kohout went on to add,

> It was among the purest and most poetic of productions. . . . [Hilar] stylized every word, every movement. In short, he culminated his search which began at the Vinohrady theatre; his *Penthesilea* and *Cid* led here. What had been experiment, here ripened to pure form. . . . *Balladyna* isn't a drama, it's a poem. And Hilar made theatre of this poem.[15]

As Hilar achieved increasing acclaim and occasional notoriety with his expressionistic productions, some critics accused him of being under the influence of Leopold Jessner, his more widely celebrated German contemporary whose name virtually became synonymous with postwar expressionism. Hilar's reply to the critical accusation was a perceptive description of his own methods and a reasonable defense of his claim to precedence in this form of staging. Citing his *Penthesilea*, *The Undivine Comedy*, and *The Cid* as prototypes of expressionism, Hilar spelled out their salient characteristics as anticipations of Jessner's later work:

a need to eliminate everything from the acting and directing that doesn't lead to the poet's final point. . . . an ideal of expressive concentration technically reflected in a sense for outline, contour, edge, linearity, slant in individual acting and the direction as a whole. . . . New Czech direction was already attempting [in 1914] a denser, simplified stage expression, as yet theoretically unformulated. . . . [Consider] Corneille's *The Cid*, which reduced scenic environment to essential furniture and the historical period to simplified costumes, created a dynamic orchestra of voices, fused actors' individualities into a single rhythmic torrent of the drama's inner passion . . . in 1918, fully two years before Jessner's Berlin debut.[16]

The production of *Romeo and Juliet*, in 1924, marked a decisive turning point. Three years after his first production at the National Theatre (*Coriolanus*, 1921), Hilar had a crowning success with Shakespeare, thus silencing those critics who still compared him unfavorably with Kvapil, for Hilar had now produced Shakespeare with greater vividness, excitement, and passion than had previously been seen on the Prague stage. It was a culmination of Hilar's highly imaginative, vigorous expressionism, but now with a human-centered and actor-centered core that anticipated the subsequent and final phase of Hilar's work. The extravagant dynamics were still present (as was the element of the grotesque in the comic servants), but now they had their roots in believable, passionate human beings, not in imposed, schematic patterns. The image of humanity began to be more complex and relative, even as Hilar still strove for maximum impact and economy in the acting. To concentrate and accelerate the force of the action, he reduced the number of scenes to eighteen by cuts and transpositions, eliminating explanatory detail, flowery description, and philosophical rambling. The key to the visual dynamics was a sustained curving, interweaving, often circular movement, with varying rhythms and intensities, and an overall feeling of carnival. Hilar's comments on the play underline his emotive, human-centered approach:

> Its meaning is the fatefulness of a family drama . . . in which parents battle with children, the ardent ones with the chilled, the passionate with the reasonable, the impulsive with the mechanical, and in which the tragedy of the everyday triumphs and shatters pure, unfettered . . . amorous feeling. A drama of love – yes – and a drama of cold reason.[17]

Romain Rolland was a visitor to Prague and saw the production on its opening night, after which he wrote the following note of enthusiastic praise to Hilar:

I have often seen Shakespeare on stage, and not only in the cold, declamatory, operatic style in which these plays are still performed in Europe. I've seen great actors in Shakespeare's play. . . . But none of these performances led me into the fiery maelstrom of Shakespeare's dramas so powerfully as your production of *Romeo and Juliet*, which was truly able to give rebirth to Shakespeare in a new form. I congratulate your actors, who were able to master their roles with such an abundance of excited enthusiasm.[18]

* * *

In May 1924, less than a month after this new crest in his career, Hilar, at the age of 39, suffered the crippling stroke that kept him away from the stage for a year and a half. When he returned he was shockingly transformed, as Frantisek Götz, his dramaturge, observed:

Before his illness he was a robust, flowering man who gave foreigners the impression of a wolf devouring life and art, work and fame from a thousand sides, for whom no obstacle is too strong to overcome, like one who actually provokes fate. . . . Illness shattered his inner equilibrium. It disintegrated his self-confidence, and under the broken visage of a nearly absolute ruler one could see . . . a visage of anxiety, inner uncertainty, timorousness.[19]

Hilar managed to regain a measure of his former energy and will, but the drastic shock had lasting effects (Plate 2). For the time being, at least, he seemed to turn inward and become more reflective, less masterful, more questioning. The stark confrontation of his own mortality seemed to make him more tolerant and considerate of others, even compassionate. The effects were also evident in his productions once he resumed a sharply reduced schedule. The choice of plays and, more important, his approach to them marked a new and distinct chapter in his career, which he himself termed 'civilism.' It was his version of what elsewhere was termed Neue Sachlichkeit, a turning away from the stylized, spastic excesses of expressionism to tamer, more understated, more sober issues and themes, to the everyday, the domestic, the personal. The change, for Hilar, had at least three sources: primarily, his own stroke and its debilitating and sobering aftermath; the sociopolitical stabilization of Europe (including the new Czechoslovakian state) after the spasms of the war and the years immediately following; and what Hilar saw as the consequent irrelevance and sterility of expressionism as a viable artistic mode. Götz offered a diagnosis of Hilar's new phase:

Sooner than Jessner and other German directors, he realized that expressionism is truly a demolished barricade which it is necessary to abandon, and he searched for new theatrical forms. He thought a

10

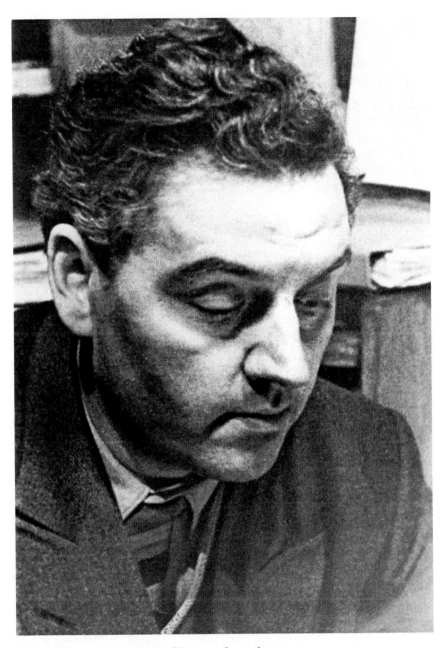

Plate 2 Hilar in his later years. Photographer unknown.

good deal of a human-centered art. Der Mensch in der Mitte became his byword.[20]

Hilar attempted to define and justify his new mode in numerous ways:

> Theatre needs a disarmament of expressiveness, a spiritual demobilization. [It is] a time of dramatic truce, a time of scenic civilism, a time of intellectual citizenship. . . . By civilism I mean the artistic expression of this spiritual calming which contrasts psychologically with the heightened feeling of war or revolution.[21]

His *Hamlet* in 1926 was a good example of his new restraint, chiefly in the lyrical and melancholy portrait of Hamlet by Eduard Kohout, one of Hilar's greatest actors. The productions of this time and beyond were notably less flamboyant, more restrained and meditative, more humanized and relatively more realistic, although still far from Kvapil's tamer, more academic work. Among the major productions of this period were Romain Rolland's *Play of Love and Death* (1925), and O'Neill's *Strange Interlude* (1930). Hilar's civilism provided a feasible approach for these productions in which, not coincidentally, the theme of mortality is strong, but not for others, like *King Lear* (1929).

As Hilar regained his former strength and spirit, however, civilism in the strict sense became too pale and calm for his innate temperament, which had to find expression in more full-blooded work. The result in some cases was spectacle at the expense of insight, as in Goethe's *Faust* (1928) or in a recurrence of the grotesque in modified form in Gogol's *Marriage* (1932). But there were also a number of productions that virtually all critics and other contemporaries regarded as the summit of Hilar's achievement: Sophocles' *Oedipus* (1932), Shakespeare's *Midsummer Night's Dream* (1933), and O'Neill's *Mourning Becomes Electra* (1934). In these productions Hilar forged a synthesis of the best elements of his earlier Dionysian creative exuberance and fantasy with increased psychological depth, complexity of feeling, and restraint in expression. Without sacrificing boldness and strength, compression and heightened tempo in staging, he seemed increasingly concerned with the deeper implications of the playwright's words and the human destinies underlying the action on stage. *Oedipus* and *Mourning Becomes Electra* were particularly impressive, the former in conveying a sense of the mythical and barbaric along with the intimately human, the latter in concentrating and condensing O'Neill's blend of antique fate and modern neurosis by selectively accentuating elements in the settings and lighting, and by increased intensity in the acting. Hilar's lifelong fascination with pagan antiquity and the modern psyche seemed to find in these two works an elemental communication or accord with his own recent vulnerability and his greater consciousness of the mystery of life and death.

The critic Rutte saw Hilar's final years as 'a loosening of civilism and a searching for avenues to a new pathos and a new romantic dimension of theatre . . . the need for a fruitful renewal by the spirit of Dionysus.'[22] Hilar's young colleague Frejka interpreted productions like *Oedipus* and *Mourning Becomes Electra* somewhat differently: 'Formerly he saw tragedy as a relation of cause and effect – but now we hear an ethical note and the ethical mysterium of theatre.'[23] The two observations point up the distinctive aspects of Hilar's final period: a revived, enriched expressiveness coupled with a more profound sense of humanity.

What further evolution might have produced – some contemporaries anticipated a more philosophical turn, others a greater social involvement – can only be guessed at, for in March 1935, not yet 50 years old, while preparing for productions of *Macbeth* and *Julius Caesar*, Hilar had a second massive stroke and died within a few days without regaining consciousness.

* * *

A closer look at some specifics of Hilar's directing, his relation to actors, and his use of scenography will contribute to a fuller understanding of his theatre. Although he introduced no startlingly new theories or methods of direction, Hilar gave serious attention to the concept and functions of the director in modern theatre, and his practices demonstrated painstaking thoroughness as well as creative fantasy. He saw the director as an artist in his own right, and in his practice was autocratic if not despotic, but he was also aware of the underlying interdependence of theatre artists: 'Today the poet inspires the director and actor, the actor the director, and the director the poet. . . . The ideal is equal value of all three, which guarantees the harmony of the result on stage.'[24] More particularly, probably because of his own literary roots, Hilar perceived a specially close creative analogy between the poet and the director:

> [The modern director] must be able to go hand in hand with the poet, but to see concretely what he sees metaphorically, to make tangible what he imagines. In a word, to be a director means to be a poet who, instead of making experiences fictive, materializes the given fictions. A poet is an artist who from the visible world creates symbols. A director is a poet who creates from symbols a visible world.[25]

Despite what would seem a sensitivity to the literary component of theatre, however, Hilar's direction often subordinated the text as literature to the text's potential theatrical values. He was consistently concerned with 'how a literary work becomes a dynamic, passionate, inspirational stage work; with what feeling, thought, rhythm, vitality, with what dramatic life a new, unstaged work is filled.'[26] His sensitivity to the dual claims of poetry and staging is evident in another remark: 'Theatricality, although it may

13

narrow the reality of dramatic poetry, on the other hand undeniably fixes it, sharpens it, exposes it.'[27] Jiří Frejka perceived a further duality inherent in Hilar's staging practice:

> This Dionysian type loves form; most of all he'd like to sculpt every feature of the face, every grimace, every stance. His two favorite words are 'pregnant' and 'piquant.' That means: form and interest – form and effect. It means more: two fundamental antitheses in his own being. The will to create a suprahumanly pure artistic whole, but on the other hand an *effect*, which prompts a crowd to applause.[28]

The will toward form was also evident in Hilar's awareness of the need for a complex interplay of time, space, movement, and lighting in giving life to a work on stage:

> This uninterrupted feeling for the plasticity and overview of the whole, this . . . wholly creative, shaping feeling for space and wholly musical feeling for time – these are general traits of the feeling for ensemble interplay, for the play of the whole, and for orchestration itself, without which a true theatrical achievement in the modern sense is unthinkable.[29]

Like Craig, Appia, Meyerhold, and others, Hilar was especially attuned to the musical values of staging, whether or not actual music occurred in a performance. As he put it, 'The essence of a dramatic effect is its musicality in the broadest and narrowest sense of the word. . . . There is an intimate and intense relation between dramatic art and musical art.'[30] Leading actor Ladislav Pešek recalled the importance of music to Hilar:

> His day begins with music. Every morning he listens to one of Bach's fugues and the toccata in D minor. . . . Music, precision, com-position, sound, this is the primary inspiration for Hilar. Every scene or sub-unit on stage has its specific rhythm. New, precisely differenti-ated, conceived to capture not the externals of reality but its inner meaning.[31]

Needless to say, Hilar's theatre was a director's theatre, in which all com-ponents were organized and shaped according to the vision and will of the director, and this made the status of his actors problematical. Severe contro-versies with actors often swirled around productions during Hilar's career, especially after his move to the National Theatre, where he inherited a corps of performers who had been accustomed to Kvapil's essentially laissez faire approach, which encouraged the development of individual egos and idiosyncrasies. Hilar himself defined the difference between the old and new theatre as the former comprising outstanding individuals and the latter an orchestrated ensemble. Hilar admitted that some of his greatest difficulties at the National Theatre occurred because many of the actors there simply weren't aware of his approach and were not able to adjust to it. Eventually most of them learned to adapt, not without considerable resentment on the part of some, and not before Hilar imported a number of his former actors at Vinohrady as replacements for those unable or unwilling to meet his standards.

A fascinating example of an actor's classic complaint is found in a formal appeal made by one of the National Theatre's actors to higher administrative echelons to remove Hilar from his position within a year of Hilar's move to the theatre:

> We're the marionettes of every healthy and sick attempt, we're asked to do this or that, we crawl into twisted stage settings even though we're uselessly straight for them, we twist our mouths with impossible speeches, our throats go dry from screaming, we climb up on various trapeze, we're modern but with our brains on a rack that cuts off all our judgment. . . . We're asked to be mere material, clay and color, sound, the final form of which can be anything, whether cubism or, by being disfigured, some sort of abortion.[32]

Not even the former actors from Vinohrady were without complaints. Václav Vydra, probably the strongest of Hilar's actors, chronically expressed his resentment at Hilar's refusal to allow an actor the freedom to develop a role, and at the prevalent belief that Hilar was responsible for the achievements of his actors. What is certain is that Hilar consistently sought, not always subtly, to make his perception and plan prevail, but that is not to say that the actors were his slaves or that he had no respect for an actor's creativity. Hilar himself counted on considerable talent, creativity, and responsiveness from an actor:

> An actor who takes over a clarified, imaginative sense of proportion from the director and is incapable of experiencing it subjectively, but returns it unassimilated and not worked over in a theatrical performance, is not a dramatic artist in the real sense of the word.[33]

Responding explicitly to the accusation of dominating actors, Hilar explained, with characteristic imagery, that it is a reciprocal process: 'There is talk of the forceful imposition of the new direction on the new actor, but it's obvious that it's a relationship of rapid oscillation in which temperaments necessarily discharge like two electric currents in a condenser.'[34] Hilar went so far as to declare that despite his detailed preparation of a *Regiebuch*, in which he indicated countless vocal and movement directions, he would nevertheless be ready to modify such preconceptions 'as soon as I observe in rehearsal that an actor's conception is in any detail more vivid, lively, artistically more truthful, and dramatically sharper than my own.'[35]

Actors and observers agreed that Hilar's basic approach to actors involved a special kind of provocation, a challenging of their habitual assumptions or patterns of thought. Rather than explain or discuss production concepts, he would 'penetrate and touch and agitate the most inner, private, fearful part of an actor – in order to upset his equilibrium and set him on the royal hunt for the character.'[36] The actors might become confused, confounded, frustrated, but these were labor pangs ultimately resulting in an authentic, richer, riper characterization. Not that Hilar refused to provide an actor with suggestions or hints, but they were notoriously metaphoric and often baffling: 'make a kind of red gesture,' 'wave with your chin,' 'be a tomcat on a roof.'

An actor like Ladislav Pešek thrived on this treatment and claimed that Hilar was loaded with ideas and promptings and generous with providing an actor with space in which to develop:

> What did Hilar ask of an actor? Fantasy and again fantasy, and naiveté. Not sobriety, not empty coloration. A Hilar actor rode on an unsaddled horse and leaped wildly and unexpectedly. Today's direction tries to suppress outbursts of passion, but Hilar wanted a free release. Detail was secondary for him. The main outline was most important. [But also] lapidarian characterization. He asked for absolute release, and constant self-control.[37]

Some of Pešek's enthusiasm may have been due in part to his encountering Hilar after his stroke, when Hilar's energy and will were drastically reduced, when he became notably more receptive to the creative contributions of others. His close associate F. Götz put it this way:

> In his last phase of creativity he developed much more human ideas about characters and no longer urged actors to schematics of simplified elements, but very intimately searched with them for ways of expressing the entire human significance of their character with all its inner fullness and dialectic.[38]

* * *

If Hilar's relationship with actors was stormy and controversial, his work with designers was consistently cooperative and fruitful. Just as Hilar provided opportunity and encouragement to a number of Czech playwrights, above all the Čapeks, he also introduced a number of new designers whose work had previously been in architecture or painting: Bedřich Feuerstein,

Antonín Heythum, Josef Čapek, and, preeminently, Vlastislav Hofman, an architect who joined Hilar at Vinohrady in 1919 for the important production of A. Dvořák's *The Hussites*. It was apparent from the beginning that the talents of each were ideally suited to those of the other. Hofman provided exactly the kind of monumental, highly expressive, bold statements that Hilar sought, and Hilar was an ideal source of stimulation and inspiration for Hofman.

Hilar's relation to scenography was a highly progressive one, starting with his aversion to conventionalized realistic and impressionistic scenery, and his dismissal of the notion that scenery exists primarily to indicate the place of action. Instead, he saw scenography as fundamentally concerned with the shaping of space and as an independent co-creator of action. His division of stage space by the use of separate lighting units was an innovation on the Czech stage, as was his organization of space to modify the movement and even the vocal delivery of actors by affecting the timing of their speeches: 'The dividing of stage space is like punctuation in the composition of a sentence.'[39] Lighting was an equally critical expressive component for Hilar. His work with it extended to various experiments with projections – *Herakles* and *The Dawns* (1920) – and his interest in stage space and movement led to his innovative use of turntables – *King Lear* (1929) and *Oedipus* (1932) – and treadmills – *What Price Glory?* (1930).

Hofman provides firsthand information on Hilar's special tastes and biases:

> He never wanted pleasing decorativeness but rather what he sought in an actor – reinforced dramatic expression and a simplified, vigorous effect, stenographic and with large dimensions. Never any fine detail, but statuesqueness . . . a form of monumentality of forgotten ages, like fate in tragedies of antiquity. After long cooperative work I recognized what Hilar wants: dark colors, restless outlines, sharp color contrasts, oblique, demolished forms always seeming old and sculpturesque . . . large planes in contrasting colors, expressive contours thrusting out from dark backgrounds . . . a feeling of dark depths on stage, of sharp outlines of lighted actors or constructions.[40]

In practice, a Hilar–Hofman stage would tend to be relatively bare, dominated by one or two carefully selected, suggestive scenic objects that were often notably enlarged and dramatically lighted, as if carved out of the surrounding darkness; for example, thrones, a graveyard wall, and central panels in *Hamlet*; a massive spiral staircase on a turntable in *Oedipus*. Only on rare occasions did the scenography in a Hilar production radically distort or eliminate recognizable objects or forms; rather, in the tradition of Appia and Craig, it eliminated secondary details and magnified essential or symbolic forms, sometimes literally in their construction or by dramatic, unorthodox lighting.

Indeed, Hilar's overall concept and vision of scenography not only reflects the symbolist heritage of Appia and Craig but anticipates Josef Svoboda:

> Let's extricate stage space from the tyranny of backdrops, battens, flats, and let's play, with the help of projectors, in pure space with pure light . . . while . . . actors move in this simplified scene in the rhythm of the performed poem. Let's attempt, not a political revolution but – with new machinery – a great revolution of spirit and poesy, thought and metaphor.[41]

*   *   *

The justification for viewing Hilar as the fountainhead of modern Czech theatre extends beyond his innovative scenography to include other directorial precedents that may now be recapitulated. In Czech theatre he established the decisive role of the director, the priority of theatre over dramatic literature, and the right of the director to edit and modify the dramatic text in order to make it viable on the stage for a given audience. He also demonstrated the vitality of nonrealistic forms and the dramatic power inherent in the contributions of related arts to the art of theatre: choreographed movement, orchestrated vocal delivery, sophisticated lighting, and sculpturesque blocking. In these and other ways, Hilar broke ground for the avant-grade directors of the younger generation, E. F. Burian, Jindřich Honzl, and Jiří Frejka, as well as the post-World War II generation of directors like Otomar Krejča and Alfred Radok.

The reactions of the contemporary leftist, anti-establishment avant-garde of the 1930s were testimony to his stature in his time. One might expect dedicated Communists like E. F. Burian and Jindřich Honzl to have little respect for the bourgeois head of a bourgeois state theatre, yet Burian expressed not only the tribute cited in the headnote to this section, but also the following, upon the death of Hilar:

> Who was K. H. Hilar? First, the greatest Czechoslovakian theatre organizer, an innovative spirit on world scale, under whose influence the entire official Czechoslovak theatre stands today, and whose creative strength is not matched by any young or old theatre worker of the Czechoslovak bourgeois theatre. With Hilar's death official theatre activity loses its profile. . . . Hilar – that is the evolution of theatre after the overthrow [of the Austro-Hungarian Empire].[42]

Jindřich Honzl, a cooler, ideologically stricter Marxist than Burian, was often critical of what he considered to be Hilar's empty rhetoric and ecstatic vagueness when dealing with social issues, yet even Honzl acknowledged Hilar's preeminence, albeit, like Burian, he qualifies his praise by identifying Hilar with the official, bourgeois theatre:

Today Hilar is our best director and all criticism and all enemies acknowledge this fact. If his productions are criticized today it is done with the awareness that they represent the best and most modern that can be expected in Czechoslovakia. . . . He is able to join elements of scenic art organically and support the entire scope of a dramatic poem in an organism that is solidly rhythmic in production. Hilar's expressionism was truly an artistic principle.[43]

Not surprisingly, Hilar's reputation plummeted in the 1950s, and he virtually became a nonperson in the new Socialist Republic with its youthful enthusiasm for Socialist Realism and its equal fervor against the former, western-oriented, bourgeois, capitalistic democracy of the First Republic. Not only was Hilar a bourgeois by class but he was constitutionally non-ideological, felt more kinship with the culture of the West than of the Russian east, and had no awe of Stanislavsky. He epitomized art that was the antithesis of Socialist Realism, and, in his position with the National Theatre, he was almost an official representative of the First Republic. Not until the mid-1960s had conditions in Czechoslovakia liberalized to the point of allowing for a tentative rehabilitation of Hilar, which took the form of a symposium of theatre critics, scholars, and artists, and a subsequent publication of its proceedings.[44] The result was an honest but cautious review and reappraisal that essentially reestablished Hilar's dominant position in the Czech theatre of the early twentieth century, and acknowledged that Hilar's expressionism modernized much of Czech theatre, especially its acting, and thereby broke ground for the new wave of avant-garde theatre.

Questions of Hilar's influence or significance in relation to the theatre of the 1960s were not pursued. Such questions began to surface later, but after August 1968 most such relatively free critical speculation was tabled indefinitely, and in the liberated 1990s critical work was primarily concerned with the post-1968 era and the present.

It was left to the memoirs of retired actors like Eduard Kohout and Ladislav Pešek to sustain the vital presence of Hilar's contribution. Pešek's summary observations are particularly apt:

every one of today's directors ought to visit Hilar's grave at least once a month and lay flowers on it. And bow to the memory of this greatest Czech director. It was he who at the cost of his life fought through the battle for the sovereignty of the director in theatre. . . . What Hilar gave to the Czech theatre, that which he gave to me, exists and will exist. A thousand-fold changed, a thousand-fold newly formed, there will always remain a bit of that embodied energy that was expended then.[45]

2

THE LIBERATED THEATRE OF VOSKOVEC AND WERICH

It would be difficult to imagine a stronger contrast within Czech theatre during the interwar years than the one between the large-scale drama productions of K. H. Hilar in state-supported, established repertory theatres such as the National or the Vinohrady, and the jazz-oriented, cabaret-like revues of Voskovec and Werich that were produced serially – and commercially – in several smaller, more recent Prague theatres.[1] The creativity of these particular artists provided highpoints of modern Czech theatre that transcended their times, even while reflecting those times in various ways.

By far the most popular and, according to many, the most relevant theatre in Czechoslovakia in the period between the wars was Prague's Liberated Theatre (Osvobozené divadlo) of Jiří Voskovec and Jan Werich. Many of its routines and songs were known by heart, recordings of its songs sold in the tens of thousands, its plays were performed by amateurs soon after they were released, and films made by Voskovec and Werich with or without other members of their company were sure-fire hits.[2] The theatre had a relatively brief but brilliant life of slightly more than eleven years. Its first performance occurred in the relatively easy and optimistic days of 1927, and its final curtain fell a scant month or two before the Munich agreement effectively terminated the existence of Czechoslovakia's First Republic in 1938.

If ever a theatre became spokesman of a generation or rallying point of a nation, it was the Liberated Theatre during its final years, as Fascism was gaining ever greater strength and arrogance in Europe. Jiří Voskovec and Jan Werich became the stuff of myth, and during the war memories of their plays and their performances contributed significantly to sustaining the morale of the occupied nation. Today they are still legendary figures for the Czechs, their names – or simply the initials V + W – more readily recognized than those of most theatre artists since their time.

During its brief existence their Liberated Theatre presented twenty-five full-length original productions, variations of a basic revue pattern which they developed into a flexible, distinctive form that moved toward musical comedy or, indeed, drama with musical interludes, with political satire as its core. For all but one of those productions Voskovec and Werich were the sole authors and librettists; they were, moreover, the leading actors, and frequently one or both of them served as designer or director.

They made their greatest impact performing the central roles in each production. Regardless of the details of a given plot, they appeared in stylized white makeup, like eternal clowns or zanni of the *commedia*, but with the difference that their comedy could be intellectually sophisticated and they themselves were highly articulate. Nevertheless, much of their charm and comic effectiveness derived from their basic stage identities as naive, earnest, good-natured, but invincibly dense personalities – grown-up but ingenuous boys trying to cope with a world difficult to comprehend.

Born in 1905, they grew up as schoolmates in Prague. Werich was the larger of the two, the more impulsive and elemental, yet he possessed remarkable grace in movement and facility in rapid, staccato speech. Voskovec, who was slighter in figure (though by no means small), more tentative and seemingly shy, suggested a certain self-consciousness and reserve. Paradoxically, however, such seeming contrasts did not create the impression of two independent or conflicting personalities; nor was one a straight man for the other (Plate 3). Instead, as their editor and long-time critic, Josef Träger, observed, it was as if one heard 'a monologue spoken by two voices at once . . . [which] showed two sides of one attitude expressed by an indivisible although doubled personality.'[3] What was true of their on stage performance also applied to their creativity as playwrights and librettists. Ranging from student lampoons to Aristophanic satire, their humor was the product of a dual artistry; two halves of a single creative inspiration.

Meyerhold visited Prague on a trip home from Paris in the fall of 1936. After seeing two of Voskovec and Werich's productions and spending the better part of several days and nights in their company, he inscribed the following in their theatre's guest book:

In 1913, my friend, the late poet Apollinaire, took me to the Cirque Medrano. After what we'd seen that night, Apollinaire exclaimed: 'These performers – using the means of the *commedia dell'arte* – are saving theatre for artists, actors, and directors.' Since then, from time to time, I would return to the Medrano, hoping to intoxicate myself again with the hashish of improvised comedy. But Apollinaire was gone. Without him I could no longer find the artists he had shown me. I looked for them with a longing heart but the Italian 'lazzi' were no more. Only tonight, October 30, 1936, I saw the 'zanni' again in the persons of the unforgettable duo of Voskovec and Werich, and was once more bewitched by performers rooted in the Italian *commedia ex improviso*. Long live *commedia dell'arte*! Long live Voskovec and Werich![4]

* * *

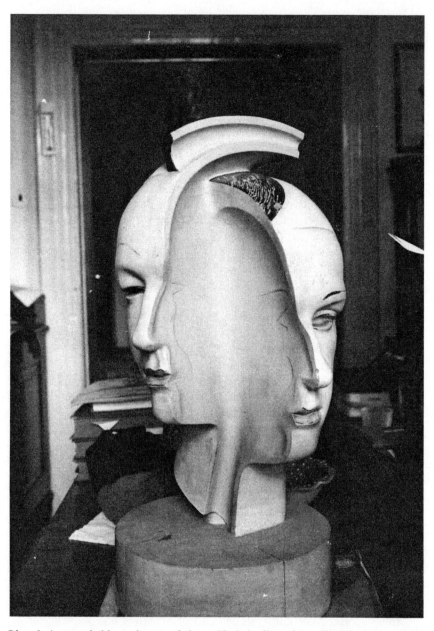

Plate 3 A remarkable sculpture of the unified duality of Jan Werich (left) and Jiří Voskovec (right) by O. Švec. Photo: J. Burian.

To determine the roots of Voskovec and Werich's theatre, one has to imagine the sense of excitement, the feeling of new beginnings and a fresh start for the Czechs at the end of World War I. They had not experienced the destruction and loss of most of the rest of Europe. War's end brought them independence as a nation – Czechoslovakia. Reluctant members of the Habsburg Empire for nearly three hundred years, the Czechs celebrated the end of the war with a reassertion of national identity.

Many influences contributed to the cultural ambience of Prague in the early and mid-1920s. Relics of the past were strongly contested by the modernistic currents of Futurism, Constructivism, and Dadaism, none of which was transplanted completely to Prague but all of which were assimilated into the Czech equivalent, Poetism, an attitude more than a tendency, much less a school. Poetism was lyrical, emotive, and gay; it was 'a way of looking at the world so as to make it a poem.'[5] Like Dadaism, Poetism exhibited an allergy to kitsch in thought, deed, and artifact, but its essentially optimistic response was a playful smile rather than a grin or a grimace. To Poetism, with which Voskovec was involved, may be attributed a considerable amount of the freewheeling whimsy that characterized much of V + W's humor.

Then, too, the good soldier Schweik himself, recently created by their countryman Jaroslav Hašek, contributed to the general irreverence toward encrusted tradition. But other forces, above all from the West, were equally influential: industry and fashion, sports and the arts. Voskovec studied for three years in France and was inspired by Apollinaire and the Fratellini Brothers, chief clowns at the Cirque Medrano. Most influential on Voskovec and Werich, however, were virtually all things American, especially American jazz and the silent film, of which they were passionate admirers. Keaton, Langdon, Lloyd, and others, but above all Chaplin, 'became Stanislavskys for the clowns Voskovec and Werich.'[6] New rhythms, colors, and attitudes were dissolving the Germanic and Slavic heaviness that characterized so much of the previous era, including its humor.

The avant-garde in Prague was centered in an informal, leftish group of poets, architects, and other artists and intellectuals known as Devětsil, of which Voskovec was a young member. One of the activities sponsored by Devětsil was an experimental theatre group named the Liberated Theatre, originally begun in 1925 by Jiří Frejka, who was later joined by Jindřich Honzl, also a member of Devětsil. Another young theatre aspirant to join the group was E. F. Burian, who had until then been a composer and musician. These three men, along with Voskovec and Werich, were to be central to the Czech theatre for the next three decades. At the time that they were all taking their first steps in theatre, Prague was dominated by Hilar's National Theatre and other institutional, traditional repertory theatres. Under the leadership of Frejka and Honzl, the Liberated Theatre performed a repertoire of international avant-garde plays in limited runs for small audiences in ill-equipped lecture and concert halls. Then, backstage tensions and clashes of temperament led to a split between Frejka and Honzl in March 1927. Honzl remained in charge of the Liberated Theatre, while Frejka, Burian, and several other actors formed a new company led by Frejka and named Theatre Dada.

That was the situation on April 19, 1927, when Voskovec and Werich, 22-year-old law students sponsored by a preparatory school alumni organization of which Voskovec was entertainment chairman, staged a very informal, amateur one-night entertainment which they themselves had written and designed. Because of its intimate scale and shoestring budget they called it (in English) *Vest Pocket Revue*, the title being an implicit lampoon of continental *revues à grand spectacle*. *Vest Pocket Revue* was an overnight sensation, eventually played over 200 performances, and became a legend in Czech theatre. It also totally eclipsed the spotty and limited successes of the original Liberated Theatre and other avant-garde groups of that time.

Both Frejka and Honzl quickly recognized the unique talents of the new team and invited them to join their already officially licensed groups. With the start of the season in fall 1927, Voskovec and Werich regularly performed *Vest Pocket Revue* as a component of the Liberated Theatre, alternating their production with Honzl's own limited-run productions of avant-garde plays, in which Voskovec and Werich occasionally took roles themselves during the next season.

Two years and five productions after their triumph in *Vest Pocket*, Honzl, who had become their director, left to take charge of drama at the National Theatre in Brno. At that point, Voskovec and Werich formally took over sole ownership and management of the theatre, which by that time had cut itself off from Devětsil. From the fall of 1929 the Liberated Theatre became the fully professional and self-supporting Liberated Theatre of Voskovec and Werich, playing in a 1,000-seat theatre in the center of Prague.

Total amateurs with no theatre schooling and virtually no previous stage experience when they put on *Vest Pocket Revue*, they were now in charge of a stable, fully professional, and self-supporting commercial operation of over 50 actors, musicians, dancers, and technical staff. Their productions, which they played eight times a week (no night off), averaged over 120 performances each (37 the shortest run, 250 the longest), in a city of fewer than a million inhabitants. A comparable average for productions in cities like London, Paris, or New York would approach 1,000 performances. Certainly no other Czech theatre group before or since has matched their success or popularity.

What distinguished their theatre and its performances? The best way to begin an answer is to refer to their own explanation of the meaning of the name of their theatre: 'Liberated from what? . . . Simply from all the extraneous freight that changed the pure, original nature of theatre . . . to the unbearable waxworks of naturalism, symbolism, pontifical mediocrities and contorted experimenters.'[7]

Instead of realism or 'contorted experimenters,' the ideal was fantasy, the poetic, lyrical fantasy of bright colors, masks, costumes and lights creating a special stage enchantment, as well as the fantasy of surprise, shock, and even aggression: 'Not boy meets girl, boy loses girl, boy marries girl. Fantasy, sir, that's theatre! Terrifying fantasy, diseased fantasy, madness. . . . Unbelievable things! Things that not even the smartest in the audience can anticipate.'[8] Love of fantasy was wedded to an instinctual love of the theatrical, sheer delight in the game of performing; theatre was for them 'a great social game.' The zest for theatricality was evident in the format of most of their productions, the frequent prologues directly addressed to the audience, the stylized clown-white makeup of Voskovec and Werich, and, occasionally, the use of theatre itself as a framing element of their plots. But laughter, exuberant, liberating, even gratuitous laughter, was the essence and final cause of their art, their game, even when their satire became most seriously engaged with grim realities beyond the walls of their theatre.

Their rejection of realism, their inherent flair for theatricality, and their delight in producing laughter were nowhere more evident than in their forestage improvisations that punctuated the action of their productions. These distinctive routines began accidentally in their very first production when a piece of scenery fell and forced them to improvise a comic exchange downstage of the quickly drawn curtain while the scenery was readjusted. In their subsequent improvisations, which became a regular, keenly anticipated part of their productions, they would make a transition from incidental participation in the action to detached commentary not only on that action but, more pointedly, on the world outside the theatre. At other times, their sallies would not be focused on the real world at all, but instead would pursue in surrealistic fashion the comic absurdities implicit in language itself, or as Voskovec put it, the 'satire of language on language. . . . On our delight in catching ourselves in the butterfly net of the abstract.'[9] Peppering their dialogues were slang, multilingual punning, and allusions drawn from classical mythology, history, and international politics. Indeed, it is not surprising that their theatre became fondly known as one for academically advanced students, for it provided a verbal feast for the alert mind. Nevertheless, it would be misleading to suggest that they played to an elite; their productions attracted throngs from all levels except the stuffiest bourgeoisie.

In each production, they retained and refined what worked best in their initial forestage improvisations, which were hastily sketched out the afternoon before the opening performance, always keeping flexible enough to allow for spontaneous topical allusions or the response of particular audiences. The success and unique effect of their forestage appearances lay chiefly in the live contact they maintained with their audiences each night. They improvised according to the emotional, psychic mood and voltage of each assembly, playing 'by ear' in relation to its responsiveness, at times overtly remarking on certain sections of the audience, at other times acknowledging their own awareness of what they were doing and, indeed, of their reputation for it. In a forestage sequence near the end of one of their last productions, *Big Bertha* (Těžká Barbora), they had the following exchange:

SECOND MERCENARY: Hold on, this isn't Eidam any longer. The two of us are here, and right in front of us is our customer, our master. [*Indicating the audience*] And right now he's waiting for his political morsel.
FIRST MERCENARY: Aha. The moment has come for keen satire to make its appearance on these boards.
SECOND MERCENARY: Of course. This is the place where two intellectual clowns play catch with a ball of abstract concepts.
FIRST MERCENARY: I see you've read the critics.[10]

The culmination of the forestage comic-satire turns was songs with lyrics by Voskovec and Werich and music by their resident composer, Jaroslav Ježek. A song usually sprang from a key motif of the preceding improvised dialogue and presented in a concentrated manner – to the accompaniment of the latest blues, foxtrot, or rumba – the equivalent of an Aristophanic parabasis: a direct, witty, often aggressive comment on a given social or political motif. It is in their songs that their most pointed, sustained sociopolitical satiric thrusts have survived, for we have in print only random samples of Voskovec and Werich's spoken improvisations, only those sections that became set. Like the plays themselves, the songs also followed a pattern of evolution: as time went on and the productions focused more and more on serious issues, the songs themselves became thematically and functionally more integrated, more consistently challenging and even tendentious in their lyrics, but without ever losing their nerve, humor, and creative fantasy. Especially toward the end, in the last half-dozen productions, many of the songs took on a rousing, morale-inducing quality to inspire a collective resistance to the imminent threats of aggression from the internal and external forces of Fascism. If one listens to contemporary recordings of those songs and is even partially aware of the times and special conditions during which they were performed, their spirit and force are unmistakable and indeed contagious.

Some of the improvisatory method of the forestage duets was evident in the general action with the cast as a whole during rehearsals. Nevertheless, the action became set during rehearsals and extemporizing during performances was liable to fine, although there was one notable exception. The final performance usually allowed for a degree of general, ad-lib improvisation in which anything went if it stayed within the frame of the play and its main action. Fans of the theatre fought for admission to the final performances, known as 'dernieri,' in anticipation of the spontaneous entertainment.

Both the tendency toward general though controlled improvisation during rehearsal and the shenanigans of closing performances testify to the ensemble rapport that existed in the Liberated Theatre under Voskovec and Werich. From all accounts the company was exceptional in its comradeship, its collective enthusiasm, its lack of dissension. Several facts contributed significantly to this phenomenon. First, Voskovec and Werich had the ability to attract a group of first-rate co-artists. Second, the performers combined a high level of skill with a variety of distinctive traits, on the basis of which Voskovec and Werich consistently wrote parts made to measure for the members of their company, frankly exploiting each actor's strengths as a performer and thereby reducing backstage resentments over casting. Third, Voskovec and Werich paid the highest salaries in Prague.

Viewed in retrospect, the form of their productions can be seen evolving from loosely structured revues toward thematically unified, plotted, integrated combinations of dramatic action, musical numbers, and improvisatory routines by Voskovec and Werich. The revue form remained throughout in the pattern of different theatrical elements assembled to make a single evening's entertainment, but the shift from random parody and musical numbers to a dramatically developed spine of action to which music and comic routines were joined is significant.

The essential point is that Voskovec and Werich's response to the world moved from delighted wonder or amazement at the absurdities of reality to a disturbed recognition of ills in their own society and even more alarming threats from abroad, and finally to a commitment to challenging and resisting those negative and aggressive forces. Never members of any party or allied with any ideology, dedicated to an autonomous world of theatre and the sheer delight of performing, they evolved into acute social critics and their theatre became a morale-inspiring force for democracy and national unity. Nevertheless, their fundamental purpose, from first production to last, remained comedy and laughter as the 'hygiene of the soul.' Their productions never lost their essential identity as works of art, as worlds of imagination and fantasy. Indeed, the tension between self-sufficient comic entertainment and socially engaged activism gives special interest to their mature productions and suggests the distinctive quality of their art. A survey of their productions will clarify the different forms and directions taken by that art.

* * *

Among their earliest productions were three pure revues. *Vest Pocket Revue*, *Smoking Revue* (May 1928), and *The Dice are Cast* (Kostky jsou vržený, January 1929) were fresh, irreverent, very casually assembled medleys of parodistic skits, the latest musical fads, and isolated songs and dances, with Voskovec and Werich basting together the elements with the slightest of plot threads. Self-conscious repetitions of the *Vest Pocket Revue* formula, the latter two revues were unable to recapture the fresh spontaneity of their first work.

Four other early plays were of two types. *Having a Spree* (Si pořádně zařádit, October 1928) was the first of their several adaptations of existing plays, in this case Johann Nestroy's *Einen Jux will er sich machen* (Thornton Wilder's source for *The Matchmaker*). The next three were original scripts that spoofed dime novels and detective stories, but proved to be misguided attempts to branch off from the loose revue form and yet achieve the success of *Vest Pocket Revue*. A more essential problem was that Voskovec and Werich played characters other than themselves, and the public was not interested. Both they and Honzl finally realized that whatever success they had previously achieved was rooted in their talents as a unique twosome playing presentational comedy that stressed their own stage personalities. And so they turned back to the revue form, but with a difference.

In practice, the new, more fully evolved and structured revue, as envisaged by them, matured over a period of three years in a series of eight productions, from *Fata Morgana* in late 1929 to *A World behind Bars* in early 1933. They called these works Jazz Revues because of the great significance of music in them and because jazz connoted for them the distinctive pulse of the postwar world. The very titles of the first and last of these works suggest the thematic distance that they spanned.

Fata Morgana (December 1929) was of particular significance for Voskovec and Werich because it marked their affiliation with a number of major co-artists. It was, for example, their first substantial collaboration with the composer Ježek and the choreographer Joe Jenčík and his dancers, who became known simply as the 'Girls.' It was, moreover, the first production for which they employed a professional stage designer, František Zelenka. Another affiliation was temporarily suspended during this and the next season. Jindřich Honzl had departed for Brno at the end of the previous season, where he remained for two years as the chief director of drama at the National Theatre. During those two seasons, Voskovec took over direction of the Liberated Theatre's five productions, a task which he obviously performed well, but which he gladly relinquished when Honzl returned in the fall of 1931.

The Jazz Revues caught on, and a basic form became established: an entertainment in two parts with a reasonably firm plot line that incorporated at least one multi-character scene of broad farce comedy, some half-dozen song and dance numbers growing out of the main action, and two or three relatively independent forestage interludes by Voskovec and Werich.

Thematically, the emphasis in their productions was on the non-erotic and the nonpolitical, as the following lyric from *Fata Morgana* makes clear:

> You may rest assured
> We won't be vulgar
> We've forbidden ourselves forever
> The erotic element.

Not knowing our way in politics
Even in the slightest
We'll avoid, willy nilly,
Political satire.[11]

Their rejection of the erotic was sustained throughout their career, probably as a result of their sense of humor, but their avoidance of political satire did not last long. During the years between *Fata Morgana* (1929) and *A World behind Bars* (Svět za mřížemi, 1933) the worldwide economic crisis made itself felt in Czechoslovakia, where rapidly escalating unemployment produced social discord. The turmoil was exacerbated not only by widespread resurgent militarism and dictatorship in Europe but also by the rise of the Nazi party in Germany, culminating in Hitler's ascendancy to Chancellorship in early 1933, with sympathetic Fascist vibrations in Czechoslovakia. A critical sociopolitical event occurred in November 1931 when groups of demonstrating unemployed workers in the northern Bohemian area of Fryvaldov were fired upon by police and military units. Voskovec and Werich, along with countless other artists and intellectuals, were appalled and outraged.

Until 1931, the revues concentrated on providing essentially escapist entertainment that only occasionally and incidentally noted disquieting social realities; otherwise, the prevailing tone was of good-humored, screwball comedy usually placed in an exotic setting: the tropics, South America, or the United States during the Civil War. But a definite progression was evident toward tighter, more controlled plot construction and also toward a relatively more artistic integration of dramatic action, character delineation, musical production numbers, and the Voskovec and Werich duet sequences. This culminated – as form – in *The Golem* (November 1931), a charming blend of romantic fable and atmosphere in Renaissance Prague, with relatively mature character interaction and sustained comic invention. In *Golem*, the revue form almost gave way to a form of romantic comedy with incidental music, dance, and satiric comment. But the Fryvaldov incident occurred during the run of *Golem* and led to Voskovec and Werich's decisive turn toward much more direct involvement with the realities outside their theatre.

The subsequent production was *Caesar* (March 1932), the first of a group of vigorously satiric productions which, while maintaining the basic Jazz Revue format, reacted with a sustained, essentially negative attack on military dictatorship abroad, various forms of contemporary Fascism, and the ills of a disintegrating domestic economy. Not until later did Voskovec and Werich devise productions that had a positive, rallying thrust. The engaged quality of their work in *Caesar* is captured in their remarks referring to that production. 'Formerly, art abandoned reality for good because it smelled. Today reality stinks and the artist must join the activists, the politicians, and the revolutionaries in order to remove the corpse.'[12]

The attack in *Caesar*, aimed primarily at the machinations of European power politics, was embodied in bizarre plots and counterplots among Caesar (based on Mussolini), Brutus, Antony, Cleopatra, and others just prior to Caesar's appearance at the senate during the ides of March. Receiving almost equally strong satiric attention were corrupt domestic wheeling and dealing in the modern parliament, depicted as the Roman senate, and the grim follies of militarism and war-mongering in general, all practiced at the expense of an ill-informed citizenry.

In *Caesar*, as in virtually all the Jazz Revues, Voskovec and Werich played characters peripheral to the main action who happen to stumble into it or be caught up by it. Usually they appeared for the first time near the end of the first act and then took the lead in a large production number that acted as a finale for the first half of the evening. In the second half they became entangled in the main action. The very last scene of *Caesar* showed the Forum being visited by a group of modern tourists, who are recognizably the characters from antiquity in modern dress. Caesar's dictatorship is ironically praised as a victory of tradition over hasty and rash progress, while Voskovec and Werich appear as news hawkers selling an 'extra' edition that headlines the latest economic dilemmas of Europe.

Although the subject matter was marked by a confrontation of meaningful issues, the form remained that of the Jazz Revue. The mixture was unsatisfactory because the theme and form were not really integrated. The satire was strong and pointed but not adequately sustained or consistent in tone largely due to the presence of elements from the nonpoliticized, escapist revues. In terms of a successful integration of subject, theme, and form, *Caesar* was actually a step backward from *Golem*.

The next two productions, which were transitional, can still be related to the Jazz Revue series but also anticipated the subsequent Political Revues. Neither was as effective as *Caesar*. *Robin the Brigand* (Robin zbojník, September 1932), a reworking of Robin Hood material, merely echoed many motifs from *Caesar*: militarism, demagoguery, social injustice, crises of unemployment and the economy. *A World behind Bars* (January 1933) was the only production on which Voskovec and Werich collaborated with another writer, Adolf Hofmeister. The result was a thoroughly unassimilated potpourri of slapstick farce, spoof of film melodramas, and sour comments on corruption and injustice in America. One of the few examples of their work that directly presents a contemporary setting and action, its cartoon-like depiction of American prohibition, cops, gangsters, and nightclub life is in the vein of Brecht's *Arturo Ui* or, with reference to Victorian England, *The Threepenny Opera*, but with very little of the coherence of those works.[13]

By the time of *A World behind Bars*, the original Jazz Revue form had been profoundly altered. Musical production numbers and casually structured comic segments had become subordinate to plots, and carefree entertainment had given way to essentially negative sociopolitical criticism. *Golem* was the peak creation of the mature Jazz Revue, and *Caesar* the first and strongest of the new pieces that tried to integrate political satire with elements of the revue form. But the new vision had yet to find appropriate new expression.

* * *

It did so in *Ass and Shadow* (Osel a stín, October 1933: Plate 4). Once again a classical source (a story by Lucian) served as a model for an assault on dictatorship and totalitarianism, this time with special emphasis on the cause-and-effect relationship between unemployment and other economic woes and the rise of political parties led by ruthless demagogues. The parallels to contemporary Germany and the rise to power of Hitler were so obvious as to draw official protest from the German embassy in Prague.

Much of profound significance had been occurring not only in Germany but also in Czechoslovakia in 1933. In January, Hitler became Chancellor and assumed dictatorial powers that spring. Later that same year the first concentration camps appeared in Germany. In Czechoslovakia, unemployment had reached its peak in February. One month earlier, Fascist groups had attempted a putsch in Brno. In October, Konrad Henlein, a German functionary living in the Czech area adjoining Germany (the Sudetenland), established a Nazi-oriented political party within Czechoslovakia to organize the Germans living in the Czech borderlands.

Voskovec and Werich drew upon many of these circumstances in writing

Plate 4 A scene from Voskovec and Werich's *Ass and Shadow* (1933), setting by Bedrich Feuerstein. Photo: Alexandr Paul.

31

Ass and Shadow, and created figures readily associable with Hitler and other Fascist types. Their fantastic plot centered on two rival political parties in the fictional land of Abdera, a so-called party of the people led by the Hitler figure and a party representing capitalist industry and wealth. Their conflict is focused on the fate of an ass that had, in turn, been the bone of contention between two very ordinary citizens, played by Voskovec and Werich, who become caught up and exploited in the struggle for power between the political parties. In an effort to save themselves, they kill the ass. The two demagogues, for whom the ass has become a supreme symbol, join forces and masquerade as the ass itself in order to exploit the people and write history as they see fit. The play reaches its climax of direct contemporary relevance in their address to the people through the mouth of the ass:

THE ASS: Fall on your knees and salute me by raising your right arms! The first Abdera is no more, the Abdera of the Ass! The second Abdera is gone, the Abdera of the Shadow! Now there arises the Third Reich! The Reich of Ass and Shadow!

THE PEOPLE: [*Saluting and yelling*] Heilos!

THE ASS: Only the ancient, pure Abderian race will live. Throw away your brains, forget to read and write, burn everything thought and written, and listen to the voice of the new, Third Abdera:

LOUDSPEAKER: [*the text is in German*] My people of Abdera! To us belongs victory and war! We gladly sacrifice the lives of millions! Away with culture, bring on cannon and gas! Down with mankind, down with the world![14]

Most of the extraneous elements of the Jazz Revues were thinned out if not completely eliminated, and the songs amounted to an often explicit frontal attack on personalities and incidents (one song ridiculed Europe's best known dictators: Hitler, Mussolini, and Dolfuss). Most of the ballet sequences were directly applicable to the key moments of the action, perhaps the most outstanding being a ballet of doctors brought in to save the dying ass. But undoubtedly the most significant difference in the total shaping of the work occurred in the placing of the Voskovec and Werich figures at the heart of the action. The two figures become representatives of the ordinary man drawn into events beyond his control but resisting and ultimately surviving by luck and native wit. Indeed, the work is closer to an Aristophanic comic-satiric play with music than to a revue.

Executioner and Fool (Kat a blázen), which opened the following season in October 1934, was essentially a spinoff from *Ass and Shadow*, dealing with the basic themes of dictatorship and factional struggles for power. Effective as it was, it did not improve on the complex achievement of *Ass and Shadow*; in fact, it marked a certain decline in its dispersal of focus and its inclusion of nonintegrated revue elements. Moreover, although theoretically central to the main line of the plot, Voskovec and Werich's roles were not integrated with the central action to the extent that they had been in *Ass and Shadow*.

The plot concerned the efforts of corrupt demagogues to assure their totalitarian grip on a highly fictive Mexico. Reference to concentration camps is but one of the reminders of contemporary actuality, but the most striking element in this work is the creation of the character Carierra, a bureaucratic nonentity who, despite himself, rises to the top of the heap. Woefully neurotic, he finds that unlimited power satisfies his aberrations which rapidly blossom into megalomania and paranoia. He declares himself Emperor and then God, before a climactic scene of madness in which he stabs himself while in a crazed dispute with his shadow. Allowing for the element of grotesque caricature, it is still a chilling image of Hitler. The play as a whole again ends on a hopeful if not optimistic note with the opposition of youth and responsible citizenry to the degenerate madness of totalitarianism.

A storm of controversy and actual riots in the theatre marked the production. Although its influence in the government was limited, the conservative, Fascistically inclined element in Czechoslovakia had attained considerable power by this time. Moreover, in this play Voskovec and Werich ridiculed the cult of national heroes and pseudo-patriotism, which also struck at some cherished ideals of the conservatives. Consequently, the demonstrations inside and outside the theatre were not too surprising. Werich tersely recalled the encounters, which culminated during the performance of 30 October 1934: 'Stink bombs, rotten tomatoes, curses, whistles, broken windows, and a great campaign by the reactionary press against the theatre and its authors.'[15]

The question of their political and ideological position confronted V + W on more than one occasion during those days and also later, even after the war. In a country where such issues were taken seriously, Voskovec and Werich seemed to embody an attitude that characterized most of the artists and intellectuals of the time. Rationally and emotionally they leaned toward the left, which represented the clearest opposition to the Fascist threats as well as a persuasive critique of many of the economic and social ills of the nation. Many of the most talented and productive members of the cultural community felt so strongly about these issues that they took what seemed a logical step and became members of the Communist Party (e.g., Honzl and Burian). But Voskovec and Werich, whether as a result of rational analysis or, more likely, constitutional aversion to any categorical, ideological commitment except to the freedom implicit in the name of their theatre, resisted all such affiliation. Their position in regard to the classic issue of art and ideology was articulated more explicitly early in 1934 and did not change in any fundamental way thereafter:

> Our mission is simple, to entertain. . . . As soon as propaganda of a certain idea intrudes into theatre, as soon as a certain ideological

tendency begins to influence theatre work, it stops being theatre and loses its most distinctive mission, an artistic mission. We regard every such dutiful subservience, whether to social need or political agitation, as artistically unclean.[16]

By the time of *Executioner and Fool*, the tension was increasing between V + W's wish to assert the sovereign value of laughter and the autonomy of theatre as theatre, and their part in the ongoing turmoil and conflict. This tension contributed to their decision to produce two conventional revues (variants of the *Vest Pocket* format). Such revues also provided them with an opportunity to exercise their comic fantasy without nailing it to politically charged issues. Not that they avoided the reality of the day; rather, they were able to attack it within the revue format in an intermittent, jabbing fashion instead of having to build a sustained dramatic action that committed itself to a full confrontation. In fact, both revues, *Keep Smiling* (December 1934) and *The Wax Museum* (April 1935), were responses to the attacks that had been launched against their theatre. Both implicitly championed the right of free artistic expression, attacked censorship, and defended the theatre against charges that the irresponsible reactionary press had been levelling against them.

Keep Smiling had as its framing action an encounter between Voskovec and Werich and the lively figures of Aristophanes and Molière, in which the masters were consulted about the prospects of satire in times of heated, often blind prejudice. And both revues hit at a number of the ongoing problems of the day, particularly those on the domestic front. It was no longer necessary to look beyond the borders to see organized manifestations of fascist, specifically Nazi, activity: Henlein's thinly disguised Nazi movement in the Sudetenland was becoming an ever-increasing force agitating for autonomy of the German population along the borders. At the same time both revues also contained numerous skits and production numbers that were relatively if not completely free of tendentiousness.

The 1934–35 season had been a strained and exhausting one. Voskovec and Werich had their fill of confrontations and decided to give up their theatre for the following season. But many people in the cultural world, including Karel Čapek, urged them to reopen their theatre in the fall of 1935 as, in effect, a service to the country. They did so with another original, non-revue work, *The Rag Ballad* (Balada z hadrů), in a smaller, rented theatre. With a smaller company and a smaller budget than usual, they deliberately keyed the production toward a tighter, more intimate, more poetic form while once again returning to the arena of political strife and contention.

Rag Ballad was a relatively serious, lyrical study of the rebel poet François Villon, who embodied Voskovec and Werich's continued battle for social justice and for artistic freedom in the face of what they called 'cultural fascism.' Comedy and song were not eliminated but were deemphasized and integrated into the main line of the action, which presented Villon as a defier of corrupt authority and a fighter for the rights of the underprivileged masses. Voskovec (in one of our interviews) looked back on the play, which had the longest run of all their productions, with mixed feelings. In retrospect he thought that they had lost something of their comic perspective and had allowed the production to get a bit heavy-handed and even sentimental. At the same time he recalled it as a beautiful production, the best that Honzl ever directed, with undeniable charm in the creation of a romantic past within a framework of pure theatricality.

The play begins in the present with a group of destitute people bedding down for the night. One of them is a student, another is an actor with a bag of old costumes and small props. They begin trying on the costumes (mainly to keep warm) and soon get caught up in the spell of make-believe. The student suggests that they improvise a play on Villon. The lights change and the characters find themselves in Villon's Paris, with new identities. The action concerns a rather one-sided conflict between the greed and corruption of establishment power, and Villon's efforts to assert the rights of the oppressed, anonymous people, as well as his own freedom of expression.

Despite the occasional shrillness and preachiness of the work, its overall quality was still comic and gay; and despite the occasional seriousness of its indictment, it was essentially optimistic in its faith in people and in the future, as the remarks of Voskovec and Werich at the time suggested:

> In today's abominable carnival of dictators, monstrous wealth and more than medieval misery . . . in the grotesque inequality between miracles of scientific reason and the depths of political fanaticism . . . there again appears to us hope for a new social order, which promises social justice as a reward to the world for the sufferings of these days.[17]

Their next production was another, more notable attempt to break away from aggressive satire, to get back to more nearly pure theatrical values, and to mount more of a spectacle than was possible in the small theatre they had used the previous year. The result, back once more in their large theatre, was *Heaven on Earth* (Nebe na zemi, September 1936) in which the central action concerned Jupiter's visit to earth and his disenchanted recoil from it. Voskovec and Werich were attracted to the roles of two notorious swindlers and built up these roles in the play.

They were aiming at a literally 'liberated' theatre, with the quality of Renaissance farce, but despite all their efforts and despite an elaborate production, it was not a success. A serious problem was the public's resentment of Voskovec and Werich playing cynical confidence men rather than embodiments of guileless, vulnerable humanity.

With the relative failure of *Heaven on Earth*, Voskovec and Werich needed a new play quickly. Their new work, *Heads or Tails* (Rub a líc, December 1936), returned to the realities of their own day, this time in an action that was a direct image of contemporary events, and that had a degree of realistic plotting that placed the work at the opposite pole from most of their previous revues. But for the interjected song and dance numbers and the several comic interludes of the leads, the work is essentially a well-constructed social drama dealing with the economic crisis, exploited and striking workers, and a threatened putsch that is foiled only at the last minute. *Heads or Tails* added elements of fascist demagoguery and an attempted takeover of government, as well as allusions to other contemporary events such as the Spanish civil war.[18]

Several of the previous works dealt with the people as gullible victims, usually off stage. In *Heads or Tails*, on the other hand, the people are the central characters, striking factory workmen who, far from being gullible or victims, ultimately save the nation from a fascist plot to take over the government. Moreover, whereas the earlier political works were strongly negative in their satire, *Heads or Tails* stresses the positive strength of democratic forces, marking a significant turn by Voskovec and Werich, which held steady in their two subsequent and final works. The time had come to stand up for those elements of society worth preserving and affirming, to rally such forces, to construct a stage action that expressed inspiration and optimism, while still accompanied by plenty of hot jazz, thematically integrated, metaphorical, story-telling ballet, and vigorous, march-like music to lyrics that stressed militant resistance to aggression.

Big Bertha (Těžká Barbora), which opened what was to be their final season in November 1937, closely followed the positive pattern of *Heads or Tails* but with several important exceptions. First, although the focus was again on a national problem, the threat was not solely from domestic forces but from the increasingly naked territorial ambitions of Germany. The reality treated by Voskovec and Werich was the patent conspiracy between Hitler and the Sudeten Nazi forces led by Konrad Henlein to force the annexation of the Czech border lands to Germany. The second important difference in *Big Bertha* was that Voskovec and Werich created a distanced, metaphoric action rather than a directly realistic one to embody the situation, which allowed more opportunity for humor and exotic charm than was possible in *Heads or Tails*.

They set the action in a mythical land of Eidam several centuries earlier and sought an atmosphere of 'old nursery rhymes or colored medieval woodcuts.'[19] Eidam, which stands for Czechoslovakia, is represented as a peaceful, rural land whose main product is cheese. Its neighbor, Yberlant (Germany), is conspiring with certain traitorous Eidamese to arrange a provocation that will justify the military takeover of Eidamese lands by Yberlant. Voskovec and Werich, once again centrally involved in the action, play two mercenaries in the Yberlant army who become entangled in the conspiracy; they accidentally gain possession of a small cannon ('Big Bertha') that was to be the crucial device in the planned provocation. Ultimately they raise an alarm as the invasion begins and help the people to repel the invaders. The decisive weapon in their victory is 'Big Bertha,' loaded with the hard cheeses of the Eidamese.

The fundamental action is of course analogous to that of *Heads or Tails*: a massive threat to the integrity of a nation is averted by cooperative, militant resistance of the people, who again become the heroes. But this time the people are treated with more humor and presented with greater color and variety than they were in *Heads or Tails*. *Big Bertha* is probably the most satisfying of the politically oriented quasi-revues, as *Golem* was of the Jazz Revues. The plot is particularly well constructed, sufficiently developed without the excessive complications that beset many of the previous plays. A particularly interesting aspect of this work was that the characters played by Voskovec and Werich became more actively instrumental in the plot as well as tougher, shrewder, and more enterprising than they had ever been before. This change, I believe, goes along with their move toward a more militant affirmation of values.

The wit and high-spirited optimism in the face of danger that characterized *Big Bertha* was sustained in *A Fist in the Eye* (Pěst na oko, April 1938) in which Voskovec and Werich recapitulated the themes of their last several productions within a mature version of their *Vest Pocket Revue* format. Almost as if they sensed that it might be their last free chance to do the type of theatre closest to them, they reverted to the form with which they began, a combination of comic sketches, bright music, song and dance, and forestage improvisations. Now the combination was clearly unified by underlying motifs, the individual elements were sophisticated and integrated, and the topical relevance of the total work was squarely on target. The handwriting on the wall became unmistakable in March 1938 with Hitler's annexation of Austria, Czechoslovakia's southern neighbor. The Sudeten Germans under Henlein were making ever more flagrant demands for territorial autonomy and even for union with Germany. And there were elements of passivity and even defeatism within the country. The times called for a collective stiffening of spirit, and that is exactly what *A Fist in the Eye* provided. The basic theme was once again the significance of the common man and the idea, as expressed in the central song, that 'It All Depends on Us.'

Voskovec and Werich once again employed the theatre as a framing element. The production began by showing the Liberated Theatre itself in a production of *Julius Caesar*. Werich entered as a legal executor named Josef Dionysos, who was there to settle various debts of the theatre. In a discussion with Voskovec, who in effect played himself, Werich–Dionysos was revealed as a fan of the theatre who begins to make suggestions for their repertoire. He stresses that more should be made of the ordinary man throughout history: not Caesars and monumental façades, but the people who, like stage braces, support those façades. The rest of the production explores that metaphor in a series of comic satiric sketches which demonstrate as blatantly as a fist in the eye the reality behind the surface of celebrated events: the decisive element in history is not the 'great man' but the ordinary, anonymous citizen.

An equally significant point was that power is essentially a figment and that one Caesar more or less makes little difference. The final production number had the entire company on stage, now in their identity as actors, not characters, joining with the audience in the last chorus of 'It All Depends on Us,' a number with the quality of a dynamic march in swing rhythm:

> To live like people, have joy from work –
> After all, it's up to us.
> To think freely, take care of traitors
> Depends on us.
> To defend our truth and judge by truth,
> After all, it's up to us,
> Not to fear truth but believe in truth,
> To fight for truth
> And win with truth
> Depends on us.[20]

Before they closed for a brief vacation that summer, Voskovec and Werich alternated *A Fist in the Eye* with *Big Bertha*. It is unlikely that any theatre anywhere ever achieved a greater mass popularity and relevance than their Liberated Theatre during those pre-Munich days of growing crisis. The Liberated Theatre became, in fact, the National Theatre. But the fall of the First Republic and the castration of Czechoslovakia followed the Munich capitulations at the end of September 1938. The dismembered, impotent Second Republic lasted until the following March, when the country became an occupied Protectorate of Germany.

In the meantime, Voskovec and Werich made half-hearted attempts to stage a revised version of one of their early adaptations, *Having a Spree*, but by then the government and ministries were filled by officials who could be counted on not to offend Germany. The production was to open on November 11, 1938, but on November 4 a decree from the Ministry of the Interior cancelled the theatre's license. The Liberated Theatre of Voskovec and Werich ceased to exist. Two months later Voskovec and Werich arrived by liner in New York harbor. They stayed in the United States until the end of the war, occasionally performing for Czech audiences, broadcasting overseas for the Office of War Information, and appearing very effectively, in English, in Margaret Webster's 1945 Broadway production of Shakespeare's *The Tempest* as the two clowns, Stefano and Trinculo.

They returned separately to liberated Czechoslovakia, Werich in early fall 1945, Voskovec in 1946. Their Liberated Theatre was formally resurrected, but except for a revival of *A Fist in the Eye*, the previously indivisible duo never performed together on stage again in one of their own creations. Their final collaboration was in an adaptation of *Finian's Rainbow* in 1948, directed by Voskovec and starring Werich. It opened shortly after the February takeover of the government by the Communist Party and the conversion of the Czechoslovak Republic into the Czechoslovak Socialist Republic. Voskovec left Czechoslovakia that same year, but Werich remained in Czechoslovakia, where he continued to appear on the stage, in film, and in television. He was awarded the official title of National Artist in 1963; more important, he remained hugely popular with the public. Voskovec, after heading his own theatre in Paris for a few years, returned to the United States and was steadily active as a leading and featured player on stage, in film, and in television, with his first name Anglicized to George. Jan Werich died in Prague in 1980. George Voskovec died in California in 1981.

* * *

It is doubtful that any more appropriate tribute to their theatre and its significance was ever composed than one by Václav Holzknecht, a contemporary, in the late 1950s:

> The intoxication lasted for slightly less than twelve years: successes, battles, fame, a rapid succession of strong impressions; they achieved a theatre that was once again a tribunal of public concern, as in the time of Aristophanes. And if Achilles when confronted with the choice between a long life without glory and a short one with glory unhesitatingly chose a short and glorious life, theirs became Achilles' lot. What if their era was a short one? They created it in the time of their youth, in the peak flowering of their personalities, in the period of their greatest personal good fortune, when a man radiates the most intense light, and they were enveloped with popularity, love, and fame. Today it is completely finished. There remains but a memory of an enchanting, new, brave theatre that couldn't be repeated, imitated, or even transferred elsewhere. It was anchored in its own time and in the youth of its creators. And so it became a part of history and a legend. And those who experienced them will never forget them.[21]

Only one point in this eloquent tribute is disputable. V + W's prototypal revues *were* 'imitated' countless times by youthful ensembles from the war years onward. Among their descendants were some of the small, unconventional studio theatres of the late 1950s and 1960s. Two of them, the Semafor and Ypsilon theatres, are still prominent in the new millennium.

3

E. F. BURIAN

E. F. Burian embodied still another type of creative personality in the inter-war era of the 1920s and 1930s. Classically educated K. H. Hilar produced the most creative, apolitical work done on the large, subsidized stages during the first Republic. Remarkably gifted student amateurs, Voskovec and Werich found the exact pulse of their times and achieved huge success in their very own *commercial* theatre, which shied away from any orthodox political commitment even as it became increasingly supportive of the leftist anti-fascist front. Distinct from all three, E. F. Burian was a highly trained musician who eventually created his own marginally financed theatre company in improvised quarters; here he championed the autonomy of art and attracted international attention with his innovative staging, even as he consciously dedicated his efforts to the Marxist-Leninist cause.

Emil František Burian, who was to become the leading avant-garde director in the Czech theatre of the 1930s, was born in 1904, the son of Emil Burian, a leading baritone of Prague's National Theatre Opera, and his wife Vlasta (née Katláková), a teacher of singing. His uncle was Karel Burian, a concert tenor. The musical environment established by his family was sustained in Burian's education: he graduated from the Prague Conservatory and subsequently completed a master's study in composition in Prague under the Czech composer J. B. Foerster. Burian eventually composed seven operas, including one at the National Theatre (*Before Sunrise*, 1925), numerous ballets and chamber works, and most of the music for his theatre productions.

If the roots of Burian's general creativity may be found in music, the roots of his social philosophy may be found in Marxism: in 1923, while still a student, Burian became a member of the Czech Communist Party. In the years of his peak theatrical activity, 1933–38, when Burian's D Theatre achieved international recognition, his art and ideology often reinforced each other, but just as often they produced conflicting tensions and, at least on one occasion, a serious crisis of conscience. His career, like that of V + W, was interrupted by World War II but continued after it. Here, I shall concentrate on his prewar activity, which represents the peak of his achievements.[1]

Burian's involvement in theatre began in 1926 when he joined the Liberated Theatre of Prague as a musician and incidental actor. The Liberated Theatre, co-directed by Jiří Frejka and Jindřich Honzl, was at that time a semiprofessional group under the influence of both the Soviet and French avant-garde. The Soviet influence was mainly evident in staging, the French in texts: Apollinaire, Cocteau, and Ribemont-Dessaignes were particular favorites. Administratively, the Liberated Theatre was a casual offshoot of Devětsil, a Czech cultural group of literati, architects, musicians, and other artists, most of whom were inspired by recently acquired national independence and the vigorous flow of fresh ideas and artistic movements from east and west after two centuries of relative stagnancy if not oppression within the Habsburg Empire. Particularly inspiring to many in Devětsil was the ideal they felt present in the youthful freshness of Soviet Communism. It was an era of fertile crossbreeding, when communism and surrealism (or futurism or poetism) were regarded as complementary rather than irreconcilable.

April 1927 was an especially auspicious month, a watershed in the evolution of modern Czech theatre. The uneasy collaboration between Honzl and Frejka dissolved, with Honzl taking charge of the Liberated Theatre and Frejka going on to form new groups. That same month, as described in the previous chapter, Voskovec and Werich opened their *Vest Pocket Revue*. Eventually Voskovec and Werich joined the Liberated Theatre, by the fall of 1929 took it over entirely, and it went on to become the single most popular theatre in Czechoslovakia's First Republic.

In the meantime, still in April 1927, E. F. Burian joined Frejka in breaking with Honzl and became one of Frejka's chief actors; not the least of his roles was Oedipus in Cocteau's *Infernal Machine* in 1928. More important, in April 1927, Burian composed and directed the first of his Voiceband productions as part of Frejka's Theatre Dada repertoire. Burian's Voiceband was a choral rendition of poetry based on the harmonic and rhythmic syncopations of jazz, a wedding of poetic text and musical expression, but without formal musical notation, for Burian wanted greater freedom and variety of vocal expression, including hissing, whistling, and other nontraditional vocalization, with percussion accompaniment. As the singular form evolved over the years, Burian added stage lighting, a certain amount of blocking, and eventually incorporated the principle of the Voiceband – musically articulated and shaped poetry – into a number of more traditionally staged productions.

In 1929, after two years of cooperative effort, Burian and Frejka went their separate ways. Frejka subsequently joined the establishment theatre, becoming a directorial assistant to the celebrated K. H. Hilar at the National Theatre in 1930 and eventually one of its trio of director-producers. Burian was hired as director of the studio branch of the State Theatre in Brno, the capital of Moravia; it was to be Burian's first real experience as a director of fully staged theatre productions. Coincidentally, Honzl was hired as a director for the main stage of the same State Theatre, but the two former colleagues had little to do with each other. Two years later, in 1931, Honzl rejoined Voskovec and Werich's Liberated Theatre in Prague as their director, but Burian remained in the Moravian province until 1932, spending the 1930–31 season in Olomouc before returning to Brno for the 1931–32 season.

Burian's productions during his three years away from Prague formed an eclectic cluster: boulevard comedy and melodrama, revivals of classics, slightly aged avant-garde (Maeterlinck, Synge, O'Neill) and several Voice-band recitals of poetry. He also appeared several times as an actor, including a role in a Brno production subheaded 'Living Newspaper,' clearly an echo of work being done by the Soviet theatre and by Piscator in Germany. More telling indications of Burian's leftist sympathies were evident in his occasional participation in political meetings and related activities of local Communist organizations, and in his productions of Brecht's *Threepenny Opera* (March 1930) and several contemporary works from the Czech left, such as Vítězslav Nezval's *Lovers from the Kiosk*, Burian's last production in Brno, in May 1932.

Burian's stance *vis-à-vis* the claims of art and politics was at best an unsettled matter and suggests an ongoing conflict of allegiances that surfaced repeatedly in his career, a conflict no doubt heightened and complicated by what even sympathetic critics referred to as Burian's sizeable artistic ego. In 1930, while a fledgling director in Brno, he wrote 'Dynamické divadlo' (Dynamic Theatre), a study in which he championed the priorities of artistry in relation to extra-aesthetic, e.g., political or tendentious, values. A sampling from the article reveals attitudes that were subsequently criticized by Czech leftist critics as bourgeois remnants of Tairov and the 1920s avant-garde:

> Before anything else, theatre is highly artistic in essence: its form or style is its decisive feature. . . . Theatre is relevant not because it presents [topical plays] but because it is sympathetic, because it provokes a human's nervous system to fellow activity. . . . Theatre is a thing of form and style. . . . As a result of theatre's becoming occupied by other than artistic questions, of dramatists and directors raising tendentiousness above creativity . . . evolution was delayed and theatre was being killed. . . . Expressive form must not be sacrificed to [biased agendas]. And then: the stage is life for its own sake . . . its boards are not life but rather a stage and nothing but a stage. And neither is theatre a political tribunal. . . . Every end or objective beyond the stage is inappropriate in theatre.[2]

Despite such pronouncements, Burian was at root also committed to the cause of militant protest against bourgeois values, capitalism, and the class structure supported by those forces. Events from 1929 to 1932 undoubtedly intensified his conviction of the rightness of the Marxist critique of the profit system: the worldwide depression had caused massive unemployment in Czechoslovakia, and reactionary forces if not Fascism were becoming increasingly powerful in the nation. Although Czechoslovakia under Presidents Masaryk and Beneš remained an island of liberal democracy in central Europe and the Communist Party was legally recognized and had members in Parliament, the prevailing strength remained in the hands of those hostile to any threat to free enterprise.

Burian returned to Prague in the fall of 1932 but could find only incidental work as a musician or director. It became clear to him that if he wanted to direct his kind of production, he would have to start his own theatre. He assembled a small group of intensely dedicated although largely amateur performers, rented what had been a small concert chamber (The Mozarteum) in downtown Prague, transformed it into a small, minimally equipped proscenium theatre, and tried to raise enough money to begin operations. Finally, with the crucial aid of a loan from Burian's mother, the theatre opened with an episodic, documentary revue, *Life in our Days*, based on a radio script by Erich Kästner. The date was September 16, 1933, less than a month before V + W opened their *Ass and Shadow*. The focus of the respective plays indicates a difference between the two theatres: *Ass and Shadow* confronts the threat of Hitler's Germany; *Life in our Days*, capitalistic oppression of the masses.

Eighteen people made up the theatre, including Burian, who provided the music on a borrowed, upright piano and also changed gels on the two spotlights the theatre possessed. A contemporary leftist critic called it the poorest theatre in Prague in terms of money, but the richest in its united élan for the work ahead.

The name of the theatre, D34, was composed of two elements, D representing the initial letter of the Czech word for theatre (Divadlo) and the number representing the year to come; the number would change each season. Burian's comments in a leaflet distributed on the day of the opening expand on the significance of the theatre's name and reveal the orientation of his enterprise:

> The numbers indicate the incessant change of actualities that the theatre will serve. The abbreviation D is for us an aggressive title, for we will be an aggressive theatre. The abbreviation D can equally stand for today as well as for laborer, theatre as well as the masses, drama as well as history. [Each of these terms begins with the letter D in Czech.][3]

In strong contrast to his statements on the autonomy of art in 'Dynamic Theatre,' other remarks and polemics by Burian just prior to and after the opening of his theatre reveal his de-emphasis of sheer artistry and a non-tendential theatre in favor of a position that dismissed so-called 'pure' art, totally rejected the conservative sociopolitical orientation and theatrical methods of the establishment theatres, decried the failure of his former avant-garde colleagues to attack the bourgeois establishment instead of amusing it, and stressed the need of a theatrical tribunal for the masses. Burian declared that his theatre would be at the center of society and categorically aligned it with the Communist critique of that society. One direct citation from May 1933 may stand for many others:

> It will be a political theatre. . . . primarily against fascism and cultural reactionism. . . . For a dramaturgic foundation, derived from a philosophic position of dialectical materialism, I plan a repertoire with an exclusively class meaning. For a core I will have the contemporary repertoire of Russian theatres. Beyond German revolutionary plays I will put into the repertoire everything in Czech literature that arose from the futile expectation of a hearing in our official theatres, and then those Czech works that will be inspired by my political theatre tribunal.[4]

Numerous assertions in that letter and in other similar statements were either to be modified or never realized, most notably the expectation of new plays sparked by his efforts. Nevertheless, the sincerity under the rhetoric was genuine, and there is no question that Burian, a product of the cultivated bourgeoisie, was consistent in damning the ills of the class system and capitalist exploitation. But what Burian's declarations at the time do not reveal is that his previously expressed feelings about the autonomy of art were never really abandoned. Eventually, he came to experience the anguish of attempting to serve two strongly conflicting ideals.

* * *

The theatre which began in 1933 as D34 lasted until March 1941 when, as D41, it was closed by the Gestapo and Burian sent to a concentration camp. The objective data about the theatre may be indicated briefly. Approximately seventy-five productions were mounted, ranging in scope from evenings of poetry presented by a few readers to relatively elaborate productions with casts of twenty or more. The number of performances varied from fewer than ten to over a hundred, with forty being an approximate average. (The performances of pure poetry had only one to four reprises.) As in V + W's Liberated Theatre, the productions were performed serially rather than as alternating repertoire, except for special occasions when a number of plays were presented in a one- or two-week period.

More than two-thirds of the productions occurred within the very limited space of the Mozarteum, which could seat a maximum of 387 spectators in front of a proscenium stage 45 inches above the flat seating floor. It was a small stage measuring 20 feet wide in the proscenium opening, 15 feet deep from the curtain line, and had a maximum height of only 14.5 feet. Additional space in front of the curtain line produced a total acting area of 360 square feet.

The company began with fewer than twenty members, including technical and administrative personnel; eventually it grew to over fifty, including: sixteen actors evenly divided between male and female; six to eleven musicians; three to seven design and technical staff; six administrative personnel; and, notably, but one director. It was an extremely stable company with very little turnover.

The theatre was not subsidized until 1938, when it began to receive a small amount from the state. Because of its shoestring budgets and the willingness of its personnel to work for minimal salaries, it could survive on less than 50 percent attendance. Despite chronic financial crises, Burian's goal was a cultural center, which he very nearly achieved with evenings of poetry, exhibitions of painting and sculpture, dance recitals, and lectures, as well as with the publication of a small but stimulating periodical bearing the same name as the theatre each season. It served as a program of most of the productions and also contained discussion of the plays, reports of related theatre activities, excerpts of poetry, and correspondence with the theatre's public. Burian and his chief technical designer, Miroslav Kouřil, also drew up three different plans for a multi-theatre complex and cultural center to be known as The Theatre of Work (Divadlo Práce). Although the projects never materialized, they did lead to the creation of a theatre laboratory for technical experimentation as an adjunct to the theatre.

The relationship between Burian and his actors was based on their commitment to a theatre of social engagement, communist in all but official designation. Burian ran a well-organized, disciplined collective. Party membership was not a prerequisite, but agreement with the 'progressive' cause was taken for granted, and all meetings ended with the singing of the *Internationale*. In theory, and to some extent in practice, administrative and logistical decisions were made by committee, but there was never any question that the chief was Burian.

Burian's view of acting was quite simply that of an artist toward one of his most valuable materials: actors could communicate the equivalent of dozens of pages of a novel by a gesture, pitch of voice, or facial expression, but they were to be nameless and shapeable means toward the director-composer's end. The director, according to Burian, is the functional center that determines the stream of action in this theatre. 'It is the director . . . who stands above all the elements, commands them, composes or, better, provides the instrumentation of a theatrical score in precise time, tempo, color, tone, harmony, and polyphonal action.'[5] It is a description that could have come from the lips of not only Hilar, but also Craig, Reinhardt, Meyerhold, or

Tairov, to name only the most illustrious of twentieth-century theatre artists preceding Burian.

In practice, however, according to the testimony of his surviving actors whom I interviewed, Burian never forced the actor to a given interpretation, did not treat his actors as marionettes, was remarkably patient and kind with them, and demonstrated exactly what he wanted only as a last resort, preferring to encourage the actors to find their own way toward the goal he sought. Nevertheless, he took pains to explain the approach to each production and what he wanted by way of interpretation. He preferred to work on stage quite early, taking only one preliminary session for discussion. He never used a *Regiebuch*, but had near total recall of blocking and other directions. He insisted on tightly disciplined, systematic rehearsals, and performances without variations, admitting that he no longer acted because he could not stand its lack of variation or improvisation. In these and other respects, of course, he resembled a conductor of an orchestra. Indeed, one of his special rehearsal techniques was to play the piano in order to illustrate or prompt what he wanted in the rhythm and tone of a speech or movement, or scene as a whole.

One of his assistants, later a great director, Alfred Radok, described to me some of the daily routine in Burian's company.[6] All actors were present at all rehearsals, even when they were not cast in the play. Rehearsals were preceded by an hour or more of vocal and dance work, the vocal often under the direction of Burian or his mother, the dance under their choreographer. Rehearsals had no set limit; everyone remained as long as Burian held out, and his energy, stamina, and élan were legendary. He would normally come to the theatre early in the morning in order to spend an hour working on the composition of an opera or other musical piece. Another hour was devoted to administrative details, and rehearsals began at 10 a.m.

Particularly noteworthy was his practice of having all rehearsals, except perhaps the very first few, conducted with full lighting and cues in order to assure the fully integrated, delicately controlled effects for which he became celebrated. His emphasis on subtle, musically shaped work with lighting had a counterpart in his stress on vocal control and precise articulation, which eventually produced a distinct speech style in most of his actors and created difficulties for some of them when they worked in other theatres later.

Production techniques remained austere for the most part, partly because of the extremely limited space and facilities, but more importantly because of Burian's elemental antipathy to naturalism and his affinity for spare, constructivist settings of authentic, often unfinished materials: lumber, ropes, straw, bare metal, coarse fabrics. This stylistic tendency had more than one cause: spatial and budgetary limitations, Soviet models, but also Burian's intense interest in the traditions of folk theatre.

* * *

Burian's handling of texts paralleled his approach to production: the writer, like the actor, was significant but secondary, a tributary artist. A striking fact is that more than one-third of Burian's productions were based on non-dramatic texts which he composed into scenarios. Moreover, it was a rare play that he did not radically edit or adapt. Part of his attitude is expressed in the following: 'I know of nothing in literature that could not be dramatically expressed. . . . But I know of many theatre plays that are unplayable on stage even though they were written for it.'[7] One of Burian's chronic laments was the lack of new scripts suitable to his vision of socially meaningful theatre, but he was not referring to completed, self-sufficient works. His premise seemed to be that the very nature of traditional dramatic construction distorted the vision of the author. He offered the following advice to potential playwrights for his theatre:

> Let the poet and the prose writer not be bound by any 'rules' other than those given by their own creative methods. First of all, let them write librettos with the full realization that librettos are what we're concerned with, and that in no way can they create the definitive form of a stage piece at their desks. With that understanding, the so-called violation of the author by the director will be irrelevant . . . and their relation will be that of librettist and composer.[8]

'Librettos' or scenario-like texts not only enabled Burian to communicate more fully the poetic essence that he found in a given work, but also allowed for greater emphasis on a particular ideological slant, whether or not intended by the original author. In the final analysis, however, ideological motivation often seemed secondary to Burian's artistic or ego-centered motivation of confronting traditional interpretations of works with his own sense of their particular truth or of using literary raw material in order to communicate his own statement or 'directorial handwriting.' Above all he wanted to express himself, to create a theatrical performance as a 'sovereignly personal expression' of his own vision. The real subject of Burian's productions was Burian himself: he is the source of everything revealed in his work, 'the noetic intermediary between the spectator and material reality.'[9] Other symptoms of the inherently romantic nature of Burian's artistry were noted by Jan Grossman when he surveyed the works especially favored by Burian in his period of ripest creativity, 1935–38:

> [They] are always highly emotive, rather spread out than concise, internally dynamic, as if vibrant. The hero is a highly individualized figure . . . in conflict with ordered society . . . who has dreams both day and night, hallucinates, and builds an unusually complex life, often on the border of the seeming and the real.[10]

47

The paradoxical point of Burian's 'dramatizations' is that the results were not dramatizations in the sense of tightly knit incidents connected to a central action, but works with a looser structure of relatively isolated but highly expressive events, which were often supplemented by additional writings by the same or other authors. In short, as Grossman observed, 'It's not a matter of the dramatization of an epic or lyric but of epicizing and lyricizing the theatre.'

Given Burian's fundamental subjectivity in handling texts and in staging them, it is not surprising that some of his productions became expressionistic or surrealistic in their effect. This characteristic of his work appeared intermittently and did not become fully evident until the later 1930s. But by that time, ironically, the criteria of Socialist Realism had begun to be applied by communist critics, and a clash was inevitable.

Possibilities of such problems seemed remote in the early days of Burian's new theatre. In theme and form the productions of D34 and D35 were in the Piscatorian vein and generally consistent with Burian's heavily politicized statements prior to the opening of D34. Whether semi-documentary assemblages of current events, original plays, 'dramatizations' of novels, or reworkings of classics (*Merchant of Venice*, *The Miser*, *The Threepenny Opera*), they stressed class conflict and capitalist exploitation with the schematism and crude caricature of agitprop theatre. The staging was simple in the extreme, but Burian already began to make occasional use of projections and a montage principle in textual adaptations and staging. These, however, were without the subjective lyricism that later developed in his work.

A witty parody of these early productions formed part of Voskovec and Werich's *Keep Smiling* revue in the Liberated Theatre in January 1935. Allowing for comic exaggeration, the following fragment provides a useful impression of this phase of Burian's work:

> The interior of a constructivistic submarine.
>
> Scene 1.
> The Miser, the Captain, Secretary, Tubercular Young Man, Proletarian Young Woman, the Miser's Daughter, Members of the Crew. All enter through the audience, line up on stage, and sing to the audience: the melody is taken from *Threepenny Opera*:
>
> We're here to present
> Topical theatre
> We'll illustrate the class struggle
> As we see it.
>
> We'll aim spotlights at each other
> And enter from the audience
> The prompter is abolished
> The critics will love it.

Lighting cables litter the floor
A fig for stage flats
Cheers for bare platforms
Away with the curtain.

We'll begin at the beginning
And play to the end
Little Emil has written some lines
The rest is from *The Miser*.[11]

By 1935, however, Burian's productions moved away from their Piscator-like, agitational phase and began to reveal a more emotive, lyrical tone. It is likely that the accords achieved between Czechoslovakia and the Soviet Union in 1934–35, plus the creation of a united front against Fascism, contributed to Burian's shift away from narrow propaganda and toward fuller artistry.

A landmark production uniting an ideologically based but humanistic theme with complex artistic expression was *War* (Vojna, January 1935). Basing his text on a collection of traditional Czech folk verse and setting much of it to his own music, he produced a powerful protest against war, with indirect but telling allusions to class struggle and economic exploitation. Drawing on the heritage of his Voiceband, he constructed a montage of scenes from village life dealing with such traditional rites as carnival, a wedding, army recruitment, and the parting of loved ones: the opening scene of carnival is balanced by the final scene of soldiers bearing home the body of their comrade and denouncing war. The authentic flavor of Burian's text was enriched by the imaginativeness of the production. Using the most ordinary materials, wooden platforms, lathing, hemp rope, straw, and thatched panels, Burian created a setting that captured the feel of the folk environment without a trace of naturalism but with great theatrical reality. Kouřil, the designer, said that they had to think realistically but achieve poetic results. On the relatively bare stage, they blended voices, choreographed movement, and music with lighting that functioned dynamically and rhythmically, softening the harsh wooden structures, casting shadows through the lathing, underscoring the emotiveness of the scenes. This is how Burian described the production:

> In its structure it is actually a ballet and poetic suite in a few movements. Not only dancers' feet but also words and verses dance in it – voice on voice and rhyme on rhyme, there are turns of assonance and leaps of metaphor. . . . The style of *War* demonstrated clean stage work . . . purified of feudal painted scenery . . . clean space for a poet.[12]

Burian's stage was rarely curtained; instead, the audience saw the stage setting when they entered. Then the stage manager would hit a gong, the lights would come up, and the stage was miraculously transformed. The highly selective settings were marked by a sense of stylistic composition, often metaphoric in form or choice of detail, often colorful, but it was in lighting and its extension in projections that Burian's theatre achieved its most distinctive expressive effects. For Burian, light was the heart of the stage and created its fluid space; lighting expressed not only external reality but also the state of the soul. Burian's work with lighting culminated in the Theatregraph, which he employed in several productions that I shall describe. It was a system of lighting, static and filmed projections, and special projection surfaces that, in conjunction with living actors, produced a synthesis further enriched by music and other sound-effects.

Whether or not they employed projections, the productions usually took the form of cinema-like montages formed on musical principles of rhythm, harmony, counterpoint. Burian himself referred to music as the hidden law of the stage, present even when it is not played by instruments. It is present not only in the text but also in mime, in lighting, in the rhythm of space, in pauses, in the melody of speech.

Jan Mukařovský, the structuralist theorist, a close observer and devotee of Burian's theatre, called music the basis of the order that Burian imposed on the potential chaos of theatre. Indeed, it was on the basis of Burian's productions that Mukařovský articulated a basic statement of structuralism as applied to theatre:

> A modern stage work appears as a very complex structure . . . that eagerly absorbs everything available from contemporary technology and other arts, but usually in order to apply it as a contrasting force: film is used to set physical reality in contrast to a nonmaterial image, a megaphone confronts natural sound with reproduced sound, the sword of a spotlight beam severs the continuity of three-dimensional space. . . . The result is that the artistic construction of today's stage work has the characteristics of a process that is protean in its changeability, that consists of a constant regrouping of elements, an agitated exchange of dominants, a wiping out of borders between drama and allied forms (revue, dance, acrobatics, etc.).[13]

Burian's productions based on poetry continued to be among his most striking, although some of them began to draw leftist criticism because of their increasing subjectivity and inclination toward surrealism, for example his productions based on the arch-romantic poetry of K. H. Mácha, *May* (April 1935), *Neither Swan nor Moon* (Ani labut', ani luna, June 1936), and *The Executioner* (Kat, June 1936).

Burian had less difficulty with a more major production significant for its fusion of ideology and creative staging, his adaptation of Beaumarchais's

The Barber of Seville (September 1936). To bring the play up to date as 'a fiery cry of accord and solidarity with the revolution in Spain,'[14] Burian added an entirely new line of action: a series of Spanish folk songs and dances presented by a wandering street singer and a chorus to evoke the revolutionary atmosphere of Spain. One completely added sequence, which illustrates the kind of supplemental, metaphoric dramaturgy practiced by Burian, was intended to echo the death of García Lorca: a special solo dance by a militant revolutionary occurred on a small, high, up stage platform; the dance was punctuated by shots, and the dancer collapsed to the floor.

* * *

Four months after the premiere of *The Barber of Seville*, Burian staged his version of Pushkin's *Eugene Onegin* (1937), in what was the most fully evolved form of his Theatregraph system of integrated lighting, projections, and live action. He had made incidental use of slide projections as early as his first production in D34, and by the spring of 1935 had begun to use occasional filmed projection as well. The first production to employ the more complex Theatregraph system was his version of Wedekind's *Spring's Awakening* in 1936.

Two things distinguished Theatregraph from ordinary projection systems in theatre. The chief technical innovation was the use of a scrim covering the entire front of the stage and serving as the primary projection surface, thus producing a simultaneous vision of projected images on the frontal scrim with live action behind it. A small, opaque, supplementary projection screen was on the stage itself, dedicated to a separate slide projector in the wings. What is often not understood about the system is that projections were not constantly employed but were used only at selected dramatic moments. In any case, the actors performed behind the scrim, with specially designed lighting that picked out only portions of the scene for illumination, making the effect of the scrim virtually disappear but still retaining its property of providing a slightly diffused visual effect. With the addition of projections, the demands on timing and balancing of lighting intensities were great, but the effect at its best was extraordinary. You could not tell, finally, whether the live actors were in front of, behind, or simply part of the projected image, enveloped in it. The images were not simply illustrational or informational; nor were they at all illusionistic, a naturalistic supplement. They functioned primarily on an emotive, metaphoric level.

> Filmed stage projection is a spatial concern, non-illustrational and non-naturalistic. Film is most valued by the modern stage for its [enlarged] detail. . . . Only detail makes stage montage possible, particularly the detail that is capable of intensifying dramatic conflict to giant proportions, and brings close to the public that which the unaided eye cannot see on the stage. . . . [Similarly,] lighting must

work with details and only seldom with the scene as a whole. The setting must not be naturalistic or illusionistic. . . . The action must be presented fluidly and almost as if in a film montage. Simply everything that functions on the stage must stem from the imagery and musicality of film criteria.[15]

The final distinctive characteristic of Theatregraph was that it used film and slides designed strictly for the given production, not drawn from stock; moreover, it employed filmed images of the very actors in the production, playing off the filmed and 'real' characters in various ways.

Burian used the Theatregraph system in three significant productions: in addition to *Spring's Awakening* and *Onegin*, his adaptation of Goethe's *The Sorrows of Young Werther* (1938). In both *Spring's Awakening* and *Werther*, the projections were clearly supplementary, of fascinating but secondary significance in relation to the more conventional, live action. In both productions it is clear that even though the projections were woven closely to the live action they could have been cut without radically affecting what remained. But that seems not to have been true in *Onegin*, in which the filmed projections and the cinematic nature of Burian's scenario threatened to make film rather than theatre the dominant, essential medium of the production.

A special feature of the *Onegin* mise en scène was a triptych approach to projections on the front scrim. The center section made use of both slides and film projection, sometimes the two together. The two smaller side sections had only slide projection, and, as an exception to the rule, these slide projections were primarily illustrational (a montage of stylized period drawings), whereas the projections on the center section were entirely and consistently for dramatic purposes. Another special feature in *Onegin* was an absolutely bare and level stage floor, but the acting space was flexibly segmented by three black curtains running laterally at different planes in the depth of the stage, thus heightening the possibilities of manipulating dramatic space and having live actors seemingly appear or disappear in the blackness, as if from or into nowhere.

To appreciate the creativity involved in this production, you must study the specially composed scenario created by Burian, the master plan for complex integration of film and stage. Four main sequences were filmed: Onegin's morning toilette, Tatyana's dream, Onegin's duel with Lensky and its aftermath of Olga's wedding, and the ball at Gremin's. All filmed sequences were laboriously shot in 16 mm black and white film on the orchestra floor of the theatre once all seats were removed. The scenario is arranged in three columns: one indicates the filmed, projected images; another indicates the live action and contains live dialogue; a third indicates all music and sound cues, including lines spoken off stage into a microphone. A portion of one sequence, Gremin's ball, illustrates Burian's multimedia method as well as the dominance of the filmed portions, live mime, and music over dialogue or text.

Filmed/Projected Image	Live Action and Dialogue	Music/Sound
469. Previous slide projection out. Tatyana and Gremin waltz toward camera.	Tatyana and Gremin waltz off stage. Onegin remains.	Crescendo
470. Tatyana and Gremin split into two pairs, then more and more pairs. Cross fade to	Onegin gazes at filmed image as if in a trance, and mechanically tears the letter.	Crescendo
471. Onegin tearing the letter.	Tatyana and Gremin dance back on and circle Onegin.	Forte
472. Enlarged detail of Onegin's hands tearing the letter.	As above.	Continued
473. Camera pans to Onegin's feet, where instead of scraps of paper, petals fall.	As above	Continued
474. Onegin takes a step and tramples petals. Cross fade to	Onegin looks at dancing pair as they move way.	Crescendo
475. A rain of confetti.	Onegin starts toward Tatyana but masked dancers waltz between them, dancing around him.[16]	Fortissimo

Essentially metaphoric in its use of detail and juxtaposition, and cinematic in its form – the structure composed of a great many relatively brief 'takes' – *Onegin* marked the furthest extreme of Burian's theatre of synthesis based on musical principles. The production indicates, also, how far Burian had moved from the agitprop topicality of D34. Indeed it is easy to miss the justification of Burian's production of *Onegin* in relation to the ostensible identity of the D Theatre as a 'political tribunal' or as a 'spokesman for the masses.' In this sense, *Onegin* is representative of many Burian productions: one has to squint at least a little in order to perceive the revolutionary or Marxist line. Nevertheless, most of the leftist critics were satisfied that *Onegin*, like *Spring's Awakening*, was condemning a system produced by class exploitation, and attacking the stifling, corrupting pressure of bourgeois values and conventions. And it is true that many of Burian's other productions expressed attitudes and values explicitly in support of orthodox Marxist premises.

Nevertheless, Burian's subjectivity and emotiveness, his incipient romanticism and fascination with expressive forms, were never far below the surface, and a combination of incidents during the 1936–37 season caused him to reveal a number of long suppressed frustrations and resentments stemming from what he considered to be assaults on his integrity as an artist. It was the great crisis of his prewar career and should be considered in any attempt to assess Burian's identity as an avant-garde theatre artist trying to work in accord with ideological principles.

The circumstances producing the crisis included news of the Moscow purge trials that began in August 1936. Closely related to the implications of the trials was the recently sanctioned 'aesthetics' of Socialist Realism propounded in Moscow in 1934, largely accepted by Czech Communist critics and applied intermittently to Burian's productions by 1935. Burian chafed at the imposed criteria of ready intelligibility and hewing to a dogmatic ideological line, both of which seemed designed to frustrate what he considered the intrinsic demands of art. Moreover, Soviet criticism of Meyerhold, long an idealized source of inspiration for Burian, paralleled the oppression implicit in the Moscow trials and in the doctrine of Socialist Realism. Having met Meyerhold during his visit to the Soviet Union in the fall of 1934

Plate 5 E. F. Burian and V. E. Meyerhold during the latter's visit to Prague in the fall of 1936. Photographer unknown.

and hearing of Meyerhold's difficulties at firsthand during the latter's visit to Prague in the fall of 1936 undoubtedly intensified Burian's disturbance (Plate 5). He went out of his way to defend Meyerhold and drew up petitions on his behalf among liberal, artistic circles in Prague, to the point of being accused of hysteria by local Communist critics. Some of Burian's most intense comments were directed against Soviet positions: he dismissed the assumed excellence of Soviet theatre in general and scorned the concept of 'Socialist' Realism as a bluff, declaring that it was really 'Soviet' realism that was being propagated – and rather stupidly propagated because it was not exportable to countries with different conditions, to countries where 'quality' was important.[17]

A particularly painful blow, which Burian must have taken as a personal insult, occurred when photographs of D Theatre productions were ordered to be removed from a Czech cultural exhibit in Moscow in 1937 on the grounds that the theatre was formalistic.

Burian's reaction to these events took several forms. In his non-dramatic writing he raked the tenets and implications of Socialist Realism, angrily mocking its presumptuousness in judging the complexities of artistic creation, and defending the autonomy of art in terms reminiscent of his 1930 comments in 'Dynamic Theatre.' He proceeded to deny the classic Marxist doctrine that class consciousness shapes an artistic work and to reject any criticism of a work of art because the art was hard to understand. His peroration was characteristic:

> He who sees in theatre nothing other than a reflection of life without artistic invention, he who would eliminate from the stage any distinctive theatrical expression of this life, he who isn't happy to be present in the audience during the miracle of the fusion of arts in the synthesis of a more beautiful and better life than the one we live, is an enemy of theatre.[18]

Burian's frustration and anger were not limited to prose essays. In *Hamlet III* (March 1937), his adaptation of Shakespeare and a novel by Jules Laforgue, he presented Hamlet as the epitome of an alienated artist in opposition to a rigid, unfeeling society (Plate 6). The depiction is of course patently autobiographical (or biographical if one applies it to Meyerhold, as well one might). Burian himself said that *Hamlet III* was 'a manifesto for the freedom of artistic expression,' and used Jacques's lines from *As You Like It* as the motto of his play: 'Invest me in my motley. Give me leave / To speak my mind.' Julius Fučík, the leading Communist critic at the time, dismissed *Hamlet III* as an attempt to justify theatrical effects as ends in themselves and to defend art for art's sake, accusations that probably corroborated the feelings of persecution in Burian's mind. 'God forbid,' Burian subsequently wrote, 'that one day an artist whom people thought they could buy for a few

Plate 6 The physical setup for the depiction of Ophelia's drowning from Burian's
production of *Hamlet III* (1937). Photo: M. Hák.

pennies lifted his head and declared art the greatest, uncorruptible, and most
moral possession of all future societies.'[19]

The following season, after several productions that once again seemed
ideologically sounder in terms of their progressive view of society, Burian
staged *Werther* in April 1938, a curious choice, considering the Austrian
Anschluss of the previous month and the mounting tensions that were leading up to the Munich crisis of September. (V + W were producing their
militant *Fist in the Eye* at the time.) In *Werther*, Burian went to the extreme
limits of the romantic subjectivity that had marked many of his plays. He
began his dramatization of this most romantic of stories with its ending,
Werther's suicide, and presented the subsequent action as the product of a
dying man's hallucinations, a shifting, confused state between the seeming
and the real, thus heightening the inherent subjectivity of the original text.
Moreover, he split the Werther character into the living figure of the story
and his dying alter ego, who accompanies the action that is presented. The
particular treatment of the story lent itself superbly, of course, to Burian's
multimedia Theatregraph method, in which dream and reality could be
blended and communicated so effectively by the combination of living actors
and insubstantial, evanescent images.

Burian explained the choice of *Werther* in terms of its author: Goethe had been denounced by the Nazis, which seemed a good reason for the Czechs to honor him. Moreover, Burian was also presumably attacking bourgeois society for killing those who would not serve it. But it is difficult not to view the production as still another form of self-expression in which Burian himself is by implication the outsider, misunderstood, driven to extremity. Moreover, the Meyerhold connection was doubtlessly a factor again: Burian staged *Werther* three months after the close of Meyerhold's theatre in Moscow. It is as if Burian felt compelled to turn inward, to return yet once again to an exposure of his most inner, personal crises as an artist. With *Werther* he reached the limit, and perhaps a catharsis. In no subsequent prewar work is the subjective element – that is, Burian's personal ego – of particular significance.

Slightly earlier in the heartbreaking year of 1938, in January, his staging of Villon's poetry *Paris Plays the Lead* (Paříž hraje prim) was welcomed for its undistorted capturing of the rebel poet's spirit. Burian's attraction to Czech folk material also continued and contributed to the united front against the Nazi threat by championing traditional, national values. At a time when V + W were performing their final two satiric revues, he achieved particular success with his *First Folk Suite* (První lidová suita, June 1938). The following year, after the fall of the first and second Czech Republics, he produced his *Second Folk Suite* (Druhá lidová suita, May 1939). Both productions consisted of three authentic Czech folk plays only slightly adapted by Burian, who, along with his audience, found great appeal and inspiration in their naive wisdom and faith. Burian's remaining prewar productions while his D Theatre was still alive are only of secondary interest except for noting his conscious choice of Czech authors, themes, and poetry, as well as his drift toward more realistic, psychologically based work that foreshadows his postwar career. His own play *Věra Lukášová* (1938) was the best example of this new interest.

In the fall of 1939, D40 began producing in a larger but hardly ideal subterranean concert hall less than a mile from the Mozarteum. In spite of Burian's overt communist affiliation and commitment against Fascism, he and his theatre were permitted to keep performing until March 1941, when the Gestapo arrested him and closed his theatre. Burian spent the rest of the war in concentration camps. One possible explanation for the unusual delay in stopping his work is that the German–Soviet agreement in 1939 may have allowed a certain amount of breathing room for artists even as anti-fascist as Burian had been. Moreover, none of Burian's productions had overtly challenged the status quo of the occupation; any attempt to do so by any theatre would have been suicidal. Like Honzl and Frejka at the time, Burian attempted to sustain Czech culture and morale by stressing works with Czech authors (e.g., Viktor Dyk, K. H. Mácha, Vítězslav Nezval, Božena Benešová) or themes that celebrated things Czech and reflected on the harsh realities of the occupation in only the most indirect ways.

* * *

Burian's complexity as an artist with a strong but sensitive ego and an often conflicting dual commitment to art and a programmed worldview makes any brief assessment of his prewar work difficult. His theatre art itself had its share of contradictions. It found equal inspiration in naive folk traditions and sophisticated technology. It exploited the resources of the human voice in the service of poetry far beyond their normal limits and yet drastically subordinated the verbal element in some of his most outstanding productions. It ranged from crude pamphleteering to subtle evocations of mind and spirit. Like V + W, he was admired by youth and by the intelligentsia, but unlike V + W he was denounced by some others as a pretentious egotist.

One thing is clear: he and his theatre were enormously influential on aspiring young theatre artists of the 1930s who came to prominence in the postwar years. Whether they worked directly with him or simply flocked to his productions, they were won over by the combination of his innovative, poetic stage art and his progressive, anti-establishment ideals. Alfred Radok, Václav Kašlík, Josef Svoboda, Otomar Krejča, Jaromír Pleskot and Luboš Pistorius are among the major postwar theatre artists whom Burian inspired, and who took his D Theatre as a model for much of their own work. His prewar artistry also made its mark abroad. E.F.B.'s D Theatre became synonymous with socially engaged avant-garde art throughout Europe and even caught the attention of American theatre practitioners and students.[20]

What remains distinct in the memory of his prewar work is the impression of an extremely gifted and industrious artist applying his multiple talents to the creation of stage works that fused specifically theatrical elements with related forms of film (frequently) and music (always) in new and striking ways. Equally distinct is the impression of the difficulties that Burian as artist had in consistently coming to terms in practice with Burian as ideologically committed fighter for social revolution, regardless of how ideal the union seemed in theory. The best known instance of the dilemma in theatre is probably that of Meyerhold, but in many ways Burian anticipated its critical, anguished phase. He was spared its brutal denouement, but lived to experience further variations of radical stress from his conflicting commitments to art and ideology in the post-1948 Communist regime. I have explored the later phases of Burian's work elsewhere, but would here simply note that, like V + W, Burian never quite found himself upon his return to Prague after the war. Regrettably, he endured more frustration and embarrassment than artistic satisfaction in his final years.[21]

4

ALFRED RADOK

His life was interlaced with tragic paradoxes. On the one hand,
Czech theatre owed few others as much as it did him for so
many truly new and inspirational impulses, from which whole
generations of younger directors drew and which helped so
many actors to an artistic rebirth. On the other hand, this same
Czech theatre gave few others as little opportunity to enjoy the
results of his work, to develop them in peace, and to live to have
them justly appreciated. In Radok's fate was something of the
fate of an outlaw, an Ahasvera; almost always he was driven
away from his work precisely at the time when it began to bear
fruit.

Václav Havel, 'Alfred Radok: an obituary'[1]

Alfred Radok, who died of a heart attack in Vienna in 1976 at the age of 61,
was the most creative Czech director of the postwar era. Briefly an assistant
to E. F. Burian, Radok in his subsequent work was influenced not only by
that major artist but also by K. H. Hilar, the earlier towering directorial
presence of Czech theatre. All three possessed an innate, intuitive sense of
theatre as an autonomous art; all three were noted for their reworking of
scripts for maximum theatrical impact; all three rejected the theatre of realistic illusion and were responsible for major innovations in total staging, in
which all elements of production are exploited to serve the director's vision
rather than to maintain fidelity to the surfaces of life.

Two of Radok's observations pinpoint his essential orientation:

The more a theatre performance doesn't resemble a photograph of
life, the more it becomes theatre.

I think of a theatre performance as a ceremony, as a kind of rite that
is presented before spectators. The spectator becomes a participant
of this ceremony.[2]

Whereas Hilar's work seemed unrelated to any worldview except that of an
artist who wishes to maximize the sheer experience of expressive theatre, and
E. F. Burian's work was heavily influenced by a Marxist worldview, Radok's
work was neither detached from issues of the real world nor aligned with any
ideology. Instead, it brought together a highly imaginative, inventive joy in

the interplay of theatre elements with a sensitive, probing conscience that sought to deal artistically with the ambivalent realities of life.

Radok's most overt but briefly experienced success was the Laterna Magika, a form of theatre descended from Burian and Kouřil's Theatre-graph. It combined filmed images and live stage action in unexpected, often poetic ways, revealing Radok's great sense of both media and their rhythmic, spatial integration. He collaborated with Josef Svoboda on this project, as he did on other theatre productions for over twenty years. Many of these productions formed peaks of postwar Czech theatre, as did a number of other productions in which Radok was joined by Czechoslovakia's other master scenographer, Ladislav Vychodil. Both Svoboda and Vychodil have testified to Radok's genius as a born theatre artist, one who could make theatre poetry out of the least promising material and for whom the contributions of a scenographer to a multilayered, complex work of stage art were as central as those of the actor. Radok worked creatively with all the media and elements of the stage; according to him, 'the text is only one melody in a total composition,' a remark that places him squarely in E. F. Burian's lineage.

Indifferent to ideology and inept as a tactician in the several kinds of politics inherent in Czech theatre after the Communist takeover in 1948, Radok nevertheless had sufficient talent and resiliency to keep in the forefront of Czech theatre for at least half his mature creative years. The other half, unfortunately, was spent in various forms of exile, both within Czechoslovakia and, finally, beyond its borders.

After having seen a number of his productions in the middle and late 1960s, I had the good fortune and privilege to make Radok's acquaintance in 1971, in Göteborg, Sweden, where he had been working since 1968 as a director in self-exile. From that meeting ensued a communication by mail, chiefly in 1974–75, including letters and audio-cassettes concerning his work, concepts, and theories. It is from that material that some of the following account derives.

* * *

When viewed as a whole, the relationship between Radok's life and his aesthetics reveals an essential consistency. His most striking techniques and forms of expression had their roots in his perception of reality.

He was born and raised in Koloděje nad Lužnici, a small town in southern Bohemia, on December 17, 1914. His mother was Catholic, his father Jewish. Radok's earliest and lasting recollections included rituals of both faiths, folk celebrations rooted in the countryside, touring farces and puppet theatre, and his mother's singing and telling stories to accompany magic lantern projections on the whitewashed walls of their rooms.

One of his retrospective remarks is especially helpful in conveying his attitude about the roots of his culture:

It is the medieval stink of witch-burning that has made our culture so rich and strong (these rituals, along with the rituals of folk theatre and those of the Catholic Church). That's how we come close to Russia and Poland – I mean, the fact of our getting our faces slapped repeatedly through history rather than the fact of our all being Slavs. It's most apparent in music, and you can see it very clearly in Chagall. The nature of Czech theatre can best be compared to Chagall's paintings, pointing out the fact that what the 'West' is lacking is the feeling of Chagall. And all of our dear Chagall originates from pain and tension.[3]

Radok had equally vivid, dissonant impressions relating to World War I: festive picture taking of young men in uniform, idealized postcards sent home from the front, and then the oval enamel photos covered with glass and embedded in a monument to the fallen that was located close to a carousel where children played. This duality of perception, a keen sense of antithetical elements, was to mark his thought and art throughout his life.

Radok never studied theatre formally, but he had the great advantage of being accepted as an assistant director in E. F. Burian's D Theatre in 1940, one of its last years of life before being closed by the German occupants in 1941. Above all he recalled being impressed by the great precision that marked the work of that ensemble, as well as by E. F. Burian's special talent for integrating varied theatrical elements (including film), all of which were dominated by the spirit if not the actuality of musical composition. In retrospect, however, while acknowledging the influence of Burian on his own subsequent work, Radok pointed out that he was temperamentally not responsive to Burian's lyrical, emotive stylization. In his mature theoretical comments, Radok took pains to disavow stylization as an ingredient in his own work, stressing instead a reliance on selected real elements as the core of his creative process in production, as I shall describe later. During the remaining years of World War II Radok did incidental theatre work, including directing, at several theatres, principally in Pilsen. More important, he stayed under cover because of his Jewish background; his father and many other relatives died in concentration camps. Radok himself spent time at a labor camp toward the end of the war.

Radok's second encounter with significant theatre art, and his first truly creative period as a director, occurred during his association with a new theatre company founded in Prague a few months after the war by a cluster of young musicians and theatre people. In the flush of enthusiasm shortly after the war, the new group was given the large, former German (Neues Deutsches) theatre. Renamed in honor of the date of Prague's liberation, the Grand Opera of the Fifth of May, as its name suggests, put most of its talents into the service of musical theatre but also had a studio wing for drama.

In this early period of his work, Radok, like his colleagues, set out to make up for the years lost in the war, to try new ideas and methods, to reject traditional patterns. Radok put it this way: 'I hurled myself at a production (and at actors) like a furious bulldog, who wants – in the name of the new, the provocative, and the original – to tear everything apart at one stroke. Almost every one of my openings provoked a scandal.'[4] Radok's most notable productions at this time included *The Merry Widow?*, *The Tales of Hoffmann*, and *Rigoletto*, in each of which he radically departed from previous models, reworking the librettos, deliberately introducing anachronisms in the staging, encouraging scenographers like Svoboda and the older František Tröster to release their creative fantasies in unorthodox ways. Underlying the productions was a spirit of extravagant parody and irony, an uninhibited zest in the sheer playfulness of theatre, pulling out all the stops to surprise, excite, and entertain the audience. The program for *The Merry Widow?* referred to the young theatre's desire to create an 'operetta dell'arte,' retaining the best of traditional operetta, its music and lyric esprit, but purging it of the 'sweet poison' of its 'false sentimentality,' its clichés and its cheap effects, all of which are associated with the unhealthy bourgeois tastes of a bygone era.

Central to these creations, perhaps more intuitively than consciously at that time, was Radok's flair for orchestrating ironic, satiric, or simply hilarious confrontations of seemingly discordant elements, whether props, characters, or special bits of business. The Merry Widow made her first entrance suspended from a balloon, *The Tales of Hoffmann* mingled elements from Radok's favorite period, the turn of the century,[5] with those of modern technology, and *Rigoletto* was staged as an opera within an opera theatre, with the audience being able to look backstage to see the performers between appearances (Plate 7). If witnessed today, Radok's work could justly be hailed as postmodern theatricalism, some forty years ahead of its time.

The great success of the youthful Grand Opera of the Fifth of May eclipsed the work of the established, traditionally oriented National Theatre opera. The awkward competition was resolved in 1948 by official decree: the National Theatre absorbed the young company along with most of its personnel, much to their chagrin. Thus began the first of Radok's three engagements in the most prestigious and venerable of the nation's theatres. The timing was not felicitous, however, for it coincided with the change of regime from the reconstituted postwar Czechoslovak Republic to the Moscow-dominated Socialist Republic. For most of the next ten years, especially through the mid-1950s, the official doctrine of Socialist Realism prevailed in the arts, and Radok's avant-garde style of theatre was an inevitable victim.

In a closed meeting of National Theatre personnel in 1949, Radok was harshly condemned for a variety of logistical and ideological faults in directing a new Czech play by Dalibor Faltis, *The Bride from Chod* (Chodská nevěsta). So heated was the meeting that Radok suffered the first of his several heart attacks but was accused of shamming.[6] It was ironic that

Plate 7 Alfred Radok and Josef Svoboda's *Rigoletto* (1947) for the Grand Opera of the Fifth of May. Photographer unknown.

his chief accuser, the head of drama at the National Theatre at that time, Jindřich Honzl, had been a leading avant-garde pioneer in the Czech theatre of the 1920s and even early 1930s. Allegiance to the Communist line, however, made him a severe watchdog of ideological correctness in later years, especially after 1948.

Radok was let go in 1949 and spent most of the next four years with a touring theatre in the provinces, assigned to producing mainly second-rate Soviet plays. Only occasionally did Radok work on a production that challenged his imagination, the most notable occurring a year after his last production at the National Theatre. It was with the State Film Theatre, a production unit set up to provide actors for Czech films. In 1950, with Svoboda as his designer, he staged *The Eleventh Commandment* (Jedenácté přikázání), an amiable but lightweight nineteenth-century Czech comedy by František Šamberk. It was the first of his productions to involve the organic integration of filmed segments with the primary stage action. As was his practice, Radok substantially adapted the work to create, on this occasion, what most nearly resembled a jolly operetta, updated to the early years of the twentieth century. A projection screen was designed into the back wall of the set, onto which were projected various specially filmed sequences involving the very characters of the play. Most often these filmed sequences revealed the characters' off stage or past actions, as a lightly ironic or downright farcical comment on their on stage actions and relations. This virtually ful-filled all the essential characteristics of what later came to be Laterna Magika save one, and that one did occur at one moment of the play when a character on stage fired a pistol at a character on the screen, who promptly fell. At that moment – in the interaction of the two media – the future Laterna Magika was born, as both Radok and Svoboda later observed. The production was a huge success with the public, perhaps because it brought a welcome dose of ingenious, escapist farce to a Czech public already into the hardest Stalinist years.

* * *

Radok had directed one film prior to this production, *Distant Journey* (Daleká cesta), in 1948–49, a powerful depiction of concentration camp life at Terezin that stressed the unwitting collusion of its victims with their fate as a result of their having refused to face the reality of the danger confront-ing them. Regarded by many as a precursor of the new wave of Czech films in the 1960s, the film won several awards abroad, but was virtually banned in Czechoslovakia except for screenings in remote provincial areas. Its fault, apparently, was its humanitarian rather than ideological view of the Holo-caust. A typical Radok sequence of ironic duality involved an international commission that came to inspect the camp, only to be shown a prearranged charade demonstrating the happy creativity of the inmates as they put on plays, presented concerts, and rehearsed dances. Once the commission left, many of the imprisoned performers were sent off to gas chambers. As a total image, it corresponded to one that seemed to haunt Radok and be character-istic of his essential perception of things. In recalling the various propaganda photographs of Hitler, he fixed on one as a classic image: a smiling Hitler bending over to accept a bouquet of wildflowers from the hands of an inno-cent little girl. For Radok this became a much more valid sign of the whole Nazi era than anything like a swastika or jackbooted storm troopers, for it captured a number of complex, dynamic realities rather than a single, static, and oversimplified symbol. At the same time, it was but a more sophisticated and mature vision of the fusion of antithetical elements that characterized his earlier farcical and parodistic work.

Radok made two other films in the 1950s, *The Magical Hat* (Divotvorný klobouk) (1952), and *Grandpa Automobile* (Dědeček automobil) (1956). Both were successful but not groundbreaking cinema comedies.

* * *

In 1954, during a political thaw, Radok was accepted back into the National Theatre, where he remained until 1959. During these years, he directed almost a dozen productions, including several in which Otomar Krejča was one of his strongest actors before becoming head of drama in 1956 and building on the demanding standards introduced by Radok. Moreover, it was during this engagement with the National Theatre that Radok did some of his most outstanding work with Svoboda, even though political pressures forced him to curb some of his exuberant theatrical expressiveness. Memorable productions included an East German play, *The Devils' Circle* (with Krejča) (1955), Lillian Hellman's *Autumn Garden* (1957) and John Osborne's *The Entertainer* (1957), starring Ladislav Pešek, an actor who had been one of Hilar's favorites. In *The Entertainer*, Radok, working with Svoboda, brought some of his most characteristic methods to fruition and indirectly made a theatrical statement of deep relevance to his time. It was the era of official optimism, when life in the new society was no longer considered liable to criticism but rather to be celebrated. Radok's production, however, suggested that all was not well, that beneath the surface a pervasive malaise existed in personal and social relations. Much of this idea is of course inherent in the script, but Radok was able to expand and intensify the meanings and suggest their applicability to his own audiences. It was a production marked by his special sensitivity to material things and their metaphoric significance in revealing layers of meaning in our lives. And it was a production which demonstrated his provocative sense of sheer theatrical creativity.

* * *

At the heart of Radok's social and aesthetic vision was his concept of *věcnost*, a Czech term that literally means 'thingness' or 'matter of factness.' It bears relation to the more familiar German term, *Sachlichkeit*, but goes beyond it. In Radok's sense, it means an ability to see things clearly, truly, unsentimentally; it implies an ability to let objects or actions speak for themselves in an understated but pointed way. It further implies that things potentially bear a number of meanings, particularly in their relation to us; that things have meaning not only on the surface but also within themselves, and that such subsurface meanings are often masked and in need of deciphering. For Radok there was also the conviction that most things, most events, bear a tension of at least two opposite poles, that things and actions – especially the countless rituals and ceremonies that make up our social life – are inherently ambiguous and ironic. According to Jan Grossman, an awareness of this leads to our 'ability to distinguish between content and form, word and deed, ideology and its actual intentions.'[7] Furthermore, as Radok said,

> It's not simply a matter of reality or truthfulness. It's related to materials, things that have a number of meanings. It is derived from the ties of a person to certain things. A director searches for precisely such things, objects which have their own significances and are capable of evoking associations. For example, the monument with photos of dead soldiers close to the children's carousel. Precision in selecting and handling such materials can express the relation of

man to such things – because we live in a common time and place
and recognize these significant things.

According to Radok, 'Our reality of life, our world, forced us to view things
and recognize them in this manner; to see more precisely, deeply, and be able
to make distinctions.'

Radok stressed that theatre should not be equated or confused with a
liberal arts college, a political meeting, a church, or a scientific institute
studying humankind or society. Nevertheless,

> We cannot ignore history or political events. Even when not directly
> discussed, they were present on stage and in the audience. . . . The
> dramaturgic selection of a play and its directorial plan was the only
> possible way I was permitted to react in the given cultural-political
> situation.

By following through with his principle of *věcnost*, by embodying it in concrete theatrical terms, Radok strove to present the complicated ties of man
to reality and satisfy his 'need to express the reality of the time in which we
live.' In preparing his directorial plan, said Radok, 'I search for *věcnost* in
the meanings of the text, in the situations of the plot, in the characters.
And I search for the methods of expressing all such meanings in time and
space.'

Reality, in the sense of real elements, materials, and actions, was always
the foundation and point of departure for Radok, rather than stylistic distortions of them. But these real elements were then organized and used in a
nonrealistic way in space and time. In particular it was the handling of props,
furniture, and other objects by the actors – often in a ritual-like manner –
that created the special stage reality Radok sought, as distinct from life
reality. 'The spectator should know that he's in the theatre' was one of his
recurrent maxims, but it is important to note that in Radok's work this did
not produce either the theatricalist flamboyance of a Meyerhold or Tairov,
or the often dry austerity of Brecht's epic theatre. Instead, it involved a
highly imaginative manipulation of real elements to create what Radok
sometimes called the reality of art, and at other times 'a theatrical ceremony,'
in which the spectator would participate, not overtly, but imaginatively as a
result of being provoked and attracted by the multiple associations and
meanings Radok derived from the interaction of theatrical elements.

A few examples from *The Entertainer* may clarify Radok's distinctive
methods. Working with a relatively bare, dark, and deep stage, Radok made
use of a series of mobile, glittering curtains as a sign of the world of the
cabaret, but these curtains rode on heavy wires that formed a network above
the stage, clearly recalling the trolley lines of a large city, an effect reinforced
by a row of street lights suspended above the central axis of the stage. The

walls of the domestic scenes were made of heavy netting in the form of enlarged embroidery, holding mementos of the Rices' theatre careers. An old upright piano with Victorian embellishment was introduced into the domestic scenes as an object strongly associated with Billy Rice, the old entertainer of the previous generation. All these concrete objects and others became rich in varied associations as the actors used them and related to them. For instance, the script merely alludes to the death of Billy, but Radok gave it theatrical reality by introducing a mimed ceremony concurrent with one of Archie's cabaret routines. As Archie paused in one routine, a set of cabaret curtains behind him opened to reveal the family in its home, standing by as four stagehands, dressed formally and wearing dark hats, lifted the piano simply but with dignity, and moved as if in a funeral procession to the apron of the stage, followed by the family. The men then slowly lowered the piano into the orchestra pit as if it were a casket, while members of the orchestra rose and stood in silence, and Archie stood at the other side of the stage and gazed into space. Without a word being said, Billy Rice had been buried in a unique ceremony blended of tangible realism and metaphoric theatricality which amplified and intensified the complex meanings associated with his death. The curtains also reinforced Archie's final exit: as he slowly walked up stage, one set of curtains after another opened before him, as if swallowing him up.

* * *

In 1958, less than one year after *The Entertainer*, Radok followed up his work in *The Eleventh Commandment* and, with Svoboda's collaboration, achieved a new peak in his creativity with the introduction of the Laterna Magika program at the Brussels Expo 58. Essentially it consisted of a revue-like format intended to present attractive images of Czechoslovak culture and industry. The basic technique of synthesizing stage performance and filmed images to create a new reality was elaborated and refined in scenarios that explored new relations and transformations of space, movement, and timing, even while providing popular entertainment (Plate 8). The introduction and ongoing 'frame' for the Brussels program involved a mistress of ceremonies and a musician, both of whom appeared live on stage and also in multiple filmed forms on three screens: a large, cinemascope-type screen up stage center, and two narrower vertical screens downstage left and right. Other, smaller screens could occasionally appear or disappear at will. The projections came from three synchronized film projectors and one slide projector. A classic instance of explicit Laterna Magika interplay occurred when the one live mistress of ceremonies and her two filmed alter-egos not only addressed the audience, but also carried on conversations with each other. This literal, overt interaction of stage and screen was modified in other parts of the program, which had images of Czechoslovak industry, history, and nature in often startling juxtaposition with live stage action, such as

Plate 8 The original Radok–Svoboda Laterna Magika production at Brussels Expo 58. Photo: Dr. Jaromír Svoboda.

three ballerinas dancing on stage to the music of Dvořák against a filmed background of a steel mill in operation.

The Brussels Laterna was a huge success, and Radok looked forward to further experiment in the related media of film and stage. As he said later, 'Laterna Magika was to be a laboratory investigating rhythm in scenic-dramatic space. Film acquired a different significance than it would have had if seen without stage action, and vice versa.'[8] Actually, Laterna Magika was an extension of Radok's basic vision and methods rather than a new concept or direction; the essence of Laterna Magika, like that of his more orthodox stagings, was the interplay and synthesis of seemingly disparate elements in a new, more complex reality with the potential of prompting recognition of significant moments in the life of a society.

Radok's artistic signature as a director lay in his counterpointing varied elements of space, time, movement, sound, music, text, and psychological motivation at significant moments, which he called 'průsečíky' (intersections, or, perhaps better, multilayered juxtapositions). In such moments he could fuse given circumstances on stage and off stage, past and present, as well as personal motivations and social forces both immediate and subtextual. Finally, Radok had a flair for embodying such moments theatrically, fully exploiting the contributions of acting, scenography, sound, and music – whether literally heard, or simply present in the underlying temporhythms of the ongoing action. The 'burial' of Billy Rice in *The Entertainer* would seem a good example.

Although he had already been working with this montage-like approach in staging for years, Laterna Magika afforded him a remarkably expressive, *added* theatrical medium, a supplementary language to convey his distinctive perceptions of human nature in social contexts and thereby to create a new, enriched artistic reality. And in Svoboda, Radok had a master designer-scenographer who was not only attuned to Radok's creative wavelengths but commanded the architectonic and technical know-how to actualize Radok's insights in stage terms. What is involved in the effective dramatic combining of stage and film in Laterna Magika is not merely the selection of well filmed images appropriate to the stage action, but a highly developed sense for the distinct semiotics of each medium, and how to combine the two media effectively in the service of a script or scenario tailored for a multimedia presentation.

Suzanne Langer's pithy comment on the problems of mixing media comes to mind as an ongoing challenge to the creators of Laterna Magika: 'There are no happy marriages in art, only successful rape.'[9] It was precisely the effort to avoid such one-sided dominance that became one of the essential characteristics of Laterna Magika. As Radok put it, 'Film must stay film, the stage the stage. Our sole focus will be on how to join the content of action on stage with the content of action on a film screen.'[10] In fact, however, the joining of 'action on stage with the content of action on a film screen' also means that neither action retains its original meaning. To put it another way, neither film nor stage action remains self-sufficient, but produces optimal results when interweaving with and affecting the other. But underlying all of these artistic and technical challenges of Laterna Magika is the need of a director-dramaturge with a special sixth sense for the potential echoes and connections among the multiple signs and perspectives inherent in life and human behavior itself, or as Shelley put it, 'the before unapprehended relations of things.' It is this sixth sense that Radok seemed especially to possess. Equally important, he possessed the ability to translate such perceptions into theatrical terms.

The great success of Laterna Magika at Expo 58 prompted ministry authorities to institutionalize Laterna Magika as an ongoing showcase for Czechoslovak culture and society; it was first set up as an experimental studio attached to the National Theatre. Radok, whose career was at its peak as a result of the Brussels triumph, was appointed artistic head of the newly established Laterna Magika organization, and it was he who supervised the first Prague program in May 1959, in effect a successful new edition of the Brussels program to capitalize on the former's acclaim. Concurrently, Radok, Svoboda (who continued as chief scenographer), and their staff were making preparations for the next program, which was to have its premiere in the spring of 1960. Ironically, however, the Laterna Magika II project resulted in a nearly terminal catastrophe for Radok.

The centerpiece of this second Prague program, which still maintained an anthology format of some half-dozen numbers, was a new piece called 'The Opening of the Springs,' based on a chamber cantata by Bohuslav Martinů using a text composed by Miloslav Bureš. To those who saw the performance in a few closed rehearsals in the spring of 1960, Radok's combining of music, film, and choreographed mime was a wondrously affecting achievement that set a new standard for the Laterna Magika productions. The short work centered on folk ceremonies marking the annual cleansing of Czech highland springs as a celebration of humanity's ties with the cyclic forces of nature. Jan Grossman's comment suggests the non-ideological, humanistic point of the piece:

> The film and stage composition and their 'dialogue' are a form of metaphoric contraction of human life, whose boundaries are love and death, and after death the beginning of new life. . . . The Laterna Magika interpretation gives Martinů's work a marvelous accent of the moral responsibility of humans to each other. The optimism of the work is deeply cathartic – purifying and impassioned.[11]

For essentially political reasons, however, the piece was not allowed to be presented publicly, and Radok was stripped not only of his artistic directorship but even of his employment with both Laterna Magika and the National Theatre.

Why? Martinů, a Czech who had emigrated to the West after the Communist takeover in 1948, was persona non grata, and the lyric, poetic nature of the piece was not judged ideologically appropriate to what was intended to be part of the Communist Party celebrations marking the fifteenth anniversary of the end of the war. Not to be ignored was also Radok's seemingly congenital inability to maneuver effectively in the swirls of cultural politics. The whole unpleasant affair also involved the breaking up of the original Laterna Magika creative team and some resentments that never really healed.[12] In the meantime, Laterna Magika was administratively shifted from the National Theatre to the Czechoslovak State Film studio, a fortuitous change in that it enabled Laterna Magika to draw freely on that organization's extensive technical resources, although little of consequence was produced for years thereafter.

* * *

Radok was given a helping hand by theatre friends, and a special phase of his career developed in the years 1963–65 when he directed at Prague's Municipal Theatres and worked with Czechoslovakia's other leading scenographer, Ladislav Vychodil. Partly because of lower budgets and partly because of Vychodil's scenographic orientation, Radok's productions there were less technically sophisticated than they had previously been, and he relied even more on ordinary materials and objects as means of expressing his special sense of the world around him. In their work together, Radok and Vychodil subordinated usual stage design or scenography to the interaction of actors with carefully chosen 'signs,' such as props, furniture, or other detailed elements of setting, each of which might take on a number of different functions or identities. It is another form of Radok's *věcnost* and 'intersections,' not as ends in themselves but as ways to reveal unexpected, ironic relations and perhaps even profound truths.

Among Radok's notable productions at the Municipal Theatres were an adaptation of a Chekhov short story, *The Swedish Match* (1961); Georges Neveux's *The Woman Thief of London* (1962); Nikolai Gogol's *Marriage* (1963); and Romain Rolland's *The Play of Love and Death* (1964). *The Woman Thief of London* offered a prime example of multifunctional furniture in the form of several large wardrobes on wheels. As Vychodil described it,

> [They] turn into little houses but then change again. They become a secret passage . . . then wardrobes again, but during the wedding one wardrobe opens and we see little girls in it waving to the wedding procession. . . . We joined in one element various functions, precisely on the basis of associations. . . . What is important is that we were able to do this without stylization. Our wardrobes remain wardrobes.[13]

In Gogol's *Marriage*, the single strongest intention was to demonstrate the appallingly raw but pretentious level of culture of the characters of the play. A proliferation of props and other objects filled the stage, but it was their particular juxtaposition and their associations that were the heart of the jest: a house with additions to make it seem more impressive; a suggestion of an outhouse containing a live goat as one of the additions; an entry where rabbits were kept; close by, two slightly raised, small platforms with 'elegant' carpets, which people were careful not to step on.

In what most Czech theatre people consider Radok's finest production – Romain Rolland's drama of the French Revolution, *The Play of Love and Death* (1964) – the stage revealed two levels, two acting areas which represented two worlds: that of the aristocrats and intellectuals, and that of the revolutionary mob (Plate 9). Compelled by the mob, the aristocrats played out their fateful game within the rough boards of a semicircular arena made to resemble a bull-ring or bear-pit, while the mob sat in the bleachers above them, observing, interfering, and finally deciding their fate. Selected props and furniture representing the ancien régime were in the pit, in dramatic

Plate 9 Radok's production of Romain Rolland's *The Play of Love and Death* (1964), with Ladislav Vychodil's setting, at the Municipal Theatre. Photo: Ludvík Dittrich, courtesy of Theatre Institute.

contrast to the crude timbers that penned in the victims, as was the often ceremonial, courtly business of the aristocrats in contrast to the coarse jeering of the masses looking down at them.

Juxtaposing the two worlds and locating them in a place associated with torment and violence was Radok's innovation, for the script called only for interior scenes dealing with the elite. In the program for the production, Radok spoke of the dual acting areas and perspectives as a staging system analogous to the Laterna Magika in depicting the relations of two levels of significance. The dual perspective added a significant dimension to the action of the play and intensified its central theme, the problematics of revolution, an issue of enormous consequence to Czechoslovakia in the mid-1960s when questions could be asked more openly. The production offered no overt dissent or easy answers, but it brought to the surface many questions and deep-rooted ambiguities about recent history with which its audiences could identify, while providing a colorful, richly textured but disciplined theatrical spectacle. Adding greatly to the production was an original musical score (several sections of the dialogue were transformed into aria-like exchanges), and sophisticated off stage sound-effects of marching feet, the roll of tumbrils, and crowd noises.

* * *

Radok's young assistant on two of the productions, *The Swedish Match* and *The Woman Thief of London*, was Václav Havel, who was concurrently beginning his association with the Theatre on the Balustrade, where he would later become internationally known for his own plays. Havel's perceptive observations during the production process of both these plays provide insight into Radok's direct work with actors, an aspect of Radok's creativity that can easily be overshadowed by the total sweep of his mise en scène. Yet his work with actors is symptomatic of his unique, total creativity.

Havel felt Radok's methods were similar to those of Stanislavsky in placing great emphasis on the actor's existential identification with the character in order to create a moment by moment living reality on stage: 'theatre in process, dynamic, existential, describable only by its own constant [state of] becoming . . . in effect, living theatre.'[14] Havel saw Radok's method as essentially intuitive, but falling into three phases, of which the first was the most extreme: ridding the actors of all accumulated habits and ingrained attitudes by shattering their shell. 'He felt he had to shake them up radically, rattle their entire psychophysical apparatus, their entire being, in order to have the shell fall away. Rehearsals were full of tension, actors unnerved, psychologically exhausted, shocked.'[15] (Radok's approach recalls something of Hilar's methods.) It was as if Radok needed to have an atmosphere of stress during rehearsals; blowups often occurred, actors were offended and stormed off stage, but after the dust settled, they were three times better than before. In the meantime, phase two involved Stanislavsky-like work on identifying with the role. Phase three was more traditional in having the director guide the actor to the most effective presentation of the character by means of blocking, expressive business, finding the most telling delivery of lines, and relating to the other actors while being responsive to the 'feel' of the audience. As Havel saw it, whereas Stanislavsky sought to awake and stimulate the actor's creative unconscious by rational even scientific methods, Radok 'awakens these or similar irrational states primarily by irrational means.'[16]

Havel also noted his larger impression of Radok's essentially unorthodox, intuitive approaches and methods:

> All the varied Radok productions had something in common: a certain magic or sorcery. An element of irrationality. The presence of the mysterious, a sense of the enigmatic. The daring to be carried along by strange and inexplicable impulses and ideas from the subconscious and fantasy, by various archetypal conceits (sometimes even Freudian symbols). . . . Obsession, passion, irony, absurdity, paradox, grimacing, despair – all this always appeared anew in one manner and measure or another in Radok's work. . . . But I would chiefly emphasize again the magic. Radok instinctively searched every action, situation, dialogue or scenic and scenographic

possibility for its magical dimension. He was a bit of a sorcerer. Even when directing the most ordinary situation in the most ordinary psychological play. Of course, he wasn't a Magus, who wants to bewitch the public and the world. On the contrary, he was a shaman, who is constantly amazed by the mystery of the world, bows humbly before it and submissively allows it free passage. He was a kind of medium of something higher, which he didn't try to say he understood.[17]

In 1965, Radok was accepted back into the National Theatre for the third time, just as Otomar Krejča left to assume charge of his own theatre, the Gate Theatre. Times had become relatively more liberal, old enemies had either passed away or lost positions of power, and Czechoslovakia turned one more corner to move toward what three years later came to be known as the Prague Spring: the experiment of 'Socialism with a human face.' The high point of Radok's last engagement at the National Theatre was another collaboration with Svoboda, a 1966 adaptation of Maxim Gorky's *The Last Ones*, a drama dealing with the disintegration of a pre-revolutionary bourgeois family in Russia. Radok's familiar methods of multilayered associations in objects, concurrent actions, and complex relations of time and space now acquired still another dimension with the Laterna Magika technique, used for the first time in a straight play. As usual, Radok significantly adapted the original script, here to accommodate filmed sequences depicting past and off stage incidents in the lives of the characters, as well as other dramatically relevant images, all precisely cued in to significant moments in the dramatic action, somewhat like motifs in a musical composition. Only one large projection surface was used, an up stage wall.

For example, as a young girl is courted by an officer, we see projected behind them on a rough wall a filmed scene of that same officer ruthlessly shooting at a fleeing captive. As a sensuous woman rises from her bath on stage and is about to be lightly slapped with twigged branches by her servants, we see projected behind her images of a manacled young prisoner about to be flogged. The filmed sequences sometimes had their partial, indirect origin in Gorky's work but more often were Radok's completely original additions. The theatricalized echoes, foreshadowings, or metaphorical reinforcements, so characteristic of Radok's work, achieved a still more sophisticated level here as a result of his employing film as yet another instrument in the performance of a serious drama. Musical comment entered by means of a frank theatrical device: a small instrumental group placed in a small alcove some ten feet above stage level in the very wall serving as the projection screen. One critic perceptively observed,

> The chord of audio-visual signs is unified by the time–space unity of the stage and cancels linear logic in the name of a multilayered,

intense experiencing of psychological processes, whose 'logic' is often illogical.[18]

*   *   *

The political and cultural climate had improved so much by 1968 that Radok was granted the title of National Artist. The man whose creative years had largely been spent in trying to maintain a precarious foothold in the turbid currents of politics and art, who had to contend with the envy of lesser artists in stronger positions, who had never remained with an ensemble long enough to apply his intuitions and theories in the sustained and systematic manner he wished, now seemed securely placed. Indeed, reliable sources spoke of his being made head of drama at the National Theatre. His most recent productions at the National Theatre were successful: Lorca's *House of Bernarda Alba* (1967) and James Saunders' *The Scent of Flowers* (1968). But that summer Czechoslovakia was invaded and occupied by its socialist allies, ostensibly for its own protection. Radok must surely have appreciated the irony of the event and especially its rationale, but his reaction – no doubt rooted in memories of suppression, rejection, and persecution that stretched from the deaths of his family in enemy concentration camps to his own encounters with insensitive, uncomprehending authority among his compatriots – Radok's reaction was to flee into exile abroad (Plate 10). He was welcomed as a guest director in Sweden and also worked in other theatres on the continent (for a total of sixteen productions), but was never in a position

Plate 10 Radok at his home in exile, in Göteborg (1971). Photo: J. Burian.

to return to Czechoslovakia. Ironically, he was about to start rehearsals of two of Havel's one-act plays (*Audience* and *Private Showing*) in Vienna when he died of a heart attack on April 22, 1976. (He had previously been scheduled to direct Havel's *Beggar's Opera* in Bergen, Norway, but the production never materialized.)

Virtually all his colleagues in Czechoslovakia whom I consulted believed that he would have had nothing to fear at home, that he would have been protected, that his position was no longer assailable. A colleague especially close to Radok flatly and persuasively asserted that his emigration was a disaster, for Radok was rooted in his Czech environment and culture to the extent that permanent transplanting was impossible. Other evidence suggests that Radok's creativity was indeed severely limited abroad because of language problems, different work habits, and a certain lack of resonance between his type of theatre and foreign audiences. Not helping matters was the fact that some of his new colleagues in Sweden were Communist sympathizers. On the other hand, to hypothesize on what might have happened had he remained in Czechoslovakia, it is unlikely that Radok would have been productive or happy in the era of imposed Normalization, even if protected from overt harassment.

The project on which he was working before his emigration was his own adaptation of Goethe's *Faust*, an activity which is both surprising and consistent. It is surprising because Radok rarely tackled an established, major classic – no Greeks, no Shakespeare, no modern giant like Ibsen, Strindberg, Chekhov, or Pirandello. Yet the Goethe project is also consistent, because it was to be an adaptation. It has been said of Radok that he – like his early mentor, E. F. Burian – always favored works that either needed dramaturgic revision, or else had a 'texture' that was loose enough to allow his kind of editing and restructuring.[19] In any case, the tentative, incomplete scenario was left behind and seems to have been lost.

Radok's observations in an interview in Munich less than a year after his departure reveal how far he had progressed from the days of *The Merry Widow?*, when he seemed primarily concerned with shocking and exciting his audience. He never lost that concern, but as his art evolved toward greater external simplicity and inner tension, his concern with its broader social context became more pronounced. In Munich in 1969 he spoke of

> the need to find certain criteria of the culture of a man or a society, to have the possibility of objective comparison – that's terribly important for our work; that's the foundation. To discover and define the moment when a society and even an individual first behaves cowardly and dishonestly. From there the road leads to a general dishonesty, which can end in political trials. It's a matter of discovering that moment, noting it and revealing it, because recognition is the first step toward warding off evil.[20]

5

OTOMAR KREJČA

> He is able to defend and put through his plans and artistic goals
> aggressively and uncompromisingly, so that he gets into con-
> flicts very often. In seeking his creative co-workers his first
> requisite is their talent and the forward thrust of their artistic
> opinions.
>
> From an official National Theatre personnel audit
> of Otomar Krejča, February 14, 1958[1]

Otomar Krejča's strength of will and stamina have played no small part in
his remarkable career. Without formal study or training in theatre, he first
became a major actor and then the most dominant Czech director of the
second half of the century, while repeatedly experiencing opposition and
setbacks as intense as his remarkable achievements. An artist of more delicate sensibility, of less rugged character and tactical strength, could not have
stood the course.

Krejča's most significant achievement occurred as the Stalinist era in
Czechoslovakia was beginning to fade. In the face of severe ideological pressures and bureaucratic constrictions, which had stultified Czech theatre as a
whole after the 1948 Communist seizure of power, Krejča and his hand-
picked team brought the National Theatre to its postwar crest in the late
1950s and thereby contributed to the unleashing of other creative forces that
made the Czech theatre of the 1960s internationally celebrated. But at the
peak of his powers in 1961, after five memorable productions, he was
pressured to resign his position as head of drama in the National Theatre.

Four years later, in 1965, he launched his own studio theatre in Prague. His
second career as artistic head of a theatre garnered even greater attention
than his achievements at the National Theatre. In the Theatre Beyond the
Gate (Divadlo za branou), he directed eleven plays in seven years and toured
throughout Europe with several of them. Yet again, however, Krejča was
stripped of a theatre. In 1972, his Gate theatre was liquidated by the regime
of the time because of Krejča's recalcitrance in publicly endorsing the 1968
Soviet-led invasion that demolished the liberalizing achievements of the
Prague Spring.

After a brief interlude at a suburban Prague theatre, Krejča was not
allowed to direct in any Czech theatre at all from 1975 to 1990. To this extent
his situation held some echoes of Radok's exile, but with fewer painful

77

overtones, because Krejča could maintain residency in Prague. Moreover, Krejča was invited to direct over thirty productions in western European theatres during those fifteen years.

Prague's Velvet Revolution of 1989 led to the government-subsidized restoration of his previous theatre in 1990. Renamed Theatre Beyond the Gate II, it mounted seven productions in three years. Then, ironically, even as Pirandello's *Mountain Giants*, his final production there, was receiving outstanding reviews, decisions were already being made to liquidate this latest incarnation of Krejča's planning and artistry, although this time for economic reasons. Gate Theatre II ceased existence at the end of 1994.

Two years later, ever resilient, Krejča was one of the candidates for the leadership of drama at the National Theatre, but youth prevailed and Krejča was at liberty – again. In 1996, undaunted at age 75, he accepted an offer to direct a major production of Goethe's *Faust*, Part One, at the National Theatre. After a rehearsal period beset with logistical and technical problems, the production opened in September 1997 to respectable but guarded reviews, although it later received several votes for the Radok award as best production of the year. As the millennium approached, Krejča was once again between engagements but poised and ready to consider options.

*   *   *

What have been the underlying elements of Krejča's temperament and attitudes? What has been his basic orientation and vision regarding theatre? In his own words a 'self-made' man, he is one whose sense of reality is seldom out of focus, one who accurately perceives who he is and in what context of circumstances and forces he is operating. Unlike his peer and sometime colleague, Alfred Radok, a fundamentally sensitive, vulnerable being, highly subject to pressures and stimuli of the moment, Krejča was always able to hold steady while assessing his artistic and career circumstances with a strong sense of practicality and reason. It is not difficult to think of Radok being at times uncertain, perhaps even self-doubting, but it is almost impossible to think of Krejča in those terms. Not that Krejča is a calculating, detached intellectual; there is strong emotion, even passion, in his analyses, his convictions, and his creative work. A born organizer, tactician, and leader, he seems always to have had a firm sense of what is right and desirable – for him, for theatre, for society. Although he joined the Communist movement, his inherent intelligence and social consciousness, his pragmatic and existential perspective, prevented him from being a 'true believer,' and instead motivated him to work from inside, through theatre, indirectly questioning the system's shortcomings and abuses.

He voiced his core conviction regarding the relation of theatre and society at the age of 22, calling for 'a raising of the stage to an ethical, socially militant necessity, to a broadly public institution, as essential as schools and hospitals.'[2] These were sentiments completely in line with the Communist view of art as a social and political instrument, but when Krejča came to apply such principles to his work as head of drama in the National Theatre during the Communist era, his implicit goal was a critique of what had gone wrong with society – and with theatre – since the Communists took over, although he never put it in those terms.

Of crucial significance was the gradual, intermittent thawing and softening of the Communist regime after Stalin's death in 1953. Until then, virtually nothing of artistic significance had been feasible since 1948, particularly in a theatre guided by the tenets of Socialist Realism. Even in 1956, when Krejča took over the reins of drama at the National Theatre, sloganeering and uncritical ideological affirmations were still the rule in public life, and simplistic realism with a politically correct message was the norm in theatre. Within this context, Krejča introduced a repertoire of mainly new plays with credible psychological and social issues accurately reflecting the tensions and stresses of contemporary life. (It was in those trying years that the internal assessment of his methods cited in the headnote was made.) In a 1959 speech in defense of his initiatives in repertoire selection and production standards at the National Theatre, he articulated his premises and policy clearly:

> We reject oversimplified visions of our life and stand for its truthful depiction in its full scope and complex problematics. . . . Such complexity is certainly not pessimistic. On the contrary it flows from the conviction that it's necessary to clarify all inconsistencies, interconnections, and problems that our society must deal with on its way to a full actualization of socialism if it truly wants to build 'a better world for better humans.'[3]

Krejča was able to back up his position not only with persuasive reasoning and forceful eloquence at top-level meetings, but also with the evidence of a series of provocative, strikingly staged new productions that swept the routine hackwork of previous seasons out of the repertoire. The way had been prepared by the brilliant work of Alfred Radok (see Chapter 4), but it was not until Krejča became head of drama that a sea-change was effected.

Nevertheless, after five rich seasons, too many conservative, entrenched forces in the politico-cultural hierarchy felt irritated and threatened by Krejča's nonconformist choices in play selection and production style. In 1961, the ideological centers of power (the 'Cosa Nostra,' as Krejča later called them) released Krejča's dramaturge, Karel Kraus, declaring that 'the present dramaturgy [i.e., repertoire] fails to assure the transition from socialism to communism, which is to occur in the 1980s.'[4] Krejča felt that he had no choice but to resign his position of leadership. He stayed in the National Theatre as actor and director for four more years, during which time he directed three major works: *Owners of the Keys*, *Romeo and Juliet*, and *End of Carnival*. Nevertheless, he was no longer head of drama, and a pattern was established: hard-won, solid achievement followed by institutional dismissal.

* * *

In what follows I should like to focus on Krejča's thoughts and practices related to the dramatic text, to acting, and to other aspects of staging. A consideration of his background and formative experiences may be the best place to begin.

Born in 1921 into a farm family of small means in Skrýšov, situated halfway between Prague and Brno, he completed his basic schooling in 1939 and almost immediately began an intensive career in theatre, first as a backstage apprentice and journeyman actor in provincial touring companies, later as a full-time actor with more stable though secondary companies in and around Prague. In four years of busy repertory theatre during the wartime era, he played in no fewer than seventy plays, including foreign classics as well as many lesser known works by Czech and foreign authors.

Before turning his attention primarily to directing in the late 1950s, Krejča benefited from working as an actor under three exceptional directors. Immediately after the war (while attending seminars in structuralist theory at Charles University) he joined the revived ensemble of E. F. Burian, whose chief characteristics Krejča later associated with 'the subordination of all means of stage expression to musical encoding. His work with actors leaned primarily on their stylized speech (under his direction) and similarly stylized physicalization.'[5] During his one season with Burian, Krejča played the title roles in *Prometheus Bound* and *Cyrano de Bergerac*, the latter directed by Burian himself.

In 1946, Krejča moved to the Vinohrady company headed by Jiří Frejka, Burian's peer from the prewar avant-garde. Krejča valued Frejka's thorough submersion in the dramatic text and his subdued but incisive, pregnant formulations containing a wealth of imaginative insights. It was in his Vinohrady era that Krejča also met dramaturge Karel Kraus, with whom he later formed a long-term creative relationship, and young director Jaromír Pleskot, under whom he performed several important roles. It was under Frejka, however, that Krejča's acting developed most fruitfully, and it was under Frejka's tutelage and encouragement in 1949 that Krejča took his first steps in directing (Gorky's *Counterfeit Money*). A fragile personality, Frejka was one of the eventual victims of the Communist takeover of 1948, and with the subsequent shakeup of the Vinohrady Theatre, Krejča moved on to the National Theatre in 1951. There he ripened his acting career and had the good fortune of working in two plays under Radok's direction before undertaking his first major directing assignments himself. Radok's work was perhaps most important for Krejča in setting very high standards for actors and employing metaphorical, consciously theatrical approaches to staging.[6]

While still primarily an actor, Krejča was named head of drama at the

National Theatre in 1956, a tribute to his talent, vision, and strength of personality. Among his first steps was the hiring of his former Vinohrady colleagues Kraus and Pleskot, as dramaturge and associate director, respectively.[7] With Kraus, Krejča formulated a strategy for lifting the National Theatre out of the doldrums. Central to the plan was the active hunt for fresh, literate, poetic *new* Czech plays that resonated with contemporary Czech life. They found them in works by František Hrubín and Josef Topol, two poets with distinctive voices even when they were not writing in verse, and in Milan Kundera, a prose fiction writer with a sharp critical sense. Three other, non-contemporary writers completed the playwrighting component of Krejča's tactical plan, or, as it was sometimes put, Krejča's theatre workshop (divadelní dílna): nineteenth-century Czech theatre artist Josef Kajetán Tyl, whose plays were traditional staples in the repertoire, Anton Chekhov, and William Shakespeare. With these plays, Krejča revitalized the routine, unprovocative repertoire of the National Theatre and established a fresh contact with contemporary audiences. With the addition of designer Josef Svoboda to his team, he also set new standards in dynamic, expressive staging making full use of Svoboda's bold, innovative scenography.

The plays themselves fell roughly into three categories, either inherently or in terms of Krejča's treatment of them. Hrubín's *A Sunday in August* (Srpnová neděle, 1958) and *Crystal Night* (Krištalová noc, 1961) were in the Chekhov mode, low-key but searching, realistic studies of contemporary attitudes and human relations with implicit social overtones. Chekhov's *Sea Gull* (1960), of course, was the thing itself, especially with its themes concerning the trials of youth and of art in the face of indifference, conformity, envy, and innate human destructiveness (Plate 11). On the other hand, Topol's *Their Day* (Jejích den, 1959), Kundera's *Owners of the Keys* (Majitelé klíčů, 1962), and Shakespeare's *Romeo and Juliet* (1963) embodied more overtly dramatic clashes of youth and human ideals pitted against not merely age but complacency and entrenched, life-denying attitudes. Tyl's two nineteenth-century plays shared this more overtly dramatic quality: *The Bagpiper of Strakonice* (Strakonický dudák, 1958), an idealized study of Czech values and attitudes *vis-à-vis* the lure of other lands, and *Drahomira and her Sons* (Drahomíra a její synové, 1960), a Romantic drama mixing history and legend, paganism and Christianity, in tenth-century Bohemian power politics. The third type of play was represented by Topol's *The End of Carnival* (Konec masopustu, 1964). Many regard it as among the great plays of twentieth-century Czech theatre for its treatment of issues at the heart of the profound shifting of ideologies, cultural values, and social patterns in the 1950s. Interweaving folk ceremonies and rituals with contemporary politics and economics in the immediate context of carnival festivities, Topol's poetic vision universalizes the harsh, real-life dynamics of the action to the level of myth.

Krejča's and Kraus's work on these texts ranged from near total fidelity

Plate 11 Otomar Krejča's first production of *The Sea Gull* (1960), scenography by Svoboda, National Theatre. Photo: Dr. Jaromír Svoboda.

(above all in the Chekhov) to varying degrees of adaptation and reshaping of the original material. In all the plays, Krejča and Kraus strove for a contemporary, idiomatic, often spare quality of dialogue, whether by using new versions of the classic revivals (Shakespeare, Chekhov, and even Tyl), or by close work with the living playwrights on their evolving scripts. Topol's *Their Day* was something of an exception in that Topol had the play in final form before submitting it to Krejča, and only small adjustments occurred during rehearsals.

In the other contemporary new works, the scripts were more thoroughly worked over structurally as well as linguistically, particularly in the Hrubín plays. Perhaps the most substantial editing and reshaping occurred with the Tyl plays. Cutting up to 30 percent of the dialogue, ridding the plays of archaisms and sentimentality, focusing the action on issues that would resonate with contemporary audiences, Krejča produced a leaner, more dramatically effective action, which often proved controversial. For example, his frank stripping of dated poetry and patriotic nostalgia in *The Bagpiper* was severely criticized by many.

As important as were such treatments of the texts, characters, and themes, it was Krejča's total staging – his mise en scène – that vitalized the playwright's literary material on stage and made it come alive in the spectator's mind and feelings. Like all great directors, Krejča was a master orchestrator of all stage elements, including the text. Less intuitive and more rational than Radok, Krejča insisted on long, thorough rehearsals devoted to pinpointing the essence of each character and its expression in precisely controlled blocking. Moreover, although these plays are rich in individual character studies, Krejča made the implicit social relevance to contemporary Czechoslovakia as important as the lifelike quality of each individual characterization. This focus has always held true for Krejča, the desired goal for each character being a thought-through, emotionally charged portrayal that clearly conveys the character's dramatic and thematic position in the play as a whole. The result is not a cluster of striking individual figures with some dimly perceived overall point, but a provocative, implicitly challenging total statement, with well-developed individual components.

The productions of these plays were also notable for their sustained, choreographed dynamism, in both the internal work of the actors and its overt expression in the sheer energy and sometimes stylized pattern of their movements, for which Krejča always sought a relatively open, sparsely furnished stage. This principle of dynamism was also evident in Svoboda's scenography. Krejča encouraged Svoboda to bring his wealth of imagination and technical mastery to the service of these works, most notably in his applications of lighting, projections, and kinetic scenery. The evocative atmosphere of season and locale was crucial to the impact of *A Sunday in August* and *The Sea Gull*. In both cases Svoboda created this atmosphere by a superb organizing of lighting in relation to the strategic positioning of physical elements such as branches and scrims.

Kinetic scenery in conjunction with complex projections became an organic part of the final stage form of Topol's *Their Day*, while both *Drahomira* and *End of Carnival* employed large, suspended, and kinetic wall-like surfaces as powerful visual adjuncts to the central stage dramas. The use of kinetic platforms and suspended panels reached its peak in *Romeo and Juliet* and *Owners of the Keys*. Scenic pieces based on architectural elements of the Renaissance shifted into various configurations to accompany the intensely physicalized play of the actors in Shakespeare's *Romeo and Juliet*, while two rolling platforms, sophisticated lighting, and strategically placed mirrors created the world of *Owners of the Keys*.

* * *

Between the termination of his work as head of drama in the National Theatre in 1961 and the start of his Theatre Beyond the Gate in 1965, Krejča continued his work as director and actor in that theatre but also undertook the guest direction of two plays at the recently formed Theatre on the Balustrade (Divadlo na zábradlí), one of several smaller, studio theatres that were to be a strong force in the surge of Czech theatre in the 1960s. The invitation to the Balustrade came from Jan Grossman, who had recently taken over as artistic head of the youthful ensemble. It was Krejča's production of Václav Havel's first important full-length play, *Garden Party* (Zahradní slavnost, 1963), that revealed his evolving thoughts concerning the type of play and theatre experience most congenial to him. On the one hand, as one critic noted, Havel's absurdist satire of bourgeois obtuseness and dehumanized conformism echoed several of Krejča's own biases, some of which could be noted in the treatment of certain middle-class characters in *Their Day* and *Owners of the Keys*. 'In this sense *Garden Party* consummates one line of Krejča's socially critical work.'[8]

On another level, however, Krejča experienced a certain feeling of incompatability with what Grossman and Havel saw in *Garden Party*. Krejča's own remarks are revealing:

> The text emerged, as far as I know, from the close and continuous collaboration of Grossman and Havel. . . . The unabashedly cabaret-like feel, verbal sleights of hand . . . and the scandalous precariousness of its allusions to political realities . . . all this was a frappant contribution to the early years of the 1960s. . . . I like to recall the certainty and pleasure with which I began to work with the actors, even though their characters may have seemed to lack 'bodies,' only being a kind of verbal schemata, montages, serially framed. . . . In those days I was used to asking plays about their standpoint toward basic human situations and states; I took their world as a total world. I intended, then, not an appeal for or against specific, relevant ideological formulas, but an 'a-historical' rooting in eternal laws of humanism and morality addressing the viewer's senses, emotions, heart, taste, as well as his ideological and political reflexes. . . . During our work, [however,] it became apparent that my poetics of staging did not adequately equip me for understanding or grasping Grossman's and Havel's concept of theatre; a theatre that places the political-appelative function of theatre before and above a philosophic-anthropological approach.[9]

Krejča had referred to his philosophic-anthropological approach in opposition to the Grossman–Havel approach in an earlier published interview as well:

> I perceived in [*Garden Party*] an effective metaphor of the whole modern world. That's the direction I wanted to send the play in . . . but I let myself be talked out of it. . . . And ever since it has seemed to me that I shouldn't have let myself be persuaded. I should have done *Garden Party* as a play concerning the whole world and all humanity.[10]

These remarks concerning a universal, philosophic-anthropological approach, made more than thirty years after the issue in question, suggest that he had come to see more clearly the broader implications of his earlier work. Similarly, his comments in 1996 on his productions of *Romeo and Juliet* and *End of Carnival* in the early 1960s define more clearly just what those productions were meant to be:

> Both productions became poetic metaphors of light and tenderness in the darkness and spiritual wasteland of those years: *End of Carnival*, the greatest postwar Czech play to this day, its humanity irradiated with sadness and the end of the 'old' days of carnival; *Romeo and Juliet* with its tragically relentless appeal to conscience, tolerance.[11]

* * *

The second main era of Krejča's career as a director began with his work in his own Theatre Beyond the Gate in late 1965 with Kraus, Topol, Svoboda, and several key actors. The theatre was housed in a former cinema converted for use by the Laterna Magika Theatre, which exploited the innovative fusion of live and filmed action developed by Radok and Svoboda. In a subterranean space not designed for live theatre, Krejča's productions successfully alternated with performances by Laterna Magika for seven years, during which time Krejča directed nine productions.

Freer to do plays they liked in the way they wanted to do them (e.g., fewer productions allowing more work on each), Krejča and his workshop team developed their productions in several interesting ways. Working during the years that witnessed an increasingly liberal regime culminating in the Prague Spring of 1968, Krejča moved toward productions that seemed less directly reflective of specific sociopolitical conditions and more concerned with either explorations of personal relations or broader, philosophic-anthropological matters, to use his later phrase. In both cases, however, realities of Czech life outside the theatre could still be read in the plays and their staging.

The freer cultural atmosphere most likely contributed to another distinct new tendency in Krejča's work in this era: an increased interest in experiment with purely formal and theatrical elements of staging, such as a use of masks and a presentational approach signalling to the audience that the company was consciously performing for them. Concurrently, Krejča's dual emphasis on a deep reading of the text and its painstaking embodiment in choreographed patterns of movement continued to evolve. An example of a transitional production was Chekhov's *Three Sisters* (1966), in which the text was scrupulously respected and deeply studied, while the embodiment on stage was partly stylized in its patterns of physical movement and rhythmic pacing. The characters were de-sentimentalized by accentuating the strained if not neurotic aspects of their personalities, which were reflected in their movements and gestures, most tellingly at the end when the sisters darted about the stage like birds trapped in a cage.

The use of masks began with Krejča's last play as a National Theatre director, *End of Carnival* (1964), which also exploited the theatricality inherent in carnival festivities and rituals. The setting was contemporary Czechoslovakia, where carnival celebrations and masquers were still in evidence, especially in the provinces. The conflict between King, a proud, independent farmer who stubbornly refuses to have his land become part of the collective, and officials of the new establishment reached a climax during the folk celebrations of Shrovetide, and the masquers became significant agents in provoking and aggravating several aspects of the conflict as they wove through much of the action, adding a ritual, mythic dimension to the socio-cultural theme of collectivization. The masquers were strongly identified with the earth, nature, and its processes as they imitated animals, trees, and the wind. This duality of identity and function – the nonhuman as distinct from the social – was echoed on another level. The masquers functioned not only as participants in the action but also as a chorus that observed and commented, thus providing a double perspective on the action. In short, Krejča used the elements of the mask in a variety of ways: as a means of enriching the stark confrontations at the core of the plot and of adding overtones of the mythic and the irrational to the social and reasoned issues of the play.

The production in which both carnival and masks appeared in their least problematic aspect was Michel de Ghelderode's *The Ostend Maskers*, a brief, very dynamic pantomimic ballet of carnival revelry with darker overtones which formed one-half of the Gate theatre's opening production in November 1965. I was in Prague at the time, and Krejča told me that the reason for his doing the Ghelderode piece as a curtain raiser was to 'warm up the theatre, to orient the audience theatrically.' Inspired by his familiarity with the Flemish spirit of carnival and the paintings of his friend, James Ensor, Ghelderode created the work in 1930 as a move toward a purer theatricality in a period when the stage was dominated by conversational boulevard drama. On the whole, the chief impression created by the production was one of relatively uncomplicated theatricality that exploited the shock and distortion inherent in the juxtaposition of boldly stylized, static masks and the capering bodies of the revelers, as well as the contrast between the masks and the actors' faces as they unmasked themselves on one or two occasions. The companion piece was Topol's new, one-act play, *Cat on the Rails* (Kočka na kolejích), which had nothing to do with masks or carnival, but focused on the conflicting sensibilities of two contemporary young lovers in an intense, physically dynamic performance. Krejča's directorial signature was also evident in his use of a fragment of dialogue from Topol's play as part of the pre-show lead-in to the Ghelderode; similarly, he used a measure or two from the pulsing music in the Ghelderode as a final sound-effect at the conclusion of Topol's play.

Krejča's employment of masks in his production of de Musset's *Lorenzaccio* (1969) at the Gate theatre was more fully the product of his own creativity. While de Musset's *Lorenzaccio* has one scene of carnival, Krejča's adaptation made the carnival a sociocultural background for the play as a whole and thus conveyed the ambience of corruption and monstrosity that characterized the society of that time and place. (The production was Krejča's strongest response to the Soviet crushing of the Prague Spring of 1968.) A few of the central characters, those possessing an element of humanity, did not wear masks at all, thus providing a perspective on the others and vice versa. The masked carnival figures never left the stage but remained to provide a sinister, semi-intelligible whispering gallery, observing and commenting on the action. The masks in *Lorenzaccio*, as well as the carnival element itself, also created a supplemental psychological, theatrical reality, the presence of which was made clear at the very beginning of the performance when Krejča had most of the actors fill the stage and don their costumes and masks in full view of the public. Taking only a hint from the original script, Krejča had allowed full play to his creative fantasy and used the mask as a crucial element the way a poet might employ patterns of imagery and instrumental metaphors to convey his vision of the world.

Schnitzler's *Green Cockatoo* (1968) is a highly theatrical play within a play that employs masks as part of its action, which takes place during the French Revolution and explores the relation of illusion and reality. Krejča enhanced its inherent theatricality by his dynamic treatment of the actors' performances. In *Oedipus–Antigone* (1971), a conflation of three Sophocles plays, virtually all the actors wore some form of conventionally stylized half-mask that suggested turbulent antiquity while also providing for ease of speech (Plate 12). The one powerful exception was Krejča's use of formalized, full head-and-shoulder masks with a texture resembling that of unglazed, greyish ceramic. Those masks were worn by the central characters after their deaths: Krejča had Oedipus, Antigone, and several others reappear on stage as ghostly presences during portions of the action following their deaths, just as he had Oedipus' children observing the action prior to their formal participation in the drama: Antigone, her sister, and their two brothers observed and responded to the action of *Oedipus*. The immobile, austere death-masks provided a notably traditional yet effective poetic dimension to the play. By virtue of those masks, the characters became dehumanized. They approached the condition of inanimate things, but by that very token they acquired a degree of serenity and permanence, a degree of the eternal. Like the figures on Keats' Grecian urn, they belonged to the ages, gaining an immortality that paradoxically can be found only in death. Here, as in *Lorenzaccio*, Krejča again had all the actors on stage at the beginning while

Plate 12 The Krejča–Svoboda production of *Oedipus–Antigone* (1971) in the Gate theatre. Photo: Dr. Jaromír Svoboda.

the actor playing Teiresias, before getting into costume, delivered the great 'ode on man' from *Antigone*.

In retrospect, Krejča's work with masks was impressive in its rich variety of forms and its intuitive exploitation of the purely theatrical. Still more impressive, however, was Krejča's fruitful integration of the mask element with the inner and outer action of a work. A mask in itself can be relatively pointless or merely a cheap effect. In Krejča's hands it assumed far greater significance. Especially in productions like *Lorenzaccio*, Krejča made of the mask a highly expressive component that became inextricably fused with others in the final synthesis of a work of theatre art.

Other notable new creative methods that developed during Krejča's work in the Gate theatre involved more radical adaptations of scripts and more striking departures from traditional realistic patterns of performance than had been Krejča's practice in the National Theatre. Critics and Krejča himself related the new approaches to montage or cinematic techniques; perhaps one might also apply the terms 'expressionism' and 'cubism.' Going beyond the usual editing and adapting of scripts that is perhaps more routine in European than in American theatre (e.g. cutting and occasional transposing of dialogue), Krejča would literally deconstruct and reassemble substantial portions of texts in an effort to reinforce and accentuate those aspects or themes of a play that he thought central to the play in his reading of it. In retrospect, Krejča put it this way:

> In those days we were testing the polyphonic and interactive capabilities of the stage. Although at times I forced the text to recall itself, and at critical moments to remind characters of their aims, deeds, lies and dreams, and to hold them in the mirror-chamber of the story, I don't think that I deformed or betrayed the poet.[12]

In productions such as *One-Ended Rope* (1967) and *Oedipus–Antigone*, the production scripts were already edited syntheses of several plays, the former drawn from many farces by Nestroy and the latter from the central three dramas involving Oedipus and Antigone. But in productions such as *Lorenzaccio*, *Ivanov* (1970), and *The Sea Gull* (1972), sections of dialogue were not only rearranged but also repeated either during a given scene or in different parts of the play; or, at times, different sections were played simultaneously. And all the characters would frequently be on the stage at the same time.

The method continued in Krejča's productions in the S. K. Neumann Theatre after the Theatre Beyond the Gate was closed. For example, in Chekhov's *Platonov* (1974), the basic text had a logical sequence of scenes – A, B, followed by C, and so on – but Krejča composed a sequence that began with a segment of scene H, followed by a segment of scene B, then a glance at scene A, before proceeding to a simultaneous enactment of scenes F and D, all the while having the entire cast on stage to present a living environment for the multiple, free-flowing action. Curiously enough, as I recall from having seen it, the result on stage was not confusion but a cinema-like montage, a challenging, sometimes irritating, but theatrically bold, powerful creation with a life of its own, providing new insights within the fictive world of the newly structured play. It was not a matter of rewriting dialogue but of reconfiguring the dramatic action in order to create new dimensions of stage reality for a given script. Krejča employed variations of the method in the other few plays he directed in the S. K. Neumann Theatre in 1974 and 1975.

Although Krejča did not really introduce this method until mid-career, he had much earlier advocated a theoretical justification of such manipulations (if not distortions) of texts, claiming it as a *right* belonging to a director. In the immediate postwar era a debate developed around the issue of a director's responsibility for maintaining fidelity to an author's intentions. It is, of course, a classic controversy that will never be resolved because the essential issues are inherently so subjective. In any case, Krejča's position at the time was clear in supporting the director's right to regard a dramatic text merely

> as material that inspires him to a new, personal stage vision. . . . The director, stimulated by the dramatist, thus becomes the new author

of the play – with only this difference – he 'writes' it with the material of the libretto provided by the dramatist.[13]

It was a position paralleling the theory and practice of Burian in the 1930s, and it foreshadowed much of what Radok was to do.

* * *

Krejča had managed to keep his Gate theatre open until 1972 despite the Soviet-led invasion of 1968 and the ensuing years of 'Normalization,' but a progressively restrictive arts policy found theatres of the sustained high quality and popularity of the Gate theatre undesirable. After the Gate theatre was liquidated, Krejča did not direct at all for two years until being allowed to work in the S. K. Neumann Theatre for a year and a half. Then, as an offshoot of economic and political negotiations between Czechoslovakia and West Germany in 1976, Krejča was officially invited to become chief director at the Düsseldorf Schauspielhaus. A deal was struck: Krejča would be allowed to maintain Czech citizenship and a residence in Prague while being granted an official visa to permit work outside the country. And so for the next fifteen years, while his name could not appear in public print at home, Krejča directed abroad, throughout much of western Europe.

Krejča's repertoire abroad focused on the classics, above all Chekhov; of the thirty-one productions he directed abroad, twelve were of Chekhov, four of Shakespeare, with Goethe, Aeschylus, Molière, Strindberg, and Beckett also figuring prominently. In the meantime, repressive conditions in Czechoslovakia slowly began to modify. The breakthrough for Krejča occurred in relation to a major Stanislavsky conference in Moscow during the 1988–89 season. Krejča was officially invited by the Soviet Ministry of Culture, which led to a series of high-level communications with Prague that provided a new status for Krejča. This eased the way for his gradual reentry into the Czech theatre world, although not as a practicing director with his own theatre until the fallout following the Velvet Revolution of 1989, when Krejča and his theatre were officially 'rehabilitated' by the new regime.

After numerous negotiations, Krejča returned as sole occupant to his former Gate theatre in the spring of 1990. The reestablished theatre, now known as Theatre Beyond the Gate II, had a life of four and a half years, during which time it produced seven productions, five directed by Krejča. In brief, although virtually all the new productions were thoroughly prepared and respectably mounted, they did not attract sufficient audiences in post-1989, liberated Prague. The entire cultural climate had changed, and with it, styles and forms of theatre. The predicament was reminiscent of the postwar experiences of both V + W and Burian in their attempts to pick up where they left off before the war.

At least two other specific factors contributed to the ultimate termination of Krejča's theatre. Although it contained numerous veterans from the original Theatre Beyond the Gate, in particular Marie Tomášová (Krejča's former Juliet, Nina, Masha, and central figure in several Topol plays), the new ensemble was neither as inherently strong as its predecessor nor as experienced in working together. Moreover, Krejča's concepts and methods had inevitably evolved and been modified.

Some of Krejča's own observations during the period prior to his first production in his restored theatre, Chekhov's *Cherry Orchard*, bear on these matters. In a talk to university drama students in the fall of 1990, Krejča stressed a non-'interpretive' approach to production: 'We don't want to use Chekhov – a great, extraordinary poet – as a springboard or trampoline for all sorts of nonsense, beginning with political theatre and ending who knows where.' Krejča expressed the same point a few years earlier, in a roundtable discussion: 'I start with the premise that the author whom I've chosen to stage isn't a dolt and that he wasn't drunk when he wrote the play. Truly. Because many [directors today] behave as if the author didn't know what he was doing.'[14] It was a sentiment he expressed more fully in the program for the production:

> My direction is changing more as time goes on, as I try for the deepest and most complete reading of a play. I try to get to know a drama from inside and to grasp it in its complete truth. . . . I don't perceive any fundamental difference between a classical and a contemporary play; it's necessary to treat the text of both with the same extraordinary care: the text is the highest law; it's not necessary to add a thing to it, or to think through what the author failed to write; what makes sense is to think through what he *did* write. On stage, we try to concretize the text, to express through another form of art, theatre, what the text 'tells' us, what we have gained from reading it. . . . The dramatist gives life to the theatre. . . . On stage, the actor makes the dramatist present . . . the actor is from the very beginning of theatre its irreplaceable essence. . . . Everything on stage happens through the actor's performance, everything is in a constant, clear, and deliberate relation to the actor.

The value placed on the work of actors was certainly not new for Krejča, but the extremely respectful attitude toward the text did seem at odds with the various liberties Krejča had previously taken in his own productions, particularly those in his original Theatre Beyond the Gate, and above all in those in which he employed his montage technique, as noted earlier. Moreover, these later observations seemed at the opposite pole from his remarks on 'režisérismus,' quoted above. In any case, his highly conservative attitude put him at odds with a tendency that had been developing in Czech theatre since the mid-1970s. Rather than working with finished scripts and presenting them in a relatively straight fashion, directors tended to work from scenarios expressing their own personal visions or concepts, or else they unabashedly adapted existing scripts according to their personal tastes. In a word, Czech theatre from the mid-1970s onward had increasingly moved toward a director-as-auteur's theatre, and audiences had almost come to expect this.

In an interview with me in December 1990 prior to the opening of *Cherry Orchard*, Krejča spoke further of his attitude toward Chekhov:

> I came to regard Chekhov's work as a kind of religion. For me, his texts are of such high quality, so rich, so infinitely broad – [they become] something like sacred script. I find in them a perfect, rich, broad image of mankind, an image of the world, a most valid anthropology – because it's an undogmatic anthropology, not anchored in any world ideological view, nor in any dogma.

In view of his expressed values and premises regarding the significance of text and actors, what of the 1990 *Cherry Orchard* production itself? It was Krejča's fifth *Cherry Orchard*, but his first in Czech (Plate 13). He rehearsed for nearly five months and had a few preview performances (Krejča called them 'rehearsals with the public') outside Prague. I had previously witnessed four or five rehearsals in November, and then attended the first preview performance in Prague, on December 1.

By today's standards and expectations the production would probably be regarded as conservative if not old-fashioned, for it was strictly faithful to Chekhov's script and revealed no fashionable ethnic, feminist, Marxist, or even Freudian tendencies. Instead, it was distinguished by enormous care devoted to the crystal-clear establishment of the central situation and characters and by equally obvious care with spatial composition, movement, and varied dynamics within a fairly narrow range. As always, Krejča embodied some of the major moments of the play in memorable stage images, above all in Lopakhin's intoxicated swinging of a chandelier to express his visceral moment of triumph as he announces his purchase of the orchard.

Krejča spoke of perceiving Greek tragedy in the play's structure. Comical or farcical elements were subordinated to an impression of the pain of change and the fear of dislocation, an impression that centered in Marie Tomášová's deeply felt, essentially somber portrayal of Ranyevskaya, a woman who seemed fated to waste her inheritance and her life. At its best the production was absorbing and thought-provoking. What was missing was a sense of spontaneity, of emotional ignition; the production ran the risk of seeming detached, statuesque, perhaps too consciously controlled and measured. And its downplaying of Chekhov's farce and tragicomic ironies ultimately deprived the audience of Chekhov's full palette and paradoxically reduced the tragic effect inherent in Krejča's reading.

I would also add that the production in its simplicity and purity had a

Plate 13 Marie Tomášová, Jan Hartl, and Milan Riehs in Act 2 of Krejča's *Cherry Orchard* (1990). Photo: Martin Poš.

definitiveness that may come to be valued most fully in retrospect. During the performance itself, the curtailing of immediate 'entertainment' and absence of any special slant was a distinct disappointment to many who – recalling Krejča's last Chekhov productions in Prague – came expecting something much more provocative. From having seen some of those earlier Chekhov productions, especially the *Three Sisters* (1966), I also noted the general absence of energized, patterned physical movement, previously almost a Krejča trademark.

The next several Krejča productions at Gate Theatre II (*Waiting for Godot*, Nestroy's *One-Ended Rope*, and Schnitzler's *Impossible Man*) fared better but did not provoke enthusiasm in audiences. Only the very last production rekindled the excitement that had once been the norm for Krejča. In the spring of 1994 Krejča and Svoboda collaborated (with Kraus, of course) on Pirandello's *The Mountain Giants*, in which Krejča once again successfully demonstrated the talents that had made him famous thirty years before – deep study of text and characterization, masterfully orchestrated, disciplined staging, plus a sixth sense for touching the nerve of contemporary issues, which had not been evident in the previous productions. Otherwise, the very nature of the play lent itself to more sheer stage and scenographic action, to which Svoboda contributed a striking use of a large semi-transparent mirror that heightened the central theme of illusion and reality. The production was a milestone for several reasons, one of them profoundly ironic. Not only was it Krejča's most effective production since his return, and not only did it celebrate the renewed collaboration of two great artists, but also it was the swansong for Krejča's Theatre Beyond the Gate II.

The play itself, a strange parable of an itinerant theatre troupe, presents new variations on Pirandello's familiar obsession with truth and illusion, mask and reality. Here it culminates in a confrontation of theatre artists with indifferent sponsors and callous audiences. It echoed the fate of Krejča's theatre and its 1994 socio-economic context almost too painfully, for one of the consequences of the new market economy was the drastic reduction of monies to support the arts. In a disturbing parallel to the fate of Pirandello's travelling players in *The Mountain Giants*, Krejča's Theatre Beyond the Gate II closed down at the end of December 1994, thus becoming the first major theatrical casualty of deregulated free enterprise in the post-Communist era of the Czech Republic.

Nevertheless, Krejča had regained his stride in *Mountain Giants*. His most recent production, Goethe's *Faust*, Part One (1997), moved even further than *Mountain Giants* in the direction of Krejča's pre-exile productions. Once again he was working with Svoboda and Kraus in the National Theatre after an absence of thirty-three years (Plate 14). As he often did in the past, Krejča cut and rearranged numerous sections of the script to strengthen certain episodes, relationships, and themes. Equally important, Krejča wanted to stage various scenes or 'beats' of the script concurrently, and also to present

Plate 14 Svoboda and Krejča during a break in final dress rehearsals of *Faust* (1997) in the Estates Theatre. Photo: J. Burian.

to the audience certain symbols or images at moments not literally indicated in the script. As he himself put it, 'Amorphous visions rapidly change into seeds of symbols, forms, images. The imagination is prompted to seek in the concrete stage elements the equivalent of literary forms, the stylistic diversity of varied verse patterns, and shifts of genres.'[15] Responding to this complex, poetic vision, Svoboda created an expressive scenographic instrument using – interactively – a huge mirror, turntable, trapdoor, painted cloths, and projections to facilitate the multiple imagery and action Krejča sought.

In its scale, its dynamics, and its elaborate orchestration of many elements, including a deeply studied text, the *Faust* production evoked memories of Krejča at his prime in such stagings as *Romeo and Juliet*, *Lorenzaccio*, and *Oedipus–Antigone*. When I saw two of its previews in June 1997, the many elements had not yet fully meshed in a fluid, coherent whole, even though many individual sequences were powerful. Any final assessment would have to take into consideration such factors as the varied strengths of the actors, the unusually daunting length of the production (just short of four hours), and the limited rehearsal time available for the precision-demanding integration of the large cast with technically complicated components of the scenography – and an extensive musical score. The reviews following the September premiere were mixed and indicated that the production still needed further ripening. Nevertheless, more than one critic's conclusion was that the return of a joint Krejča–Svoboda project to the National Theatre was a revelation of a theatre experience lately in short supply. As one critic said, the production has

> an admirable grandness of scope, something we do not often encounter today. We have a reasonable amount of interesting and decent 'small theatre' activity available, but what are we to make of a theatre that despite today's all-engulfing smallness once again strives toward a large format, a theatre that not only leads us beyond the borders of the everyday, but also – above all – transcends us in attempting to create a distinctive version of age-old poetic visions?[16]

From the understated, finely shaded production details and the total fidelity to the text evident in the 1991 *Cherry Orchard* to the broad scale and vitality of the 1997 *Faust*, Krejča displayed a spectrum of his mature artistry working within new, often problematic circumstances. As late as the spring of 2001, *Faust* was still in the repertoire, but Krejča had no ongoing tie to the National Theatre or any other theatre. As was true so often before for Krejča, the future was open.

* * *

Any overall assessment of Krejča's significance to Czech theatre must remain tentative, but Václav Havel's observation in 1969 still has validity as one thoughtful attempt to describe the essence of his theatre:

> How might we summarize the characteristic signs of Krejča's aesthetics? I would say, in a unique and interesting union: on the one hand, the efforts of a non-thesis theatre, a theatre of rich and multi-leveled import, which in complex structures very sensitively mirrors a whole range of movement in human sensibilities and renounces all schematic interpretations of the world; on the other hand, a sustained desire for perfection, leading the actor to animate worked-out, thought-through stage concepts, visions, and intentions, the precision of which is rich and sometimes even ornamental.[17]

6

GROSSMAN, MACHÁČEK, SCHORM

Three major Czech directors of the late twentieth century

I would like to supplement the previous studies of Hilar, Burian, Radok, and Krejča with a briefer look at three other Czech directors of lesser prominence but of uncontestable importance in defining the best of Czech theatre in the second half of the twentieth century, especially in Prague. I have made various references to them in previous chapters and there will be some other references to them in the remainder of the book, but I believe that their work warrants a more detailed account here.[1]

The death in February 1993 of director Jan Grossman, Václav Havel's chief collaborator in the 1960s at the Theatre on the Balustrade, was a severe loss to Czech theatre in the era of reorganization and reorientation following the Velvet Revolution. Grossman died two years after Miroslav Macháček, major actor and director at the National Theatre since the 1950s, and only a bit more than four years after Evald Schorm, freelance and youngest of this triad of significant theatre directors. Although they did not gain as much attention as their countrymen Alfred Radok and Otomar Krejča, these three directors nevertheless helped to create and keep alive the high standards of Czech theatre before and after the Prague Spring of 1968. A brief survey of their careers is a reminder of the range and quality of Czech theatre in the second half of the twentieth century, when the arts were heavily subsidized but ideologically and bureaucratically restricted by the Communist regime.

An important literary critic, theorist, and editor, Grossman (1925–93) entered the world of theatre shortly after World War II as a reader at the National Theatre in Prague. Later, after working a few years as a dramaturge at the State Theatre in Brno, Grossman returned to Prague in the early 1950s as dramaturge and occasional director for E. F. Burian's revived D34 theatre. But Grossman's most significant theatrical activity occurred first as dramaturge and then as director and head of drama at the Theatre on the Balustrade in Prague during 1962–68, years when the nation moved from the restrictions of a rigid Communist system to the enlightened Prague Spring of 1968 and its motif of socialism with a human face.

Grossman brought a sense of literary discipline and structure to the theatre, formulating an artistic policy that gave the theatre a special identity. In this he had the good fortune of working with Václav Havel, who was resident playwright and later dramaturge under Grossman. Grossman's program at the Theatre on the Balustrade created a theatre of conscious 'appeal' to its spectators. The productions were carefully conceptualized and theatrically inventive models of social, political, psychological behavior that confronted the audiences with implicit questions regarding the society in which they lived. The plays, which tended toward absurdist satires, were mostly original works, such as Havel's first three full-length plays (*The Garden Party*, *The Memorandum*, directed by Grossman, and *The Increasing Difficulty of Concentration*) or Grossman's provocative adaptation and direction of works like Jarry's *Ubu* cycle and Kafka's *The Trial*. All these productions brought the theatre sustained success at home, international attention, and tours abroad.

Both Grossman and Havel resigned from the Balustrade theatre for nonpolitical reasons even before the Soviet-led invasion and occupation in August 1968. Nevertheless, for the next twenty-one years, because of his implicitly critical, liberal artistic profile, Grossman was restricted to directing abroad or in peripheral but progressive Czech theatres to which he brought his distinctive style. Until 1974 he directed abroad, chiefly in the Netherlands and Switzerland. The years 1974–82 saw his return to directing in Czechoslovakia, although it was limited to provincial theatres, chiefly in Cheb and Hradec Králové. Finally, from 1983 to 1988 he was able to direct in Prague again, but only in the peripheral S. K. Neumann Theatre, where Otomar Krejča had spent several seasons in the early 1970s. His hard-earned return to prominence was capped in the spring of 1989 when he was allowed to return to the Balustrade theatre as a guest director of Molière's *Don Juan*, which proved to be one of the outstanding productions of the Prague season.

Fact became more dramatic than fiction when, after the Velvet Revolution swept the previously jailed dissident Václav Havel to the presidency of Czechoslovakia at the end of 1989, Grossman staged Havel's previously banned *Largo Desolato* at the Balustrade in April 1990, even persuading President Havel to provide a recorded voice-over narration of the stage directions as part of the performance. Later that same year, Grossman once again became head of drama at the theatre, and in the summer of 1991 he was named its artistic director, although not before a bitter internal power struggle with the actors, who wanted the theatre to adopt a more commercial orientation in the post-Communist era (Plate 15). In that same summer of 1991, he was officially granted the Doctor of Philosophy degree from Charles University; it was a degree he had earned in 1949, but it had been held up for forty-two years by his tacit refusal to compromise with Communist cultural authorities.

A patient, gentlemanly intellectual, but painstakingly persistent in his staging demands, Grossman's work was marked by a thorough, philosophically slanted analysis of the text, a selection of telling stage images, and a

Plate 15 Jan Grossman with playwright-dramaturge Karel Steigerwald at the entrance to the Theatre on the Balustrade (1990). Photo: J. Burian.

precisely defined mise en scène that sought to reveal the socially relevant motifs of the play rather than Grossman's subjective 'take' on it. Nevertheless, Grossman's work was often marked by personal directorial touches in staging. In his production of Albee's *Who's Afraid of Virginia Woolf?*, which I saw in 1988, I was struck by his use of loud recorded chimes to signal entries, moments when characters hurled objects in rage, and, at end of the play, four or five large golden rubber balls tossed on stage from off stage (to signify this has been a playroom for infants?). Another example of Grossman's stage imagery was the interpolated use of a tattered, obviously stage-shop-constructed plague memorial as the central acting space for the Balustrade *Don Juan*: Don Juan and Sganarelle lived within the lower parts of the lathing and papier-mâché construction, while the vertically segmented levels and small ramps allowed for a dynamization of the action as Juan and Sganarelle confronted the other characters of the play. Using Havel's own recorded, off stage voice reading the initial stage directions in the production of *Largo Desolato* was a more capricious, witty conceit.

Grossman directed three other plays at the Balustrade, a new play by the theatre's resident playwright, Karel Steigerwald – *Alas, Alas, Fear, the Noose, and the Pit* (1990), Havel's *Temptation* (1991), and Alan Bennett's *Kafka's Dick* (1993), his final work. In the fall of 1992, before his death, he had invited a bright new director to work in the Balustrade theatre. Petr Lébl had gained notoriety with his amateur, fringe productions, but Grossman obviously recognized a special talent in him. The following spring, Lébl not only directed a production at the Balustrade theatre but also successfully competed for the position of artistic head after Grossman's death. From 1993 to 1999, Lébl's often controversial productions brought the Balustrade new fame.[2]

* * *

Like Jan Grossman, Miroslav Macháček and Evald Schorm endured various forms of restriction and oppression during the Communist years, primarily in being prevented from working steadily at their art and craft because they would not adapt to various pressures and demands from official authorities. Macháček (1922–91), a major actor as well as director, was banished from work in Prague during the 1950s and then prevented from directing during most of the 1980s. Schorm (1931–88) was restricted to itinerant and intermittent work in theatre after his successful career as a film scenarist and director (e.g., *Enough Courage for Every Day*, 1964) in the Czech New Wave era was terminated as part of the purging of liberal forces following the crushing of the Prague Spring. Despite these forced gaps in their creative efforts, each made his mark on Czech theatre.

Macháček worked in several provincial theatres as well as Prague's Municipal Theatres before being brought into the National Theatre as both actor and director in 1959 by Otomar Krejča. His most notable productions for the National Theatre included *Oedipus Rex* (1963: see Plate 16), the Čapeks' *Insect Comedy* (1965: see Plate 17), *Henry V* (1971), *School for Scandal* (1972), the Czech classic, *Our Swaggerers* (Naši Furianti, 1979), and *Hamlet* (1982), a straightforward but powerfully affecting production that remained in the repertoire for six years. Macháček also acted in some of these productions (the Tramp in *Insect Comedy* and the First Player in *Hamlet*). Luka in *Lower Depths*, Shakespeare's Henry IV, Macbeth, and Tybalt were some of his other major roles in the National Theatre and other Prague theatres. A choleric, intense, often sarcastic and goading personality, Macháček was above all an actors' director who sought out the passionate core of a drama's confrontations. Not inclined toward avant-garde experimentation in staging, he nevertheless worked fruitfully with Josef Svoboda, infusing the latter's often abstract, metaphoric sets with a richly textured, vivid humanity in the give and take of the actors' performances. In a Macháček production, the characters were almost always more colorful, broader, more intense than one anticipated they would be.

Macháček's uncompromising, fierce commitment to the spirit of independence led logically enough to his becoming the chief spokesman for the Prague actors and ensembles who played a central role during the turbulent demonstrations, strikes, and debates of the Velvet Revolution.[3] His last

Plate 16 Miroslav Macháček's production of *Oedipus Rex* (1963) at the National Theatre, with Svoboda's scenography. Photo: Dr. Jaromír Svoboda.

work in the theatre occurred less than a year later, as Serebriakov in *Uncle Vanya* (1990), which was preceded by his final direction, Shelagh Delaney's *A Taste of Honey* (1988). Both productions were in the National Theatre.

* * *

Evald Schorm's personality and directing style were the opposite of Macháček's. A handsome, tall man, quiet, reticent, and gentle, he worked best by indirection. Rather than exhort his actors like Macháček, or provide subtle analyses like Grossman, he would seemingly throw up his hands and

Plate 17 Macháček's production of the Čapeks' *The Insect Comedy* (1965) in the National Theatre, with Svoboda's tilted mirrors. Photo: Dr. Jaromír Svoboda.

declare he did not know what a given moment meant or how to handle a difficult sequence, thus appealing to the actors for a special, intimate artistic collaboration, to which most responded enthusiastically. Again unlike Macháček, most of whose work was for a single company, the large, institutional National Theatre, Schorm worked primarily with a number of relatively small studio theatres, such as the Drama Club (Činoherní klub), the Balustrade theatre, Ypsilon Theatre, Theatre on a String (Divadlo na provázku) of Brno, and the theatre in Ústí on the Elbe.

All these ensembles and other even smaller groups keenly anticipated his guest-directing visits, for he seemed to bring a breath of simplicity and purity with him, a disarming modesty that hid the intense, perceptive study he devoted to each project. Among his outstanding productions for studio theatres were his own adaptations of novels, such as *Crime and Punishment* (1966, his first stage work, for the Drama Club) and *The Brothers Karamazov* (1979), for the Balustrade theatre. Other highly regarded works were *Othello* (1979) and *Macbeth* (1981), each of which revealed a taste for stylized experimentation, such as the use of mattresses in *Macbeth*, and the Kabuki elements in

Plate 18 Evald Schorm and Svoboda during a final rehearsal of *The Magical Circus* in the late 1970s in New York. Photo: J. Burian.

the costuming and acting of *Othello*. His *Hamlet* (1978), for the Balustrade theatre, was another very expressive, unconventional, and sharply critical production in the era of Normalization. It is described more fully in other chapters.[4]

Schorm's work was not restricted entirely to small-scale studio work, however. His most lasting affiliation was with the Laterna Magika Theatre ensemble, headed by Josef Svoboda, who saw in Schorm's film and theatre expertise an ideal source of creative contribution to the complex mixed media form of Laterna Magika (Plate 18). The most successful of Schorm's six Laterna Magika productions were *The Magical Circus* (1977), *Night Rehearsal* (1981, a probing critique of eroding ethical values in Czechoslovakia during that era), and the lavish spectacle of *Odysseus* (1987: see Plate 23, p. 120). He also directed a number of opera productions, including some with Svoboda, chiefly abroad. Indeed, his last directorial work was the National Theatre production of Beethoven's *Fidelio* in 1988. Nevertheless, it is as a director of more intimate, psychologically centered works drawing on the actors' distinctive talents that Schorm will probably be longest remembered.

As the Czech theatre reformatted and reoriented itself in the 1990s, these three artists, among the few remaining survivors of the high-water mark of the Czech theatre of the 1960s, were sorely missed.[5]

7

JOSEF SVOBODA

Among most theatre followers throughout the world, Josef Svoboda is the best known and most highly regarded Czech theatre artist of the past half-century.[1] Born in 1920, he is now among the most senior of major Czech theatre practitioners, one of the dwindling number of those who launched their professional careers in the 1940s, during or immediately following World War II. Despite stresses and pressures of many kinds, he is probably the sole leading artist to have worked without interruption in Czech theatre since the 1940s. Like a self-regenerating natural force, Josef Svoboda not only survived the strains and traumas of his homeland in those years but also achieved a world reputation.

His work has been applauded on the stages of major theatres throughout Europe, including Britain, and in the United States and Canada, as has his exhibition work in World's Fairs and lesser expositions. His directorial collaborators have included such figures as Laurence Olivier, Wolfgang Wagner, Götz Friedrich, Giorgio Strehler, John Dexter, and Roland Petit. He has received international awards and honors from theatre organizations, art academies, and architectural institutes, honorary degrees from universities, and the French Légion d'honneur. The sheer quantity of his output challenges credibility – over 700 productions of drama, opera, and ballet since 1946. Of more significance, however, is that his work – his 'scenography' – altered and expanded the parameters of twentieth-century stage design.

Many references to his specific productions and artistic collaborations in Czech theatre are to be found in preceding and subsequent chapters. In what follows, I shall try to describe in more detail his distinctive talents and contributions not only to Czech but also to world theatre, including a more detailed account of the development of his and Radok's Laterna Magika.

* * *

Svoboda was born in 1920 in Čáslav, a small Czech city some 50 miles east of Prague. After acquiring the skills of a master craftsman in his father's cabinet and furniture-making establishment, he went to Prague in the late 1930s to study art history and philosophy at Charles University. But

European history intervened, and by the end of the war Svoboda had shifted his studies to interior architecture and become associated with several young theatre groups. By 1948, he was concurrently chief designer and technical supervisor of a major Prague theatre and a full-time student of architecture.

At the present time, Svoboda is a creative artist still actively engaged in his career, working at home and abroad. From the early 1950s to the mid-1970s he was the chief designer as well as chief of technical operations at the National Theatre, and from 1969 until 1990 a professor of architecture in Prague's School of Applied and Industrial Arts, from which he himself had graduated. Now over 80, he remains artistic head of Laterna Magika, today's descendant of the 1958 innovation he produced with Alfred Radok. Svoboda has been in charge of it since the early 1970s.

Svoboda's name is chiefly associated with a full-scale artistic exploitation of the latest mechanical, electronic, and optical devices (many of which he and his staff developed themselves), with the so-called kinetic stage, with wide-ranging use of sophisticated lighting and projection techniques, and with radical assaults on the limitations of the still dominant proscenium theatre.

In this and other respects his work recalls the ideal of the artists of the Bauhaus school of the 1920s: a synthesis of art and technology. His work has also been related to that of such giants of modern stage theory and practice as Appia, Craig, and Piscator, as well as the Soviet avant-garde of the 1920s. All such associations, however, still require considerable qualification to define his talent.

He is, for example, less a theoretical visionary than was Appia or Craig, but he surpasses them in his mastery of sophisticated materials and techniques as well as in sheer practical experience. Many of his productions recall the emphasis on scenic dynamics and the stage-as-mechanism evident in the early post-revolutionary work of the Soviet theatricalists Meyerhold and Tairov, but Svoboda's greater technical sophistication and less tendentious approach provide a generally subtler, more emotive experience. Similarly, although some of his most audacious work in the fusion of film and stage relates to the earlier work of Piscator, Svoboda has attained a more complex level of creation with a hybrid form combining actor and screened image.

In Czechoslovakia itself, Svoboda could draw on a rich, architecturally grounded stage design tradition. Influenced by avant-garde staging in both western European and Soviet theatres in the early part of the twentieth century, the Czech theatre consistently incorporated expressive stage settings as an integral component of production, as a subsequent chapter on Czech designers will illustrate. Indeed, it took the lead in this regard during the 1930s as repressive political forces gained strength elsewhere in Europe. Svoboda absorbed much from the work of several important earlier Czech designers, especially Vlastislav Hofman and František Tröster; others he admired include Antonín Heythum, Bedřich Feuerstein, František Muzika, and František Zelenka. All but Muzika were trained as architects. E. F. Burian was a special influence by virtue of his provocative avant-garde theatre and his innovative work with lighting and projections, especially in his Theatregraph, a prototype of Laterna Magika.

More than anyone else in modern stage design, Svoboda has embodied a union of artist, scientist, and professional theatre worker. Technically a master of his complex medium, thoroughly conversant with the realities of theatrical production – the pressures of deadlines, budgets, personnel super-vision, and inter-artistic cooperation – he is essentially a superb theatre artist applying his creative imagination to the scenic fundamentals of space, light, and movement. He comes closer than most to embodying Craig's ideal of the 'artist of the theatre,'[2] as well as Piscator's and Brecht's hopes for 'a theatre that would truly belong to our century.'[3]

The term 'scenography' is a loaded one for Svoboda. In its historic sense, scenography for Svoboda relates back to the Renaissance and Baroque mas-ters, such as Serlio, Sabbatini, Torelli, and the Bibienas, men who were archi-tects and engineers bringing scientific method and technological expertise to the service of scenic art. Conceptually, a scenographer is not merely a visual artist interested in creating pictorial effects or backgrounds, but one who has mastered the principles of design in relation to one of the 'harder' discip-lines, such as painting, sculpture, graphic art, or, above all, architecture, for the scenographer's primary challenge is that of defining, controlling, and transforming space, dramatic space: stage space which accommodates a given production and no other. Equally important, however, his scenography is flexible and adaptable, like an instrument in an orchestra: at a given point in the performance it may dominate, but at another point it may virtually disappear, depending upon the guiding concept of the production and its director-conductor.

Scenographers should also be able to think as a director; they must be concerned with the ways in which their scenic proposals will *function dramat-ically* in the evolving stage action. Scenography is not concerned with scenery as mere decor or as a static illustration of place. A stage setting should be a dynamic, transformable component of the total dramatic action, very much an 'actor' in the performance. In Svoboda's words,

> I don't want a static picture, but something that evolves, that has movement, not necessarily physical movement, of course, but a set-ting that is dynamic, capable of expressing changing relationships, feelings, moods, perhaps only by lighting, during the course of the action.

Svoboda also has a rage for order, for the laws that underlie his work. His feelings about music are significant in this respect:

I admire its order, its purity, its cleanness – this is what I would like to establish in scenography. I know it's impossible but at least I want to aim for it. I'd like to eliminate dilettantism and make theatre truly professional. Scenography is a *discipline*. I've been pursuing an ideal for [over fifty] years: precision, systematization, perfection, and control of the expressive means available to scenography, even the ordinary means. Why shouldn't this age make the most of its technical developments as previous eras did? That is, the machinery of the baroque era, the electric light at the turn of the century.

A scenographer, according to Svoboda, must master the 'expressive means' of his day. As the Renaissance sculptor knew the medium of stone or metal, the scenographer must know the contemporary techniques, materials, and technical devices – kinetic mechanisms, light, sound, pictorial techniques of projection by means of film, TV, or slides, or laser and hologram technology. Only then may a wonderful thing happen: these materials and techniques may become a source of inspiration. But these expressive means should remain nonintrusive, nondisruptive of the main action of the play, virtually nonevident; they must serve the production as a whole and be used only when dramatically necessary.

An example of what he considers to be the essence of scenography as distinct from stage design is found in the projected but unproduced version of Goethe's *Faust*, with Alfred Radok as director in the late 1960s. The production concept involved the dual identity of Faust's domestic servant and Mephistopheles; an instant distinction between the two identities became crucial. The setting would consist of a huge room virtually empty except for the thousands of books lining its walls. Svoboda's chief scenographic contribution would be invisible: a floor designed to produce either a heavy, hollow sound of steps or else absolutely no noise, depending on who walked on it and precisely where he walked. As Svoboda describes it:

> The servant walks to the door, and we hear the hollow sound of his steps in the vast room. He turns just as he reaches the door, and starts back – and suddenly – silence! – and we know, instantly, that it's the devil. Nothing is visible, but this is scenography and is what I think sets me apart from most other designers. It is scenography raised to scenographic direction.

*   *   *

Svoboda's relation to his work and to the Communist regime needs some comment. How did he, unlike most prominent theatre artists, manage to survive and remain productive through all the stresses of the Communist era? Fundamental to any answer is that stage design/scenography is inherently less vulnerable to censorious monitoring than a playscript or a directorial interpretation of a playscript; moreover, a scenographer does not carry the high profile of a playwright or director. Beyond that, he was protected by the growing international acclaim for his work (including strong admiration of his work in the Soviet Union); finally, the state reaped a substantial portion of Svoboda's hard currency honoraria for his work in the West.

He joined the Communist Party shortly after the war primarily for tactical reasons, as a way of strengthening the work of the theatre he was with at the time. In doing so, he was also motivated by his belief that the Communist program was a rational one that paralleled his own attitudes. His sociopolitical outlook always favored free enterprise and free expression, but was opposed to any system that tolerated hunger among its people. He believed that socialism, ideally, assumes the responsibility of caring for all its citizens. Like most of his colleagues, however, he perceived that the honeymoon under the Communist regime was over and that the system was a disaster during the deadly show trials of the early 1950s.

Svoboda consistently strove to remain apolitical, in so far as that position was possible. Neither a practicing Communist nor a dissident, he remained in the Party primarily because he wanted to be able to do his work under optimal conditions. Like other Czechs he had learned how to sidestep, evade, and outwit the wartime German occupiers; the practice carried over into the hard Communist years. He avoided involvement in Party matters, meetings, action groups, and so on. Unlike many colleagues even more disillusioned than him, he was fortunate in never being forced to provide overt support for the Party or overt condemnation of the dissident movements.

In many respects, the Communist regime was generous to the arts, but almost always at a heavy price. Svoboda was not spared some harsh reprisals. For example, in the wake of the Warsaw Pact invasion of 1968 many people were pressured to make overt declarations of approval of the invasion; Svoboda did not do so, and one consequence was his being stripped of his function as chief of technical operations in the National Theatre, although he stayed on as chief designer.

He could easily have secured lucrative, permanent employment beyond the iron curtain from the mid-1960s on, but Svoboda chose to retain his base of operations and his home in Prague. In staying, he was able to exert some resistance to the system from within by his scenography, which in many productions helped to embody metaphoric opposition to the prevailing regime. As head of Laterna Magika, he was also in a position to shelter numerous politically vulnerable theatre people who otherwise would have been without work, for example Evald Schorm, who directed several Laterna productions in the 1970s and 1980s.

Not the least of his reasons for staying was also his intense identification with his native culture – his 'cradle,' as he has put it. Svoboda's feeling for his roots – personal and professional – is particularly apparent whenever he speaks of his feeling for Czech history and culture, as well as his early years and experiences. His love of nature, his respect for craftsmanship and order, his feeling for raw materials, like wood, that serve theatre, and his acute responsiveness to the properties of space and light were all part of his boyhood in Čáslav.

Writing understatedly of his critical decisions at the end of the war, Svoboda recently observed:

> Like most of my generation I believed that after the war it would be possible to build a better world, in which liberated art would reign. Like most of my generation I experienced disillusionment and dis-appointment, and like most I accepted November 1989 as a relief and a new promise.[4]

Indeed, in the hectic early hours of the Velvet Revolution, Svoboda put the quarters and facilities of his Laterna Magika theatre at the disposal of Václav Havel and the Civic Forum movement. Typically, it was done without fanfare.

*　*　*

Since a number of his productions are noted elsewhere in this book, I should like to conclude this chapter on Svoboda with a closer look at a few charac-teristic examples of his scenography from his early, middle, and late years.

At least brief documentation should be provided for some of Svoboda's freshest, least inhibited, perhaps most extravagant creativity released after the war and most fully expressed in variations on the principle of surrealistic collage. Perhaps the single best example was the Prague production of *The Tales of Hoffmann* in 1946, his first work with Radok and his first big post-war production (Plate 19). Carrying on the tradition of the 'liberated stage' of the prewar avant-garde, both Czech and Russian, the production was deliberately unconventional in its use of fantasy and conscious theatricality, starting with Radok's adaptation of the text, which had the action begin in a theatre costume room. Subsequent action developed in a fantasy space with several acting areas juxtaposing traditional period atmosphere with blatantly modernistic components.

The key was a liberated imagination, which makes everything possible. A character arrives in a mini-auto; fifteen duelists accompany a duel; a white cyclorama shifts to a black one. A large, suspended sphere opens to reveal Antonia, who sits on a chair more than 6 feet off the floor. Her gown falls to the floor and is drawn by a funeral wagon and a rocking horse; the whole effect is surrealistic. As the opera draws to a close, the gown lifts up and reveals an old theatre curtain that ends the whole opera.

A later, mid-career production embodying a high degree of conscious theatricalization was the culmination of Svoboda's use of theatre itself in

Plate 19 Alfred Radok's prototypal postmodern version of *The Tales of Hoffmann* (1946), with scenography by Josef Svoboda, in the Grand Opera of the Fifth of May. Photographer unknown.

his designs. The Prague *Don Giovanni* (1969) was a production that by its very nature must remain unique (Plate 20). The central concept arose from the collaboration of Svoboda and his long-time colleague Václav Kašlík. Svoboda had designed numerous productions of *Don Giovanni* previously, both in Czechoslovakia and abroad, but this one was to be different:

> My primary goal was to express the unique Prague-ness of the work. The design was deliberately nonrepeatable, with meaning only in Prague; specifically, I saw the opera in the context of the Tyl [Estates] Theatre, where it had its original premiere.

Svoboda extended the Mozartian-era decor of the auditorium itself onto the stage to form the very setting of the opera's action. The opera that was written in Prague, for Prague, and had its premiere in Prague in this very theatre under Mozart's own direction, was now performed not only in that same theatre again, but also within a setting that duplicated the interior in which it was originally performed. The effect was dense and powerful; it was theatre in theatre, *transcended*. And surely the stressing of Prague's unique cultural treasure was not coincidental less than one year after the Warsaw Pact invasion.

Plate 20 The Václav Kašlík–Svoboda *Don Giovanni* (1969), National Theatre. The mobile boxes separated to reveal a backdrop of Mozart's time. Photo: Dr. Jaromír Svoboda.

Svoboda's remarks suggested additional implications inherent in his concept:

> I deliberately used aged, period, somewhat deteriorated theatrical objects, props, even chandeliers, from Mozart's time, and deliberately revealed old painted backdrops and curtains between the boxes on stage or else as total backdrops. I wanted to evoke the feel of an old eighteenth-century theatre – the feeling of the 'ghosts' of theatre. A person with imagination really feels the ultimate significance of a curtain; a theatre; a stage; an auditorium; and their relationship – the significance and strength of theatre in the evolution of society.[5]

As late as 1991, Svoboda was still demonstrating what could be done in a nontraditional theatre space, this one the main chamber of a converted bank in Antwerp: a large open space with three levels of galleries around its perimeter. Most productions staged there take place on a stage at one end of the open floor area, but for Max Frisch's *Biedermann and the Firebugs*, the decision was to use the central area for a form of arena staging and then stage

111

the attic scenes on a gridwork of stretched steel cables at the level of the second gallery – a 'layer cake' approach to central staging. Before the play started, the grid above the central acting area was covered with Studio folio, a gray, translucent plastic material; as the play began, this folio burst into flame (via film projection from above) and then was aggressively stripped away while oil drums were noisily rolled around above the audience. Subsequent scenes also took place on this upper level. The whole grid measured 8 meters by 16 meters; the cables were 5 millimeters thick and formed 8 × 8 centimeter squares, quite adequate to support the actors. The grid was suspended from above by several rows of thin cables sufficiently separated to allow free movement by the actors.

Svoboda's inventive use of mirrors has enriched many of his productions. A notable one, Svoboda's second *Insect Comedy* (Ze života hmyzu, Prague, 1965), directed by Miroslav Macháček, combined two huge slanted mirrors tilted over the stage, the main part of which was a turntable with variously patterned cloths (one for each act) on its surface (see Plate 17, p. 102). The combination of the rotating turntable and the multiple, constantly altering reflected images of its surface created a kaleidoscopic, virtual space capturing the teeming insect world of the play. It was a prime example of Svoboda's kinetic, dynamically alterable scenography.

Two late variations of mirror-scenography could be seen in the 1990s. Svoboda's production of Verdi's *La Traviata* (1992) employed one huge mirrored surface tilted over a very wide stage on which were many layers of painted cloth scenery representing the scenes to follow. The initial, top layer was a painted curtain from Verdi's era. The mirrored reflections formed the background of each scene as each layer was stripped away.

Svoboda's more recent production, Goethe's *Faust*, with his veteran colleague Otomar Krejča (Prague, Estates Theatre, 1997), once again made use of a large mirror and a turntable (Plate 21). This mirror is circular, mobile, and semi-transparent, so as to function at times like a scrim; the turntable has a rectangular opening in its center, thereby allowing the mirror to reflect not only the surface of the stage but also the various actions and scenic elements located below stage level – including projected images onto the substage floor; and the opening in the turntable is spanned by a *Biedermann*-like gridwork of cables, which enable actors to walk or even lie on its surface for still more complex visual imagery in keeping with the different layers of reality in Krejča's concept of the work.

A notable use of untraditional projection surfaces which in themselves create a spatial scenography was present in Chekhov's *The Sea Gull* (Louvain, 1988). *The Sea Gull* production was Svoboda's fifth version, and the first he had done with a director other than Otomar Krejča. The scenography was austere, abstract, and yet remarkably lyrical. It consisted of the lightest, silky nylon drapes suspended in various configurations above the floor; most hung some 4 centimeters above the stage level, and it was easy to walk

Plate 21 The Krejča–Svoboda production of Goethe's *Faust*, Part One (1997), National Theatre. Mephistopheles is seen reflected in a mirror suspended above the stage; the actor is actually lying down some twenty to thirty feet up stage of the standing Faust. Photo: Hana Smejkalová.

through them as well as to 'use' them occasionally, as when Nina wrapped herself in one while referring to herself as a sea gull. They were sensitive to the lightest breeze and were almost always in some motion from strategically placed fans. 'They became alive, contained an energy, a fourth dimension. It would have been stupid without the movement. Moreover, they also suggested the period of the play,' Svoboda commented. The ceiling was of the same material and diffused the light rays sent through it. Projections were minimal, such as a suggestion of leaves in the first act. Contrasting with the abstract nature of the drapes were naturalistic elements such as the unfinished floorboards, actual leaves, and actual water as rain in the last act. Some thirty years earlier, in the initial Krejča–Svoboda *Sea Gull* in Prague, the impressionistic mood was more realistically captured by brilliant, intense streams of light passing through leafy branches suspended above the stage (see Plate 11, p. 82).

Three strongly contrasting productions suggest the range of Svoboda's inventiveness and creative imagination: a realistic play infused with cosmic overtones, a large-scale, technically complex opera, and a classic Czech folk comedy.

The challenge in staging Paul Zindel's *The Effect of Gamma Rays on*

Plate 22 Svoboda's scenography for Paul Zindel's *The Effect of Gamma Rays on Man-in-the-Moon Marigolds* (1972), directed by Jaromír Pleskot, National Theatre. Photo: Josef Svoboda.

Man-in-the-Moon Marigolds (Prague, 1972) was to capture both the commonplace realism of the play as well as its transcendent implications (Plate 22). Svoboda's solution was abstract and powerfully metaphoric: thousands of small spheres literally filled the stage space around a grittily realistic selection of household furniture and props. The small spheres suggest many things – cells, molecules, structures of order and energy, and, finally, mystery; their massive repetition is finally what is decisive thematically and scenographically. The lighting could reinforce the presence of the spheres almost overwhelmingly or else make them virtually invisible.

Svoboda has collaborated on three complete cycles of Richard Wagner's *Ring of the Nibelungen*, in London (1974–76), Geneva (1975–77), and outdoors in southern France (1988), respectively. A pictorial-architectonic mix distinguished Svoboda's scenography for his most recent version, in the ancient Roman theatre in Orange. By means of contemporary hi-tech scenography, a setting for Wagner's nineteenth-century *Ring* was created within a two-thousand-year-old classical theatre – a remarkable juxtaposition, but also fusion, of cultural resonances. The *scaenae frons* of the Roman theatre was respected and made visible on various occasions during the production. 'I wanted this magnificent wall to be part of the production,' said Svoboda.

The image of a circle (or, indeed, ring), a sphere, a 'world' was the essence of the central scenographic components: a suspended quarter sphere, the complete steel circle/ring that formed its base (35 meter diameter), and the semicircular concave stairs below them. All these were also echoed in the circular seating of the musical orchestra. Partially transparent pliable sheeting lined the semi-hemisphere, thus facilitating a variety of projections that imaged the world and the heavens as the total environment of Wagner's epic music drama; four diapositive projectors and two 35 mm film projectors provided the projections. The scrim-like quality of the sheeting also enabled the Roman wall to be seen and serve as still another poetic perspective on the action of the opera. Exposed lighting units mounted on the circle extending the base of the semi-hemisphere heightened the air of conscious theatricality.

* * *

The simplest of these three productions was a nineteenth-century Czech classic, *Our Swaggerers* (Naší furianti), by Ladislav Stroupežnický, directed by Miroslav Macháček (Prague National Theatre, 1979). The stage depicted the black silhouette of a church steeple and village buildings against the sky. From the audience view, it seemed, logically, that a two-dimensional cutout of the village was placed somewhere forward of a cyclorama. In reality, however, it was not the village skyline that was a cutout form, but the bottom of the cyclorama. The village silhouette was actually empty black space. Why? Besides being a novel optical design illusion, it enabled actors and furniture to move on and off stage easily from a black void in the rear. It was a classic example of Svoboda's ease in shifting from elaborate hi-tech wizardry to minimalist ingenuity when circumstances prompt it, e.g., a directorial concept, low budget, or need for efficient, quick changes of scene.[6]

The austerity and technical simplicity of the scenography for *Our Swaggerers* lie at the opposite pole from most productions of the Laterna Magika, the production system employing – simultaneously – live performers with projected filmed images. I have already described its origins and essential characteristics, especially in Chapter 4 on Alfred Radok. Now, I shall trace its evolution from 1959, when Radok's association with it was terminated. First, however, a brief description of Polyekran, a cousin of Laterna Magika, is necessary.

Polyekran was the creation of Svoboda and Emil Radok, Alfred's brother, for a second and distinct Czechoslovak public relations visual 'show' at Expo 58; the word means 'multiple screens.' Its essential difference from Laterna Magika was that Polyekran was based on fixed screens of different shapes and sizes distributed variously in space, with no stage action or live performers. The interest lay strictly in the shifting collage of varied images projected onto the screens by a battery of film and slide projectors to the accompaniment of sound-effects and music. Although Polyekran did not involve an interplay of stage and screen, live and filmed action, some of its principles and techniques were eventually absorbed by Laterna Magika.

After Radok's departure, Svoboda stayed on with Laterna Magika to work with another of his early colleagues, composer and opera director Václav Kašlík, on a production of Offenbach's *Tales of Hoffmann* (1962). This version with Kašlík was notable in being the first Laterna Magika production of an opera or, more broadly, of an already composed dramatic work. Otherwise, in relation to the earlier Laterna Magika productions, it made relatively more use of stage components and the live action within them, including live singing. The production drew a mixed reaction, but in retrospect was regarded as insufficiently unified or adequately balanced in its combining of stage and film. Of course, it is this central problem of overall synthesis that still challenges those who work with Laterna Magika today.

What Radok, Svoboda, and others had originally envisioned as a long-range goal for Laterna Magika was the employment of its principles and techniques for major dramatic texts already written or yet to be written; that is, taking substantive works with a considerable textual component and reconfiguring them into Laterna Magika form. Radok had envisioned productions of Romain Rolland's *The Play of Love and Death* (which he eventually staged with great success as a straight theatre production) or a new scenario drawing on materials from the Eichmann trial. In actual practice, however, these visions or goals became compromised in varying degrees by the Laterna organization, sometimes almost totally. During the next ten years (the balance of the 1960s and into the 1970s), when Svoboda had little to do with the operations, efforts to approach the original ideals tended to be shortchanged by the new Laterna Magika producing teams, who turned out several fairly banal revue-type works emphasizing visual spectacle or sight gags for the tourist trade, none of which marked any real progress over the original productions.

In the meantime, even before the initial shift from the National Theatre, the Laterna Magika and the Polyekran processes had begun to be used by *other* theatres, specifically as components worked into what would otherwise have been regular productions of plays or operas. The results were not full-fledged Laterna productions, but in addition to employing some of its techniques they also achieved some of the basic intentions of Laterna Magika, such as creating a new theatrical reality possessing artistic seriousness and a distinct relevance to its audiences. The most notable of such productions were designed and technically supervised by Svoboda.

For example, as early as the fall of 1959, even before Laterna Magika II, Svoboda and Otomar Krejča staged an original play by Josef Topol, *Their Day*, in the National Theatre. They used a modified Polyekran projection system in conjunction with the main, live stage action. The projected images were mainly used as environmental background and indirect comment, while the Laterna use of the same characters on stage and in the film was minimal, as was the direct interplay between stage and screen. Another Laterna characteristic was that the screens could change size and position, as well as disappear and reappear.

In the same vein of non-Laterna Magika productions using Laterna principles and techniques, a very significant innovation occurred in the Boston Opera Company's production of Luigi Nono's *Intolleranza* (1965), directed by Sarah Caldwell, with projections and scenography by Svoboda. It could be considered a Piscatorian production in its emphatically propagandistic focus on social and political abuses, but its theatrical embodiment was clearly the Laterna Magika form, with one major novelty and advantage: the employment of live *television* projection as well as film and slide projection on multiple screens. One of Laterna Magika's chronic problems, indeed limitations, was its binding of the live performers to the fixed timing and rhythms of the film projections. By supplementing several film projectors with several live television projectors and monitors not only on stage but also off stage in interconnected locations, a much freer and more expressive staging was possible. A live chorus in an off stage location could be projected onto an on stage screen in relation to on stage action; the same technique would apply to the live projection of an on stage performer or even to a live projection of the audience itself at decisive moments in the on stage action.

Perhaps the most satisfying large-scale employment of Laterna elements in a straight dramatic production occurred with the reunion of Radok and Svoboda in staging Gorky's *The Last Ones* at the National Theatre in 1966, briefly described in Chapter 4 on Radok. In many ways, it was a masterful descendant of their prototypal, pre-Laterna production of *The Eleventh Commandment* (1950). Svoboda's scenography facilitated the Laterna Magika approach, as well as Radok's intersection technique, mentioned earlier. Only one large projection surface was used, an up stage wall. In one scene, for example, the projection of a wrongly arrested student is juxtaposed with the home life of the despotic but guilt-ridden police official responsible for the student's torment. In another scene, a careerist officer's true character is revealed by a projected image of his off stage actions in relation to his stage presence as a proper suitor of the police official's daughter. Both examples underline the critical Laterna characteristic of implicit if not actual interaction between screen image and live action. It is this inherently dramatic interplay that sets Laterna Magika apart from both Burian's Theatregraph and the earlier projection work of Piscator.

It was the last Laterna Magika-type production for the Radok–Svoboda duo. In August 1968 the Moscow Pact military forces invaded Czechoslovakia; two days later Radok and his family fled the country. Particularly poignant in the context of Laterna Magika, Radok had been adapting Goethe's *Faust* for possible Laterna production when the Soviet-led invasion occurred. He never completed the project.

Several other non-Laterna Magika productions designed by Svoboda within the next few years resembled those just mentioned in their use of

Laterna practices. Carl Orff's *Prometheus* (Munich, 1968) used the live tele-vision technique of *Intolleranza* in a more restricted but powerful manner. At certain moments, a live television image of Prometheus' face was simul-taneously projected onto the surface of the stylized rock to which he was pinioned on stage. For two other operas, L. J. Werle's *The Journey* (Hamburg, 1969) and B. A. Zimmermann's *The Soldiers* (Munich, 1969), Svoboda's scenography filled the stage with large cubic structures in and on which con-siderable action occurred, accompanied by large-scale, multiple projections of a documentary type, keyed in to heighten the impact of the music and libretto. In neither of the last two operas, however, did the projected images directly connect or interact with any on stage character or action as they had in *Intolleranza*, *The Last Ones*, or *Prometheus*. In this and other respects, the guiding antecedent was Polyekran as much as Laterna Magika.

The next major development in the history of Laterna Magika itself occurred in 1973 when it returned to its former status as a studio of the National Theatre and was put under Svoboda's control. This assured its ongoing experimental nature as well as high technical and design standards, for Svoboda is eclectic in his tastes and indefatigable in his pursuit of new expressive means. Although he continued his scenographic work in other theatres in Prague and throughout Europe, he also handled most though not all of the scenography for Laterna Magika. Since he took charge, it has produced over fifteen productions with many variations in choice of subject, staging space and format, and in the relative roles of text, scenography, live performance, and projection techniques. For example, in the last half of the 1970s, three productions of full-length stories were aimed at audiences pri-marily though not exclusively at children. The most successful of these, *The Magical Circus* (Kouzelný cirkus, 1977), has played internationally on tour and is still in the repertoire, having passed its 4,000th performance in 1995. Both scenario and direction were by Evald Schorm. Svoboda and others attribute its popularity to its universal, accessible storyline and gently rueful theme (two circus clowns in a lifelong pursuit of an unattainable, idealized Venus figure), and an effective balance between filmed and staged action.

In 1981, for the first time, Laterna Magika staged an original full-length, scripted drama written expressly for it. It was Antonín Máša's *Night Rehearsal* (Noční zkouška); in 1987 he wrote another, *Vivisection*. Both were intimate in scale – contemporary, realistic, psychological studies, with socio-political overtones – and both were crafted with Laterna Magika in mind as part of their original concept, although they echoed *Intolleranza* in using live television projection. Moreover, both used a metatheatre approach in situat-ing their respective actions in a place of performance, and both toned down the sheer element of visual spectacle in projected images; stage action and dialogue were central. The former play was a critique of contemporary social patterns of irresponsibility, as seen in the self-serving activities of the com-pany members, which had prompted their director to call a special, night rehearsal. Onstage action was supplemented not with film but solely with live television images projected onto a large on stage monitor to reveal backstage incidents as well as multi-angled shots of on stage action. The television cameras on stage were dramaturgically justified by situating the action of the play on a theatre stage having a special rehearsal of a current production with the rehearsal being shot as part of a television documentary on the fictive company. Directing *Night Rehearsal* was Schorm, whose sensitive work on some half-dozen Laterna Magika productions between 1975 and 1987 came closest to filling the void created by Radok's departure.

A similar socio-ethical theme formed the core of Máša's second custom-made play for Laterna Magika, *Vivisection*, which focused on ruinously irresponsible ecological policies of the state as demonstrated in their effects on one official's family. Once again, the action occurred in a performance area, this time a studio of a television station which was investigating the case, thereby justifying the presence of television cameras, projectors, monitors, and larger screen surfaces to show previously shot news reports. The use of live television (although film was used as well in *Vivisection*), the theatrical settings, and the air of contemporary actuality of the subjects made both productions very successful with the public, and suggested that this sort of smaller-scale, more realistic, non-spectacle work might be a viable alternative path for Laterna Magika. That it did not become so is most likely related to Laterna Magika's need for large audiences and high box office income to offset its massive, ongoing expenditures for equipment, technical processes, and salaries. Spectacle will draw more spectators than straight drama, in Prague as well as New York. The production was directed by Máša himself.

In striking contrast to the contemporary realism and studio scale of the two Máša productions was Laterna Magika's most spectacular production up to its time, Homer's *Odyssey*; adapted and directed by Schorm, it opened in 1987 and is still in the repertoire. Although deliberately designed for performances in large theatres or cultural halls, and deliberately intended to appeal to a mass audience who might like to break away from their television sets to see an adventure spectacle on a grand cinemascope scale, Laterna Magika's *Odysseus*, like the Máša plays, also leaned toward a humanistic, ethical message, related here to matters of fidelity, responsibility, and endurance as depicted in Odysseus' indomitable efforts to return to his home (Plate 23).

The fabric of this adaptation is an anachronistic, postmodern blend of antiquity, twentieth-century history with emphasis on barbaric warfare, and contemporary lifestyles. The film and staging techniques also reflect today's postmodern methods: fast cuts, multiple images, a mix of classic documentary film montage with almost cartoon-like animated footage, surrealistic images, startling contrasts between panoramic shots of the sea or cosmos and enormously enlarged close-ups. Two unconventional projection surfaces are used: a large, curving, and slanted cloth loosely attached to a scaffolding-like wall (the cloth at times is pulled away to allow movement on

Plate 23 A technical rehearsal of Laterna Magika's *Odysseus* shows the large sloping projection surface and the multi-purpose raft, here tilted up to reveal its trapdoor-plank that extended the raft's functions. Photo: J. Burian.

the scaffolding) and a smaller, mobile surface that is actually the bottom of Odysseus' raft, which is tiltable and suspended from the flies and able to move laterally from stage left to right and back. Complementing the filmed portions very effectively is a complex sound and music score, as well as vigorously choreographed, dialogueless on stage action. (The only speech one hears is in brief, occasional voice-overs in ancient Greek.) Particular attention is given to the interplay of the live and filmed forms of action, but not to the degree of the earliest Laterna Magika productions; in this production, the filmed portion functions as an expressive, atmospheric background as well as an occasional active, dramatic partner in direct interplay with the on stage performers.

The three productions that followed *Odysseus*, though not as broad in scope, continued the trend toward familiar classics or other well known subjects aimed at adult, international audiences seeking a healthy dose of spectacle in their entertainment. All three formed part of the 1990s repertoire with *Magical Circus* and *Odysseus*. The one Laterna Magika production directed by Svoboda himself, *Minotaurus* (1989), had as its basis Friedrich Dürrenmatt's poetic narrative of the Cretan legend, which emphasizes the pathos of the Minotaur's abuse by humanity. The audience heard parts of

Dürrenmatt's narrative by means of a prerecorded voice-over prologue, and then at a few points in the action. The prime focus was on a dynamic three-performer dance drama which took place within a stylized, labyrinth-like space flooded with rapidly changing, expressionistically distorted images projected onto its curving walls and other screens in accompaniment to an aggressive sound-score.

A Play about the Magic Flute (1992) was the first Laterna Magika production after the Velvet Revolution of 1989 and the separation of the Laterna Magika organization from the National Theatre to become an independent, self-supporting unit under the Ministry of Culture. Flute presents virtually the whole of Mozart's opera except for passages of nonmusical dialogue, interludes, and some musical repetitions. The libretto has been somewhat modified, which accounts for the title, A Play about . . .. No singing occurs on stage; instead, live choreographed, mimed action accompanies a specially commissioned, full orchestral sound-recording of the opera sung in German, along with a sustained series of filmed images echoing elements in the opera itself. Many of the filmed characters, topographies, architecture, and sculpture (as well as some modern newsreel footage of humanity's destructiveness) are stylized in various ways to remove any suggestion of literalness. The organization of the stage space is highly conventional and austere: unlike the unorthodox projection surfaces in Odysseus and Minotaurus, two large, parallel classic projection surfaces face the audience frontally, one behind the other. Both are made of scrim-like materials, thus allowing live action not only in front of them but between and behind them – 'action in depth,' as Svoboda put it. Otherwise the stage is empty and makes no attempt to mask its bare walls, lighting instruments, and catwalks.

The next production was Casanova (1995), based on an impressionistic scenario drawn from Casanova's writings and other historical sources, the storyline being Casanova's progression from innocent boyhood to jaded old age, his life a vain pursuit of erotic pleasures. In several respects Casanova represents a culmination of Laterna Magika tendencies after Vivisection: increased attention to elements of spectacle at the expense of a character-oriented storyline, increased importance of projected imagery over stage action (except for considerable dance), decreasing attention to a dramatic interplay between stage and screen, and virtual elimination of speech on stage or screen (the Minotaurus voice-overs and the Magic Flute libretto notwithstanding). Temporarily, at least, Svoboda and his staff seem to have opted for highly recognizable titles and treatments that are likely to appeal to international audiences without the complication of verbal communication. Moreover, it is as if the increasing sophistication of cameras, projectors, and new fabric and synthetic projection surfaces were an irresistible incentive to more extravagant visual display, which unfortunately is sometimes conducive to producing a feeling of sensory overload.

In Casanova, Svoboda is able to work with remarkably versatile new electronic projection equipment that goes far beyond the simple film and television projectors and screens used earlier. Electronic disks and computer chips instead of film or video-tape, portable television projectors that are as flexibly directional as follow spots once were, and a large, universally kinetic mirror that also functions as scrim and projection surface – all these and a state of the art multitrack stereo sound-system make available a dazzling palette-cum-keyboard. But despite individual sequences of remarkable inventiveness, interest in the core of potential drama becomes in part attenuated, in part distracted, by the unrelenting blitz of images and sounds.

The most recent Laterna Magika production, *Riddles* (Hádanky, 1997), is live dance with projected backgrounds, with virtually no interaction of the two media and no dramatic action, but a series of game-like episodes related to various art forms.

Laterna Magika has for years been the most profitable theatre in what is now the Czech Republic. While still technically under the Ministry of Culture and performing in the National Theatre's New Stage (Nová Scéna), for which it pays rent, it has continued to be self-supporting primarily by playing very effectively to the tourist market. It is clear that Laterna Magika's efforts to mine the possibilities in the interplay of film and stage will continue in the twenty-first century.

Although it is difficult to generalize, a few main observations may be worth noting with regard to its evolving identity and practices. In retrospect, Laterna Magika and its spinoffs have had three main 'faces':

- an ingenious, provocative mix of live and filmed action, with maximum explicit interplay, mainly as light, informative entertainment as seen in its early anthologies or revues of short pieces
- an effective blend of live and filmed action in the service of substantive works with a strong action-character-text basis, drama or opera: *Intolleranza, The Last Ones, Magical Circus, Night Rehearsal, Vivisection*
- heightened spectacle with a dramatic core of varying strength and a textual component that is token or nonexistent: *Odysseus, Minotaurus, Magic Flute, Casanova*.

In terms of the aesthetics of joining film and stage, Laterna Magika has developed from a direct and strongly metaphoric interplay between live and filmed action, to a less tightly interconnected relation of the two media, in the process losing some of the unique impact of the film–stage symbiosis, but gaining more flexibility in communicating the 'message' presented by each.

From subjects and scenarios that were ingenious, entertaining skits or etudes, Laterna Magika progressed to full-length, serious dramas, operas, and literary classics, almost always with ethical themes with implicit comment on contemporary social tendencies. *Riddles*, the most recent work, marks a break from that pattern, perhaps only a temporary one.

This prompts a final, tentative observation: although Laterna Magika's enormous potential as multimedia theatre is strongly dependent on technical mastery of stage and film, most of its notable creative achievements have been rooted in imaginative dramaturgy and direction, the hallmark of which was stamped by Radok. Until a new Radok emerges, further positive evolution along lines other than technical seems unlikely.

* * *

Svoboda is of medium stature and gives an impression of restrained alertness, of energy banked and well controlled. Occasionally, his manner may even convey an impression of mildness and a certain remoteness, but such impressions are superficial and finally misleading, for Svoboda is a man of glowing intensity once his interest is aroused and he warms to his subject. Then his features become animated, his eyes brighten, and his voice suddenly acquires added range and expressiveness. With a spontaneous, intrinsically histrionic flair he often proceeds to reinforce his verbal account with dynamic gestures and movements as he strives to communicate the precise, essential quality of a given production and the concept it embodies. Such movements reveal how deeply rooted in feeling and, indeed, passion is Svoboda's creativity, and how important a role the intuitive plays in shaping his art.

Although he places enormous emphasis on the need of a disciplined, methodical, logical foundation for true creativity, and consistently applies scientific principles and hi-tech innovation to his work, Svoboda also remains something of a mystic in his sensitivity to the latent forces within the interplay of space, time, movement, and light on stage.

The elemental, intuitive state that underlies even his most complex, calculated efforts was perhaps best expressed in an early 1990s French television feature devoted to Svoboda. Its final moments show him sitting in the empty orchestra of the State Opera, where he began his professional career in 1945 as a member of the Grand Opera of the Fifth of May. As the lights gradually darken, we hear his thoughts via his voice-over:

> When I sit alone in a theatre and gaze into the dark space of its empty stage, I'm frequently seized by fear that this time I won't manage to penetrate it. And I always hope that this fear will never desert me. Without an unending search for the key to the secret of creativity, there is no creation. It's necessary always to begin again. And that is beautiful.[7]

8

TWENTIETH-CENTURY CZECH SCENOGRAPHERS IN THE INTERWAR ERA

As I briefly indicated in Chapter 7, an artist like Josef Svoboda did not develop without earlier roots, without previously established standards, without a tradition.[1] These antecedents for Czech theatre were found in the 1920s and 1930s, when Czech theatre also achieved international recognition. It did so not only because of Karel Čapek, K. H. Hilar, and E. F. Burian, and ensembles like Burian's D Theatre and the Liberated Theatre of Voskovec and Werich, but also because a group of notable designers contributed to the formation of dynamic, provocative theatre on both establishment and avant-garde stages. In this chapter I shall describe some of the work of these often neglected contributors to modern Czech theatre. I have had to be selective. For every one of the artists that follow, at least two or three others of consistently high quality might have been mentioned.

What are some of the chief characteristics of modern Czech scenography before World War II? Most apparent is a consistent rejection of illusionistic, descriptive realism, naturalistic detail, and historical, academic accuracy. In this the Czech theatre echoed progressive theatres in the rest of the western world, which, in turn, were profoundly in the debt of pioneers like Adolph Appia and Edward Gordon Craig. But the Czech theatre was also sensitive to the turbulent dynamics of the larger world of art: the salvos and campaigns of the cubists and expressionists, the futurists, constructivists, and surrealists found an alert response in Czech scenography. These and other contemporary artistic forces mixed and sometimes fused with comparable Czech movements to form some of the distinctive styles of Czech designers.

The rejection of conventional realism also had a more abstract corollary. The work of these designers and their theoretical speculations on that work (the Czechs are rarely content with artistic creation itself; they feel compelled to analyze and rationalize it) reveal an increasing confidence in the aesthetic validity of stage design or scenography as an art possessing its own autonomy, its own principles in the fictive world of theatre. Certainly the Czechs were not the first or only theatre artists to arrive at such views, but the extent to which they articulated ideas of the unique identity of stage design is striking. A Czech designer whose career began toward the end of the period under consideration, František Tröster, expressed many of these attitudes when he later wrote:

> Painting in the 1920s relinquished its pictorial aspect, and so did architecture. The effect on theatre design was a suppression of decorative forms, a subordination of form to function, a dramatic function ... a liberating of theatre, its theatricalizatlon, its distancing from the non-aesthetic level of life.[2]

In terms of actual production, the immediate issue became one of space in theatre, more specifically the implications of dramatic space: space for the actor and his expressive movement, space modified, expanded, intensified by new materials and techniques to enhance the particular concept underlying a given production. The question of space related to two basic approaches to the design of a setting, that of the painter and that of the architect. Both deal with space but with notable difference of concept and technique. Almost without exception, the leading Czech designers of the 1920s and 1930s were highly trained, practicing architects or painters. For many of them theatre was not a sole, or even primary, activity. To put it another way, most were not full-time, professional stage designers. None, in fact, was trained for stage design as such. Their rigorous training in painting, fine arts, and architecture gave them a discipline, a mastery of necessary crafts, and a broader perspective on stage design as an art.

A foreshadowing of later developments and a milestone in the evolution of modern Czech scenography was the 1914 Prague production of Viktor Dyk's *The Coming to Wisdom of Don Quixote* (Zmoudření Dona Quixota), designed by František Kysela (1881–1941). Here for the first time in Czech theatre was a decisive break not only with traditional realism but also with the rather tame, atmospheric impressionism that was its successor. The reality of theatre as conscious artifice was underlined by the stylized frame of the setting as well as by the deliberate stylization and disproportion of the actual setting itself in relation to the human scale of the actors. Three ornamental portals filled the regular proscenium arch, each of them with drapes to reveal or close off what lay behind them. Backing these arcades were painted exterior drops of charming simplicity and no trace of realistic detail. Between the painted drops and the front arcades were simple, mostly two-dimensional, stylized objects or indications of locale that ignored illusory perspective and realistic proportions. The result was a clean-cut, lyrical elegance achieved by essentially a painter's means.[3]

Dominating Czech stage design and scenography during the entire period between the wars was Vlastislav Hofman (1884–1964), by training and talent both painter and architect. While steadily engaged by the two leading, official theatres of Prague (the National Theatre and the Municipal

Vinohrady Theatre) he also functioned as a municipal architect, graphic artist, and designer in industrial arts. Of enormous significance to his work was his sustained association with Karel Hugo Hilar, the most forceful, innovative, far-ranging director-producer of large-scale theatre in Czechoslovakia in his own lifetime. Hilar raised Czech theatre to world standards, and Hofman contributed in great measure to that achievement. In turn, many of Hofman's most impressive works were obviously prompted by suggestions from Hilar.

Both men were essentially expressionists by artistic temperament, and that powerful shaping force was rarely absent even from their most controlled work in this period. As Hofman himself put it, 'It is necessary to transgress prescribed "appropriate limits" constantly, in order to achieve artistic truth.'[4] His career evolved through numerous phases and his work never became set in any single manner, yet his stamp is rarely hard to discern: a heightened expressiveness that often approaches a distortion of form reminiscent of the Baroque, a tendency toward weightiness, mass, and powerful contrasts. There is about his work and that of Hilar a sense of hypertension, of extravagance restrained with difficulty.

A fruitful tension existed within Hofman between the painter and the architect, the one alternately tempering and prompting the other. Viewed as a whole, his work from 1919 through the late 1930s moved from vivid, essentially two-dimensional pictorialization, to a more restrained, puristic, partially constructivist period in which architectonics of space dominated the painter's vision, and eventually culminated in what he called 'constructive realism,' a form in which functionalism and constructional simplification were united with elements of reality according to the special laws of theatre space. Hofman's own remarks from an article, 'Constructive Realism,' are useful in defining his position:

> The contemporary stage setting is an artificial reality which exists for its own sake and only on the stage. It is also, however, an indication of nature and reality. For this constructional handling of exteriors and interiors, which always means a handling of constructional stage space, I use the relatively unfamiliar term, a 'montage of reality.' It is a matter of reality on stage, of reality as it were assembled from real elements, as much as possible not painted. . . . The word 'montage' because suggested indications of reality are placed constructionally in space.[5]

Hofman's first production was *The Hussites* by Arnošt Dvořák, an historical drama directed by Hilar in 1919. The main elements were still painted backdrops, but instead of realistically depicting a given locale, Hofman created powerfully expressive, distorted paintings that seized upon and intensified the dramatic high point of each scene. His treatment of clouds is

126

especially striking. In this and other productions, his desire for maximum expressiveness extended to his design of costumes and makeup, for he realized that without comparable heightening of these elements the setting would be too far out of scale with the actors.

Hofman's evolution toward simplified, more abstract settings was already evident in *Antigone* in 1925; the use of geometric solids brings Appia to mind. A further development occurred in *Hamlet* (1926), directed by Hilar, in which open space replaced solid matter as a dominant. Hofman referred to the evolution as one from 'complicated disturbance, which dominated expressionism, to constructional simplification and plainness in the handling of things,'[6] a difference of tendencies evident in comparing *Hussites* with *Hamlet*. A term often applied to this phase of Hilar's and Hofman's careers was civilism, its implication being a toning down and cooling off from the highly charged, frequently overwrought extremes of wartime expressionist hysteria giving way to increased social stabilization in a period of peace.

Sparse, simple units of furniture and properties were assembled on low, two-step platforms backed by various combinations of tall, silver-gray screens. This basic scenic arrangement alternated with expanded scenes for which larger architectural units provided a more massive background. Lighting played a crucial role as it carved actors and environment out of the surrounding darkness. Color was virtually absent: black, white, and gray are dominant.[7] (See Plate 44, p. 171.)

A 1928 production, *Crime and Punishment*, clearly illustrates Hofman's essential architectural orientation in the various acting areas distributed in space to serve the many locales of the action (Plate 24). Four years later, Hilar and Hofman collaborated on what many regard as their supreme achievement, *Oedipus* (1932). Hofman referred to *Hamlet* as a stepping stone toward *Oedipus*, and indeed the latter did provide a more distilled, more metaphoric stage image in architectonic terms, a prime illustration of what he referred to as constructive realism: the combining of pure architectonic functionalism with elements of reality in an austere but powerful dramatic image. The setting consisted of a massive double set of stairs that spiraled upward from downstage ground level behind the columned entrance to the royal palace to reach the top of the entablature above the columns (Plate 25). The entire structure was centered on a turntable 12 meters in diameter, thus allowing for striking entrances and exits, countermovements of chorus and principals, and a supremely dramatic moment at the end of the play when, in Hofman's words,

> Oedipus, blinded by his own hand, voluntarily leaves his home for the unknown, mounting slowly, step by step, during the turning of the set, until he reaches the top, where he stands during the complete darkening of the scene, alone, sharply lit, like an outcry of fate.[8]

Plate 24 Hofman's drawing for *Crime and Punishment* (1925) in the National Theatre. Photo: J. Burian.

Lighting, as well as the restricted use of kinetics, played a vital role in the production, as Hofman's description of the end of the play suggests. A special effect was achieved by cutting holes in the risers of the stairs to allow for spotlights behind the steps, which suddenly illuminated actors during certain entrances and exits.

Hilar's last major production before his death, and his last production with Hofman, was O'Neill's *Mourning Becomes Electra* (1934). A contemporary review referred to Hofman as a 'dramatist among designers,' an epithet warranted by his dramatically charged, monumental set which suggested a partial return to his expressionistic architectonic period. The setting was marked by isolated, sometimes distorted segments of reality placed against black drapes. Columns and doorways were major plastic elements, and lighting was again a key dramatic component.

Hofman continued to design for over twenty more years, but his vital, genuinely creative years ended with the 1930s. His subsequent work, despite occasional flashes of his old power, became increasingly academic, conventional, and literal, especially during the postwar years that saw the imported doctrine of socialist realism dominate the Czech stage. His

Plate 25 Hofman's spiral stairs for Hilar's *Oedipus* (1932). Photo: J. Burian.

masterful architectonic sense was never lost, but all too often it was merely architectural without being dramatic. In the twenty-odd years of his prime creativity, however, he explored the full spectrum of major movements of modern art as reflected in theatre, with the exception of surrealism. During those years his intuitive sense of theatre rarely abandoned him, and he never fully broke away from his inherent inclination toward expressionism.

* * *

In relation to Hofman, Bedřich Feuerstein (1892–1936) represents a more restrained, lighter, often wittier version of an inherently expressionistic designer with strengths as painter and architect. By training and profession an architect, he was never regularly attached to any theatre, and he spent extended periods of time away from theatre work entirely. Most of his designs were for the establishment theatres in Prague, but a few of his outstanding settings were executed for a leading avant-garde group, something that was never true of Hofman. Feuerstein lived abroad on numerous occasions: as a student in Paris, later again in Paris as an assistant in an architectural atelier, and from 1926 to 1930 in Tokyo as an architectural assistant in an American firm. Although his theatre designs show a progression toward greater simplicity and lightness, his inner state apparently developed otherwise. Despondent over repeated rejections of his

129

architectural proposals in various competitions and lack of recognition of his work, he took his own life in his mid-forties.

Several characteristics remain fairly constant in his scene design: a disciplined architectonic sense of space and order that is softened and lightened by curved motifs, decorative treatment of the frames of his sets, frequent use of warm, bright colors, and a recurrent appearance of draperies; occasional warping and twisting of lines and forms that reflect tendencies in expressionist painting; and a rather consistent treatment of space by means of two-dimensional layers or planes with distinctive outlines rather than by means of plastic forms, reminiscent of Cézanne (Plate 26). Like Hofman, Feuerstein tends to fill his stage with his sets, pictorially if not structurally. On the other hand, he could never be accused of the heaviness or excessiveness that sometimes seems the corollary of Hofman's powerful scenic imagery; Feuerstein's work always shows impeccable taste and proportion.

Some of his most interesting designs were done in the early 1920s, before his long sojourns abroad. Elements of cubism and expressionism appear in his first setting, for the original production of Karel Čapek's *R.U.R.* (Prague, 1921), to which he was invited on the basis of his friendship with the Čapek brothers. Here the architect in Feuerstein clearly dominates the painter, despite his use of a bright palette of colors: the geometric precision of lines and

Plate 26 Bedrich Feuerstein's setting for Jaroslav Vrchlický's *Love and Death* (1923), in the Vinohrady Theatre, directed by Bohuš Stejskal. Photo: Courtesy Theatre Collection, National Museum.

curves, and the obvious use of three-dimensional forms reveal his professional training and also go hand in hand with the modernistic, mechanistic motifs of the play.

Both Molière's *Imaginary Invalid* (Prague, 1921) and Marlowe's *Edward II* (Prague, 1922) reveal fundamental similarities of style: deliberate distortion of line and form, extensive use of drapes, and firm architectural groundplans with a painter's sense apparent in the working out of details. Differences include the relative openness, sparseness, and architectural dominance of the *Edward II* setting in relation to the flats, wings, and backdrops that fill the sets of *Imaginary Invalid*. Each design retains remarkable stylistic consistency. The design of *Edward II* stresses the motif of elongated Gothic arches, while that of *Imaginary Invalid* is almost a caricature of baroque waves and curls. *Edward II* is austere in its suppression of color except for occasional accents in banners or a single drape, while *Imaginary Invalid* is marked by bright, dashing color. The striking distortions and deliberate disproportions of form in both settings no doubt reflect the expressionist leanings of Hilar, the director of both productions, as much as they do Feuerstein's own inclinations.

Feuerstein did six productions for one of Czechoslovakia's most celebrated avant-garde groups, the Liberated Theatre of Voskovec and Werich, under the direction of Jindřich Honzl, the Czech theatre's leading theorist-director. By the time Feuerstein contributed to their productions, their satire was becoming increasingly focused on the harsh political realities of the growing fascist threat to European democracy. Feuerstein's setting for *Ass and Shadow* (Prague, 1933) is an interesting combination of comic incongruities and disturbing threat. Disjointed columns and cartoon-like properties are in comic accord with disproportions of scale (the dwarfing of humans by objects), but a huge hand gripping a dagger that is plunged into the earth strikes a sinister note that suggests Feuerstein's sympathetic echoing of surrealistic elements. That same year he also designed *Lovers from the Kiosk*, by Vítězslav Nezval, for the National Theatre. Its assemblage of varied elements captures the witty, capricious tone of the play very effectively.

* * *

Although Antonín Heythum (1901–54) was also an architect, his career represents a departure from those of Hofman and Feuerstein. He was, for example, instrumental in the initial efforts of several important avant-garde theatre groups in Czechoslovakia and never severed connection with such non-official, experimental ensembles, continuing to work with all of the major avant-garde directors not only in Prague but in other Czech theatre centers as well. Nevertheless, his range extended to work on many productions in establishment theatres throughout Czechoslovakia, including Prague's National Theatre under the direction of Hilar himself. Heythum's peripatetic tendencies were also reflected in his designing of several Czech pavilions at international fairs, such as the Brussels World's Fair in 1935. Moreover, it was while he was in charge of a Czech cultural exhibit in London in 1938 that the Munich crisis occurred and subsequently led to Heythum's emigration to the U.S.A. After redesigning the Czech pavilion at the New York World's Fair in 1939–40, he worked with Erwin Piscator at the New School in New York in 1940–41, designing a production of *King Lear*. Thereafter he devoted most of his efforts to teaching industrial arts and design and to innovative projects in urban planning and conservation. From 1942 to 1952 he taught at major schools including California Institute of Technology, Syracuse University, Columbia, and Harvard.

Heythum's particular signature in stage design is a remarkable economy of expression, a feeling for open space defined by a minimum of structural elements, and an abundant store of wit and gaiety. Although he was highly responsive to color in stage design, he is, in almost all other respects, the antithesis of the designer as painter. It is easy to label much of his work as constructivistic, but his use of color, varied and occasionally graceful forms, and humorous accent is incongruous with the strict models of that movement. By the same token, the geometrical, structural purity of his work as well as its airiness are in striking contrast with most of Hofman's and Feuerstein's work. On the other hand, Heythum's designs rarely achieve the power of Hofman's best efforts or the emotive depth and texture of Feuerstein's.

Writing in 1932, Heythum defined his attitude toward the problematics of his vocation. Like many others, including Hofman, he identified space rather than scene painting as the essential element of a stage setting. True scene painting, according to Heythum, lies in music and mainly lighting. His subsequent remarks clarify his particular view and methods:

> Theatre is a world unto itself. Real things do not belong on stage, for the stage has its own scale, unlike that of real life. Theatre asks for pure settings – that is, a spatial montage of objects. . . . In the meantime, the traditional stage inventory needs to be adapted. We remove the canvas from flats and leave the empty, sight-conducive wooden frames. We wash off the pictures painted on drops and let them function as cloth, velvet, curtains, what they really are. . . . We use lighting not merely to illuminate the stage but to divide it spatially. We use stage machinery to make the setting mobile, as a direct part of the action. The turntable turns as part of the play and the frontal set is revitalized by a masterful play-in-space, or spatial play.[9]

Heythum's setting for O'Neill's *Desire under the Elms* (Prague, 1925) was often reproduced in theatre publications. Its skeletal framework allows for the maximum of visible movement, simultaneous action, and open, airy design. Although it closely follows O'Neill's own stage directions, it eliminates virtually all elements of solid surface.

Aristophanes' *Thesmophoriazusae* (Prague, 1926) shows one of Heythum's most definitive constructivist adaptations. Extremely abstract, a loose collection of steps, scaffolds, ladders and frames of unfinished wood painted a bright red against a white background, it is a setting at its most functional and nonrepresentational (Plate 27). Additional distinctive touches are the contrasting accents of repeated circles (a hoop-swing and a painted bull's target), a small Chinese lantern, and a dangling rope, all of which offset the severe plainness of the setting. Very similar to this set were Heythum's creations for Molière's *Georges Dandin* (retitled *Circus Dandin* by its Prague director, Jiří Frejka, 1925) and Ribemont-Dessaignes' *Mute Canary* (Prague, 1926), all of these productions being among the earliest efforts of the Liberated Theatre before the arrival of Voskovec and Werich.

Another of Heythum's comments provides a further rationale of his method:

> The stage in today's theatre is a showcase, an eternal temporary expedient which is conducive to painter's errors struggling with the three-dimensionality of the stage. The fundamental requirement is that the structure of the setting satisfy the conditions of space, to

Plate 27 Antonin Heythum's constructivist setting for Jiří Frejka's production of *Thesmophoriazusae* (1926), by Aristophanes. Photographer unknown.

which are joined the dimensions of time and the actor's movement in space.[10]

A modification of the extreme austerity of some of Heythum's early settings was evident in *The Fateful Play of Love* (Lásky hra osudná, Prague, 1930), by the Čapek brothers (Plate 28). On a low, two-step platform were placed a stark staircase and two offset parallel panels of different dimensions which partly sandwiched the staircase. Five parallel ribbons dropped down loosely to form a swag before being attached to the top of the downstage flat. They and the stylized sky with stars and moon added a distinctly lyrical, graceful touch that is a little unusual for Heythum but in fine harmony with the *commedia dell'arte* nature of the script.

Further modification was evident in one of Heythum's most successful creations, *The Merchant of Venice* (Prague, 1931). Skeletal frames were present but they were occasionally supplemented by flats that formed walls of buildings: the effect, while still stylized and abstract, moved toward increased representationalism. Another significant addition was the loose-drape hangings that were lowered to cover buildings and thus indicate shifts of locale. Of great design importance were the textures and the bright, cheerful colors of the materials and fabrics covering the various structures: brown velours, red velvets, blue canvas, yellow waxed cloth, and rough burlap. A further

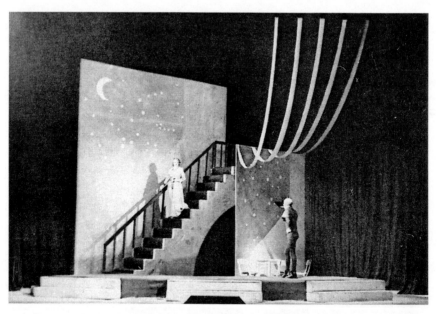

Plate 28 Heythum's setting for the Čapek brothers' *The Fateful Play of Love* (1930), National Theatre Studio production, directed by Frejka. Photographer unknown.

lyrical touch occurred with projections of Botticelli's *Three Graces* and *The Birth of Venus* that enhanced the romantic atmosphere of the Belmont scenes.

* * *

A fine balance between a painter's sense of color and imagery and an architect's sense of spatial composition is what is most impressive about the work of František Muzika (1900–74). Muzika's one hundred or so production designs include some that are based primarily on painted flat surfaces, some that are almost purely architectonic and lack color, and many that provide a synthesis of the two approaches. In most cases, however, one is aware of a moderation, a poise that gracefully restrains a rich pictorial imagination. What is also apparent is his ability to make a strong poetic statement with the most limited means. There is much in his work that suggests a fusion of Heythum and Feuerstein: the former's lightness, economy, and spatial openness; the latter's expressionistic imagery and stylistic purity. He shares with both an aversion to literalism or illusionistic scenery.

Trained as a painter both in Prague and Paris, Muzika came under the influence of the major forces in modern art: expressionism, cubism, surrealism. Formalism, a talent for pure design, is a notable feature in his settings. Toward the latter part of his association with the stage, the surrealistic mode becomes increasingly apparent, dominating his architectonic concern for stage space with a highly charged pictorial expression of recurrent dreamlike, distorted forms and images. In 1947 Muzika gave up stage design but continued as a painter.

Muzika's strong sense of spatial form and design is clear in his original rendering for V. Vančura's *The Alchemist* (Prague, 1932). Subsequent revision eliminated the baroque curls and put more emphasis on the varying vertical levels. A clean geometric precision marks the set. The many scene changes in the play were effected by rotating the set on a turntable and adding supplements for given scenes.

The surrealistic phase of Muzika's scene design work, hinted at in his *Hamlet* (Brno, 1936), is vividly evident in Bohuslav Martinů's opera, *Julietta* (Prague, 1938), directed by Jindřich Honzl in the National Theatre (Plate 29). The opera deals with a man's search for a girl whose image once enchanted him. His obsession is conveyed by having her dream image appear mysteriously, hauntingly in recurrent guises, blending with natural surroundings and buildings. Muzika's rendering captures the lyrical distortions of fantasy and dream. Features of landscape acquire bizarre shapes, overlap, and dissolve to form new images. It is a highly poetic vision communicated essentially by a painter's means, yet the visual effect is strongly spatial.

* * *

With the arrival of František Tröster (1904–68) in the 1930s, the Czech stage

135

Plate 29 František Muzika's interest in surrealism was evident in the National Theatre production of Bohuslav Martinů's opera *Julietta* (1938). Photographer unknown.

received a new surge of creative energy and experienced a significant expansion of its limits. Tröster was a scenographer, not merely a designer: following up some of Heythum's ideas, he consciously worked with the stage as a stage, as an instrument, which is to say that he was aware of its unique principles and laws of spatial scale and proportion, of its potential for dramatic, theatrical expression by means of movement (materially or by means of lighting and projections), and most fundamentally by means of alterations of space. As he said in the late 1930s, 'The foundation of stage action is space. The stage itself is a hollow cube into which it is necessary to place artificial space, dramatic space.'[11]

In many respects Tröster was a successor to Hofman. Like Hofman, Tröster was trained as both painter and architect, but of the two it was architecture that dominated his vision of the stage. Like Hofman, Tröster devoted virtually all of his creative energy to theatre. Like Hofman, too, Tröster was at his core an expressionist, a designer with a degree of creative fantasy that needed to transform surface reality radically in order to express itself. The director with whom Tröster worked most often, Jiří Frejka, referred to the special form of staging that he and Tröster evolved as 'hyperbolic realism,' and explained it this way:

> What shall we call today's form? Perhaps something like hyperbolic realism. It steps before the spectators from the darkness of absolute space. It relates to external reality but its speech is hyperbolic; it abbreviates and condenses.[12]

What are the differences between Tröster and Hofman? The painter in Tröster added a more poetic, lyrical quality to the essentially architectonic nature of some of his settings, whereas in Hofman the painter found expression by more literal means: scene painting. Tröster was, moreover, of a later generation, and more attuned to the possibilities of new technology: kinetics, new materials, lighting, projections. Perhaps of even greater importance was that Tröster was so closely associated with a director of Frejka's stamp: a sensitive, lyrically endowed, essentially lighter and more pliant sensibility than Hofman's co-creator, K. H. Hilar. That may help to explain Tröster's higher degree of poetic expression, liveliness, at times fancifulness. To return to fundamentals, both Tröster and Hofman are marked by a great creative vitality that seeks expression in powerful stage images organized in space. Like Hofman, Tröster also consistently transgressed 'appropriate limits' to achieve artistic truth.

Writing in retrospect, Tröster provided another comment on 'hyperbolic realism' as he defined his own brand of stage space and suggested his relation to Hofman. He speaks of his experience as an urban architect-engineer in Algeria in the 1920s, where particular aspects of the terrain led to architectural plans based on ramps and podiums, with foundation and superstructure conceived as interpenetrating bodies. Tröster transferred some of these concepts to the stage and says he regards them as his contribution to the Czech theatre. He then adds:

> I believe that I embodied this objective as precisely as Hofman, before me, organized architectonic matter and, by editing it, arrived at his definitive form of functional stairs that were capable of dramatic action. But between the 'internal function' of interpenetrating bodies on the one hand and a staircase on the other is an essential difference. Hofman organized matter according to an architectonic order on stage, a classical order. He organized active matter within passive space negated by darkness. On the other hand, my interpenetrating ramps and slabs were essentially but a skin that enclosed space, which was primary, active, and changeable, as if it were made of elastic material. Into this 'envelope' is pressed dramatic space, and

I would say that there must be a precise amount more of it than of actual space, a degree of overpressure that this 'envelope' can still contain but that reveals itself in the composition and abnormal structure of the 'Envelope.'[13]

A sampling of Tröster's work in the 1930s illustrates several variations of his sense of dramatic space.

Lope de Vega's *Fuente Ovejuna* (Prague, 1935) was Tröster's first production in Prague. The intention was to capture the harsh reality of a troubled land, not a picture postcard vision. The set was placed on a turntable, which had a significant dramatic function beyond merely mechanical movement to indicate a change of scene. Instead, the movement was intended to bring the actors closer to the audience, or distance them when that was appropriate. It was an attempt to approximate the film technique of a close-up. Tröster expressed another aspect of the production and thereby indicated his view of stage reality:

We placed a living tree on stage, added straw, real things, and emphasized their structure. We projected film on to the rough surface of the wall. Nevertheless, it was not naturalism. Not even illusionism. From real elements we composed a new reality that could exist only on the stage and be truthful only there.[14]

Still another distinctive artistic technique – interesting in theory and practice – was developed by Tröster and Frejka. It consisted of what Tröster called, 'dramatic planes or levels that we provide ... to show the actor from "unreal" angles above and below him, in effect from all sides, and that have the resonance of sounding boards.'[15] A striking example of this technique is found in *Julius Caesar* (Prague, 1935), one of the most celebrated Frejka–Tröster productions (Plate 30). It is reminiscent of the Hilar–Hofman productions of *Hamlet* and *Oedipus* in its complete elimination of the painted, conventionally pictorial scene, in its definitively architectonic treatment of space and matter, and above all in its creation of dramatic space.

First, Frejka sought to disturb the traditional separation of stage and audience by breaking through the framed opening of the proscenium. The stage was extended beyond the proscenium, over the orchestra pit, by means of a curved, raked platform, thus also making it possible for actors to approach closer to the audience. Behind the raked forestage a series of variously angled levels or slabs were placed on a turntable. In certain positions of the turntable, these levels rose upward at an angle of 30 degrees toward the audience, so that actors who ascended the level from behind could suddenly appear over the edge of the level with strong effect. But most dramatic was the juxtaposition of actors and huge sculptured pieces that towered over

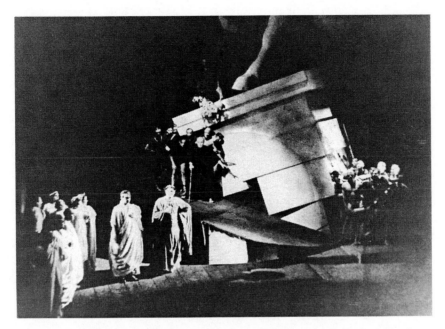

Plate 30 František Tröster's starkly expressive scenography for Frejka's *Julius Caesar* (1936) in the National Theatre. Photo: Aleksandr Paul.

them at precarious angles. Tröster's explanation of the setting and its function is illuminating:

> We were concerned with expressing instability by means of large broken slabs which bore gigantic sculptural pieces terminating somewhere high above the proscenium arch: Caesar enters from the circus and stands under a huge statue of a horse, actually under his uplifted hoof. Caesar is dwarfed by the discrepancy of scale, but the crowd greets him stormily. The deliberately contrived angle of vision from which we view Caesar and the tragedy as a whole is not a symbol but a point of view or attitude toward the whole.[16]

The deliberate disproportion of actor and scenery or property recalls similar instances in Feuerstein's settings for *Imaginary Invalid* or *Ass and Shadow*. In Tröster's *Caesar* the effect is heightened by the three-dimensional sculpture in addition to the tilted angles employed.

An unusually fine, early example of kinetic scenography closely integrated with the on stage action of actors occurred in the Frejka–Tröster production of Gogol's *Government Inspector* (Prague, 1936). The scene is Khlestakov's tipsy entrance into the chief of police's home after a day spent drinking with the chief and his colleagues (Plate 31). The desired effect was a heightening of the intoxicated state of the group. Tröster explains how he responded to the challenge:

> The entrance of Khlestakov and his companions begins by their coming through small doors placed at the depth of the stage. Then other 'drunken' doors ride in from above and below, and finally a huge sofa rises up from the orchestra pit and Khlestakov falls into it. At that moment the phantasmagoric dance of doors froze.[17]

Tröster continued to design throughout the war years and after, in fact until shortly before his death in 1968. In 1945 he was a co-founder of the university-level school of fine and performing arts, Akademie Múzických Úmění, and headed its design division until his death. His work achieved

Plate 31 Tröster's setting for Gogol's *Government Inspector* (1936), directed by Frejka in the National Theatre. Photo: J. Burian.

international recognition in 1959 when he received the first prize in scenography at the São Paulo Bienale. Yet it is questionable whether Tröster has received the degree of general recognition that he warrants, perhaps because his career was split by the war years, perhaps also because he was in official disfavor in the 1950s due to his lack of compromise with the approved doctrine of socialist realism. In any case, just as he may be viewed as a significant successor to Hofman, he cannot be ignored as a major foreshadower of the postwar surge in Czech scenography. Many of its achievements may be traced to Tröster's prototypal work with Frejka. Not only his actual production achievements but also his concepts were ahead of their time. His remarks in 1937 have a prophetic quality and indicate that his orientation was precisely in line with that of subsequent developments in scenography, including the work of Svoboda, who briefly studied with Tröster:

> Film reveals the detail of a tear-drop. The theatre discovers the same – in so far as it is possible in terms of its technical and dramatic essence. An originally flowing action is interrupted. The action, actor, and even property approaches or withdraws. It is a persuasive sign that the evolution of theatre space will be influenced by new technical inventions in optics, lighting, as well as discoveries of new materials.[18]

* * *

Another distinctive foreshadowing of Czech scenography of the 1960s occurred in the D36 Theatre of Emil František Burian. As already noted in previous chapters, Burian was above all a poetically endowed theatre artist who constantly experimented with theatrical synthesis, a form of production in which text, acting, lighting, music, and other production elements are variously and flexibly modulated – like a musical score – by the master creator, the director. The concept was first articulated by Craig, but Burian was one of the few, and probably the first, to apply it consistently and systematically. In this he was served not only by a relatively stable acting ensemble but also by a faithful staff of capable designer-technicians, chief among whom was Miroslav Kouřil (1911–84).

Burian created scenarios for each production, which allowed him to give full rein to his multiple talents. His productions were not without flaws: occasional indulgence in lyrical pathos and sentimentality, a certain overdoing of some scenic or textual or acting 'effects' that bordered on preciosity. In spite of the occasional flaw, he created some of the most notable experimental theatre of the 1930s, not only in Czechoslovakia, but also in all of Europe.

Burian and Kouřil had to work in deplorably inadequate surroundings, a small concert hall (the Mozarteum) with a raised, usable acting area of less than 35 square meters, a small proscenium opening, and no fly space (Plate 32). The challenge to ingenuity was unmistakable. One relatively traditional

Plate 32 E. F. Burian's *First Folk Suite* (1938). Photographer unknown.

example of how the challenge was met by Burian and Kouřil was evident in the production of Beaumarchais's *The Barber of Seville* (1936). Kouřil's setting was based on a practicable larger-than-life image-symbol of the body of a guitar lying athwart the proscenium opening on an oblique angle down over the edge of the forestage, with the upper part of the torso elevated by several risers on the stage proper behind the proscenium (Plate 33). Complex area lighting helped shape the stage space, and abstract projections were used on a partially closed front curtain to add texture. It was a clever, metaphorically based solution typical of others by Kouřil.

The most impressive scenographic innovations of Burian's theatre, however, were based on lighting, projections, and, finally, on the fusion of projected image and stage action in the Theatregraph, which has been briefly described in Chapter 3 on E. F. Burian. The name 'Theatregraph' was defined by Kouřil:

> It is theatre with static and film projection, coherently and dramatically integrated into the directorial-scenographic conception. It depends on the state of film technology around 1936–38 and the discovery of transparent projection screens covering the front of the stage and allowing for a simultaneous viewing of the actor and the filmed image on the screen.[19]

Plate 33 E. F. Burian and Miroslav Kouřil's *Barber of Seville* (1936). Photo: Otto Skall.

What might have been added is that the actor seems enveloped by the screened image, not simply placed next to it. The technique was fully used in three productions, the first of which was Wedekind's *Spring's Awakening* (1936). The front of the stage was covered by a transparent gray scrim on which both film and slide projection were used (Plate 34). A smaller, opaque screen was placed at an angle in the up-left part of the stage and received frontal slide projections from off stage right. The floor and rear of the stage were covered in black, with a masked opening at the rear of the stage for entrances and exits. Even without projections, ingenious lighting from both sides of the frontal scrim provided a number of poetically suggestive effects, from a hazy sense of distance and the gradual emergence or disappearance of a character in the darkness, to the lighting of selected details: an actor's face or hands, depending on the balance of intensities of the different area and spot lights. Space and visual composition were flexible, modulated, and dynamic.

Projections enriched this already imaginative scenography. Central to this system were projections that were only incidentally used to illustrate locale or provide information (i.e., Piscator's method). Much more important in Burian's theatre was their metaphoric, dramatic use to convey the emotional atmosphere of a scene in a number of ways: recalling a previous event,

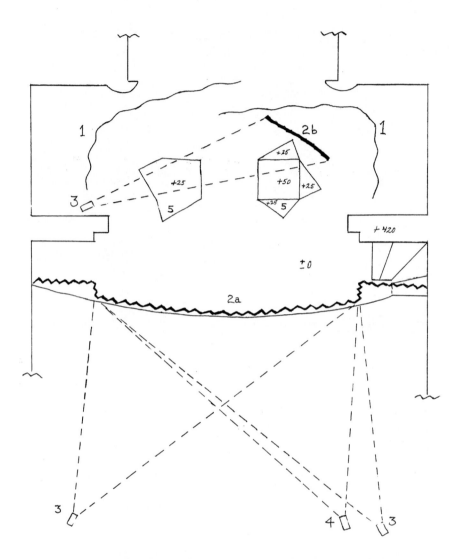

Plate 34 Ground plan of Burian's D37's Mozarteum stage and auditorium set up for the Theatregraph system as used for Wedekind's *Spring's Awakening* (1936). 1 – black drape cyclorama; 2a – front projection scrim; 2b – opaque projection screen; 3 – slide projectors; 4 – film projector; 5 – elevated acting platforms, height in centimeters. Proscenium width = 6 meters.

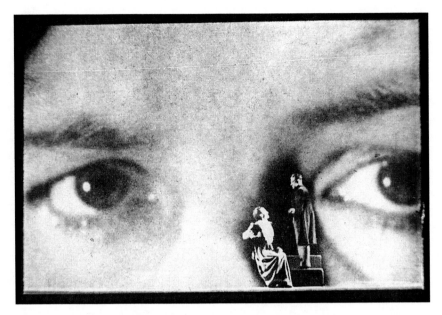

Plate 35 An example of how a scene from *Spring's Awakening* was handled by the Theatregraph system. Photo: Otto Skall.

revealing the state of mind of a character, substituting for live actors, providing perspectives and suggesting relationships not spelled out in the text (Plate 35). The legacy of expressionism was still alive in this technique.

At its most essential the production was based on the precise rhythmical integration of actors and projected images. Although much of the action of the play occurred without projections, maximum spatial and aesthetic effect no doubt occurred when live actors and multiple projected images were simultaneously visible. The synthetic nature of the technique is most apparent in the scenarios that have survived, such as the one for *Eugene Onegin* (1937), which clearly indicate in separate columns the text, the live action, the projected image, and the live or recorded sound. (See the example in Chapter 3 on E. F. Burian.) Other details are worth noting: the live action and dialogue on stage were intelligible and coherent without the projections, which were dramatic supplements; on the other hand, the filmed images made no sense without the stage action, although they may have possessed a certain aesthetic interest of their own. The films and projections were specially made for each production, not taken from any stock material. Particularly striking effects were based on the projection of magnified details in disproportionate relation to the live actors. Rear projection was never used.

Goethe's *The Sorrows of Young Werther* (1938) introduced a few variations. The sole projection surface was a frontal scrim that consisted of two parts that overlapped in the center and allowed an open passage for actors, who could perform in front of the scrim as well as behind it. The stage itself was broken up into acting areas at various heights, much more so than in the previous two productions of Theatregraph. Only static slides were used for projection; sometimes negative images underlined the feeling of cold and desolation.

Considering the complexities of the Theatregraph technique, a critic at the time wrote:

> E. F. Burian most dexterously abused film for theatre ends. He often used film as a document, not a historical or objective document but a theatrical, fictive one. . . . It is no longer a question of film, but of a new material for the scene designer, material from which one cannot separate the director.[20]

The question of sources and influences in connection with the use of film in theatre is more tangled than one might at first assume. With regard to Theatregraph one inevitably thinks of Piscator's work in the 1920s as well as Radok's and Svoboda's work culminating in Laterna Magika in the early 1960s. Numerous distinctions can be made, but for the purposes of this survey Kouřil's observation seems a just one:

> Laterna Magika is to Theatregraph as today's jet is to Blériot's first flying machine. Technically and conceptually, they are of the same birth: theatre based on lighting. They contrast by differences deriving from the development of technology during 30 years. Both are simply the fruit of modern efforts to solve for the second and third time the artistic equation THEATRE–FILM, which was first solved by Piscator.[21]

Burian's and Kouřil's scenography based on a complex, lyrically based synthesis of elements produced new ways of dealing with stage space dramatically. Their methods were certainly the most unconventional in Czech theatre up to their time, but their activity was essentially still of the same kind as that of the others I have described. The Czech word for what we call design is *výtvarnictví*, which means an active shaping or forming, whether it be of plastic matter in space, pigments on canvas, drawings on paper, or space, matter, and light on stage. All of these men were shapers and formers in this sense. The range and variety of what they shaped and formed, how they did so, and with what degree of distinction is impressive. A tradition was established and, indeed, carried on directly by some into the postwar era.[22]

9

CZECH SCENOGRAPHY SINCE 1968

A younger generation

A consideration of several Czech scenographers from the second half of the twentieth century makes clear that the tradition described in Chapter 8 was carried forward vigorously, not only in the work of Josef Svoboda but also in a number of his younger contemporaries and those of the following generation. In this chapter I shall focus on four of these artists and mainly on their work up to the 1990s. What was true in Chapter 8 is also true here. I have been selective, and many others who have also done outstanding work might have been included here.

In no way clones of Svoboda, Tröster, or other Czechs, these younger designers reflect broader movements and changes in theatre practice within Czechoslovakia as well as in the world beyond its borders. Their work in the 1970s and 1980s cannot be divorced from the cultural generation gap separating those artists who reached artistic maturity before the 1960s from those whose professional work in theatre did not begin until the mid- or late 1960s. The former, for example, Svoboda, are essentially in the tradition of stage design or scenography as an art, an art which plays its role in the total synthesis of theatre but can also be appreciated for its own values of line, color, pattern, and total poetic statement.

As a result of the social, political, and economic upheavals of the 1960s, however – above all the trauma of the 1968 Soviet invasion – Czech theatre as a whole underwent a radical change as the decade ended. In the ensuing era of Normalization, not only was the basic repertoire curtailed to safe classics or works of neo-socialist realism, but also staging practices reverted toward a neo-conservatism. In reaction against this tendency, theatre artists who were not tied to the mainstream of institutionalized, large-scale repertory theatres deliberately pulled back to the most basic, human-centered elements of theatre, as if rejecting the officially sanctioned, traditional forms associated with a repressive political and cultural system. In other words, they were less likely to think of their work as 'art' than as a scaled-down, functional ingredient in productions that stressed collective improvisation, spontaneity, intimate contact with audiences, and socially relevant motifs.

Needless to say, the work of this group of younger stage designers also reflected movements in theatre and art beyond the boundaries of Czechoslovakia during the 1960s. Happenings, environmental theatre, pop art, found art, and Grotowski's 'poor' theatre all contributed toward radically simpler, nontechnological methods of staging in which the actor would dominate and traditional scenography would either be eliminated or become minimalist in its application. Small spaces and improvised facilities became a desirable norm, and in Czechoslovakia 'action' scenography became a byword.

What is 'action' scenography? Essentially, it is scenography which virtually ceases to exist independently of the actors and their stage business. The new ideal becomes an active, creative interplay of actors with seemingly random and neutral objects, props, platforms, and other materials. In Czechoslovakia itself, prototypes might be found in the work of Antonín Heythum during the 1920s and 1930s. In fact, some of Svoboda's own work anticipated the mode, for example, *The Mill* (1965), or *Mother Courage* (1970), or even certain aspects of *The Entertainer* (1957).

It is against this background that the work of the following selected scenographers is best considered.[1] They vary in their ages and quantity of experience, but they are professionals whose talents have been demonstrated in a rigorous repertory system that even in smaller theatres mounts at least six premieres each season in addition to some ten productions from previous seasons. Some are freelances but all have been resident designers for at least part of their careers. While sharing a number of characteristics, each has developed individual methods and qualities. Moreover, each one, being an artist, has not restricted his or her work to mere functionality, but has found ways of distinctive expression without dominating a production. And several have indeed begun to question whether it is not time for scenography to assume a more prominent role in productions once again.

Jaroslav Malina, born in 1937 in Prague, is the elder among these younger scenographers, and his work may be seen in part as retaining some qualities of expressive design while turning to untraditional materials and stressing function over decor. At first a student of painting and ceramics, he went on to formal training in scenography under František Tröster at Prague's theatre academy DAMU in the early 1960s, as did numerous other designers of Malina's generation. Until 1980, Malina was primarily associated with the regional theatre at Liberec; then, after two years at Hradec Králové, he became a freelance operator. He was a gold medal winner at the Novi Sad Triennial (Yugoslavia) in 1984, and has participated in several Prague Quadriennals. In 1982 and again in 1987, he lectured and exhibited his work in the U.S.A., also designing productions at the University of Kansas and San Francisco State in 1987. In the 1990s he joined the faculty of DAMU, and in 1996 became rector of the several Prague academies of performing arts.

Central to Malina's work is the principle of contrast, especially between the real and the artificial, between authentic materials and conscious artifice; for example, making use of real tree trunks and branches, but painting them a decidedly non-natural color. Objecting to what he calls 'one-dimensional' stylization – a unified, consistent modification of reality – he tries to create a heightened theatricality by calling attention to discrepancies between natural objects and their conscious manipulation on stage.

For years he created set after set from ingenious, functional exploitations of cloth. For the non-musical dramatization of *Jenůfa* (1986), Malina placed artificially colored slim birch trunks on stage and then created the different scenes by stretching a long, wide band of cloth in varying configurations around the trunks. In *Troilus and Cressida* (1979), the stage was covered with huge pieces of cloth attached to ropes and pulleys, an iron mattress frame served multiple functions, and a net containing the debris of a corrupt civilization hung above the stage. An even greater ocean of cloth, painted, translucent, and often back lit, formed the concave surfaces for Dostoyevsky's *The Insulted and Injured* (Cheb, 1984), creating cave-like alcoves as well as floor, ceiling, and walls, and stretching out into the audience, attached to the balcony lighting units (Plate 36). In contrast, cloths tautly stretched by cords attached to iron frames formed the oppressive walls of *The House of Bernarda Alba* (1980).

Alternatively, not only was cloth tautly stretched over the stage to form ceiling pieces, but also two layers of cloth covered a thick styrofoam sponge

Plate 36 Jaroslav Malina's scenography for a dramatization of Dostoyevsky's *Insulted and Injured* (1984) in Cheb. Photographer unknown.

floor for *A Midsummer Night's Dream* (1984), with holes in the top layer of cloth allowing characters to crawl between the layers and emerge from them. Quite different was the treatment of cloth for *Mother Courage* (1977): various cables with hooks were attached to other cables strung above the stage. A large tarpaulin-like cloth was hooked on different cables for different scenes, thus dividing the space in various ways. The cloth also served a number of other functions, such as a chute for Katrin's fall after being shot and later her shroud.

In most of these examples the cloths were either undyed or lightly painted to create some texture, but in Nezval's *Manon Lescaut* (1982), seven huge silky drapes each of a different intense color were suspended over a pyramid construction of basic platforming assembled in view of the audience; scene changes consisted of the separate cloths being dropped down to cover the platforming. In Büchner's *Leonce and Lena* (1976), brightly painted soft cloths billowed over frames to enclose the various scenes. Malina's own comments on his attraction to cloth are found in an exhibition catalogue:

> I regard cloth as closest to man ... the intermediary between the human body and the external world. It's pliable but it can also be stiff, transparent or opaque; it can merge things or be wrinkled, be beautiful or repellent. And it's actually relatively inexpensive and storable.

Not that Malina is addicted to novel applications of cloth. For example, in two productions at Prague's National Theatre, Malina used very traditional stage flats and drew on his painter's love of color in striking ways. For *Love's Labors Lost* (1987), he assembled as a background a series of tall, mobile flats with irregular shapes suggesting the crowns of trees. The tops of the flats, however, were of plain translucent canvas to suggest something like clouds, while obviously remaining flats; the lower sections were covered with vividly painted papier-mâché in the form of floral reliefs. In *Miss Julie* (1988), similar but lower and even more vividly painted flats formed the encompassing background to a wall-less kitchen, creating the floral atmosphere of midsummer eve in the manner of the youthful work of Edvard Munch, according to Malina (Plate 37). In contrast, an earlier production, Howard Barker's *The Claw* (1985), was based on an abstract, hard-edged construction of metal frames, metal barrels, and transparent plastic.

In these and other works, Malina made no effort to hide the necessary technical components, which were usually rather simple, almost as if deliberately 'home-made,' in contrast to the usually elaborate, sophisticated equipment of many theatres, which he finds too standardized. Ideally, he says, he would like to design settings that could exist anywhere, independent of stage technology.

As if to demonstrate that he cannot be pigeonholed, he took a new turn in

Plate 37 Malina's setting for *Miss Julie* (1988) in the New Stage of the National Theatre. Photo: J. Burian.

one of his later productions, *Merlin* (1988), a metaphysical fantasy by the East German writer Tancred Dorst. Here cloth gave way to oxydized metallic walls and a very large, kinetic metal ring with lighting units (à la Steven Spielberg's *Close Encounters of the Third Kind*), which also served as King Arthur's roundtable. In speaking of the production, Malina observed:

> The tendency for years has been to do simplified theatre in reaction against grandiose theatricalism and imitative decoratism. By now it has perhaps become too simplified, even boring. Here in this production we could again attempt a great theatricality, theatre of greater effect, a greater 'show.'[2]

Two examples from his work in the 1990s illustrate this move toward greater theatricality. For a National Theatre revival of the Čapeks' *Insect Comedy* (1990), he created a scene based on eight large metallic rings retreating up stage to form ribs of a tunnel-like space; everything else was a black void except for flown-in pieces to represent abstract clouds or textures. It was hard to avoid the overall effect of a large empty space, despite attempts to fill it with ingenious gadgets and machines used by the characters. Much more successful was his set for Shakespeare's *Cymbeline* (Zlin, 1996). Here he had a stage within the stage: a grandiose Baroque proscenium frame with period painted scenery behind it was installed on the regular stage. Occasionally it could turn so as to reveal its bare canvas and wood construction for comic, ironic effect, reminiscent of the Radok–Svoboda *Rigoletto* (1947: see Plate 7, p. 63).

* * *

If Malina incorporates both traditionally expressive and more recent minimalist tendencies, Jan Dušek, born in Prague in 1942, leans more consistently toward the latter. Dušek came to formal scenographic study after five years of very practical experience as a scene builder and painter for Prague's famed Barrandov film studios and also for one of Prague's municipal theatres. At DAMU he was one of the last to complete his studies under František Tröster, in 1967. (Tröster died in 1968.) Dušek then spent six years in Ostrava theatres, before moving on to Brno and eventually freelance work since 1974. In 1972 he won the gold medal for scenography at Novi Sad; since about 1980 he has been on the scenographic faculty at Prague's DAMU, thus carrying on the tradition established by Tröster. Still another of his activities is exhibition designing, which has taken him to many parts of Europe.

Most of Dušek's work places greater emphasis on functionality and relatively less on expressive decor than Malina's. Dušek focuses on the reality of the stage and strives, as he puts it, 'to create space for play, for drama,' likening stage action to the play of a child with wooden blocks, with the wooden blocks taking on an infinite number of identities and functions. He rarely creates scenography that can stand on its own as an indication of environment, much less as stylized decor; instead, he prefers scenography that forcefully interacts with the actors. Two things continue to fascinate him: 'using ordinary things with traditional associations in new and striking ways,' and scenography 'that can't be totally planned in advance, only prepared to a certain extent,' the rest evolving with the dramatic action. By the same token, he likes to work with directors who try to maintain something of the relatively unfinished quality of rehearsals in the performance itself.

Two Shakespeare productions illustrate his bare bones approach on certain occasions. The First Quarto *Hamlet* (1978) at the Balustrade theatre, directed by Evald Schorm, consisted of vertical panels of buckram material lining the three walls of the stage and providing ideal positions for eavesdropping that would be evident to the audience; the panels were progressively torn down during the performance as visual reinforcements of the action. Only two other scenographic elements were used: a number of skeletal cubes were stacked in a variety of ways to function as furniture and even Ophelia's grave; and a camouflage net hung above the stage for most of the play and was yanked down to form a shroud over the dead bodies at the final curtain. A *Macbeth* production (1981), also directed by Schorm in the

Balustrade, keyed to the image of karate fighters in movement and costumes, made use of mattresses with hooks that were tossed during the action and stuck to the walls that were hung with netting; one side of the mattresses had the stuffing coming out, to help form an image of Birnam Wood.

Somewhat more elaborate was a production of *Mother Courage* (1986). On a small turntable Courage's wagon itself remained stable but served different functions when disassembled for certain scenes, for example becoming the hut onto which Katrin climbs toward the end of the play. Similarly, in a production of *War and Peace* (1986), the tall backs of chairs were painted to represent soldiers; knocked over in the battle scenes, they became casualties of the war.

Like Malina, Dušek also feels that the time may be ripe for scenography to become more visually expressive again, to play a greater role in a performance. Particularly in light of the prevailing literalness of television scenography, Dušek thinks, theatre should be more imaginative and bold. By the same token, although much of his work stresses the virtues of minimalism, Dušek enjoys working with productions demanding a larger scale. For the surrealist opera by Martinů, *Julietta* (1982), he created a large ship's profile out of latex stretch cloth and attached it by ropes to other objects on stage, again creating a setting that could readily change during the flow of the action. Later, he fabricated larger-than-life pop art figures that could be yanked out of cardboard boxes for *The Threepenny Opera* (1987), such as Queen Victoria triumphantly appearing at the end of the play (Plate 38). Even more monumental was his scenery for *Danton's Death* (1989) in the National Theatre. The setting gave the impression of a period stage with painted perspective scenery depicting larger-than-life neo-classical arched entrances, but here as a box set rather than one with wings. A large net was suspended above, with bits of stage scenery debris in it. An elevated podium with stairs and wheels to facilitate its movement was often used for formal speeches but also for sheer emphasis by the actors at certain moments. A similar purpose was served by a diving board type of plinth emerging from high up stage left, reachable by ladder. Colors were reduced to the white–gray–black range, as if in an engraving. Effective lighting changes provided vitality and variety; and enlarged shadows were cast on the rear wall from special spotlights in the bottom part of the orchestra pit.

Even in his more minimalist vein, Dušek often seizes on a stage image that is not only functional but also richly metaphoric and thereby visually striking. For *Long Day's Journey into Night* (1983) Dušek constructed a simple framed background of panels and a doorway (Plate 39). But each panel consisted of transparent plastic with several layers of irregularly torn, soaked paper lightly pasted to the back of the plastic. Testing revealed that the paper would gradually dry and peel away from the plastic, with one panel being bare by the end of the first act and the rest by the end of the play, thus graphically reinforcing the progressive stripping of the souls and defences of

Plate 38 For the finale of Brecht's *Threepenny Opera* (1987) in Brno, Jan Dušek created a giant Queen Victoria. Photo: J. Burian.

Plate 39 Dušek's scenography for *Long Day's Journey into Night* (1983) in České Budejovice. Photo: J. Burian.

the characters. An added dramatic touch was the mirror effect created by the bared panels as well as the ability to see the characters before they entered the main acting area. Similar scenography occurred in Alexander Vampilov's *Duck Hunt* (1985), a work during which a steady rain falls. An unfurnished room is backed by frames with inclined plastic panels that have been white-washed from the back. Tubes released light streams of water down the back of the panes, leaving black streaks at first, and eventually clearing the panes completely, enabling the audience to see threatening figures behind them.

* * *

In western theatres known to us, the role of women from the late seventeenth until the twentieth century was that of seamstresses, actresses, playwrights, and – rarely – theatre managers. It was no different in Czech theatre, and it took Czech women somewhat longer than their western counterparts in the twentieth century to extend their theatre work to costume design and, eventually, stage direction. Scenography in the sense of *stage* design was among the very last professional theatre activities to be entered by Czech women.

Two women scenographers have drawn most attention in recent Czech theatre: Marta Roszkopfová (b. 1947) and Jana Zbořilová (b. 1953). Products of different schooling in different parts of the Czech Republic, sharing certain stylistic characteristics but essentially distinct in their total stage imagery and resultant effects, they are now in mid-career and have made their mark in a field still dominated by men. A consideration of their backgrounds, range of work, and scenographic orientation will help clarify the special qualities of their contribution to contemporary Czech theatre, as well as their distinctive features *vis-à-vis* each other.

Costume design was the primary activity for each in the early part of her career, and the high quality of each one's work was rewarded by the gold medal in costume design each won at the Novy Sad (Yugoslavia) Triennale, Jana Zbořilová in 1981, Marta Roszkopfová in 1984. Nevertheless, each has preferred to do scenery and costumes together as one unified design project, which is what now happens most of the time; occasionally one or the other may still do only costumes, but hardly ever has either one done only scenery. As usual in Czech theatre, stage lighting is also their responsibility.

Although each has done from 150 to 200 professional design projects, Roszkopfová has worked with a relatively smaller number of theatres and directors than has Zbořilová. Beneath this quantitative, surface difference lies a more personal, temperamental distinction. By her own account, Marta Roszkopfová finds scenography an intensely subjective, philosophically provocative activity most satisfying when undertaken with a few tried and true directorial collaborators, largely in one theatre center. While Jana Zbořilová does not represent an opposite extreme, she brings to mind a somewhat cooler, more detached approach, ready and able to deal with a wide variety of ensembles and individual artists.

To generalize from examples of their work itself, it is clear that both reject realistic, decorative, or traditional painterly scenery, but both also usually steer away from use of architectonic, technical elements, and neither one cares for projections. Instead, both seem attracted to relatively open stage space, and special treatment and distribution of real, functional objects within that space. In this sense, they both fall within the 'action design' category, although both, especially Marta Roszkopfová, often transcend that category.

Given these tendencies in common, differences are equally apparent. While Roszkopfová is more readily associated with medium to large proscenium stages, much of Zbořilová's work has been marked by her early and occasional ongoing association with small, non-proscenium studio stages. Moreover, Roszkopfová's work often conveys a sense of boldness, power, and sheer material presence compared to Zbořilová's relatively more spare, skeletal, open creations. As one critic noted, Roszkopfová tends to add on, while Zbořilová takes away. Another preliminary, overall observation is that Roszkopfová's work often tends toward themes of a darker, harsher, more aggressive tonality to which she responds subjectively, whereas Zbořilová seems more at home with lighter, more ironic and witty material that she treats with relative objectivity.

Finally, for the moment, each has a distinct 'signature' element in her choice of scenic materials: Roszkopfová admits to finding the varied use of very tangible, hard-edged panels or boards a significantly expressive scenographic component, while Zbořilová seems drawn toward varied use of suspended or draped cloths and fabrics, akin to Malina's practice.

The specific training and early professional experiences of each undoubtedly affected their stylistic evolution, especially Roszkopfová's. Her pre-professional schooling concentrated on textiles, and before going on to theatre design training she worked for a year in the workshops of the Slovak National Theatre in Bratislava. From 1968 to 1973 at the academy of arts in Bratislava (VSMU) she studied scenography under Ladislav Vychodil and costume design under the leading Slovak designer Ludmila Purkynová. Especially interesting is that Roszkopfová then spent an additional year in Warsaw at the academy of fine arts studying scenography in the studio of Józef Szajna, the major Polish designer-director who had collaborated closely with Jerzy Grotowski as scenographer on the former's *Akropolis* (1962) before going on to stage his own memorable productions (e.g., *Replika*, 1972, and *Dante*, 1974), which stressed baroquely expressive, nightmarish visions rooted in his own concentration camp experiences. Much of Roszkopfová's dynamics and imagery seem indebted to her exposure to Szajna, who, as she noted in an exhibition flyer, 'tormented us toward independent directorial thinking . . . and strong metaphoric expressiveness.'

In contrast to Roszkopfová's varied training, Jana Zbořilová's might seem almost routine. She spent her high school years at the central school of design in Prague before progressing in 1972 to the five-year Prague theatre academy of arts (DAMU), where she had traditional training in stage and costume design from designers who had themselves been students of František Tröster. Even before completing her study, however, she was already working with one of the seminal studio ensembles of the post-Prague Spring era, the Theatre on a String (Divadlo na provázku) of Brno.[3] This experimental, improvisation-based theatre became her professional cradle, although for the first seven years of her professional career (1977–84) she was essentially a freelance artist who also worked elsewhere, even abroad.

In the meantime, in 1974, directly after her year with Szajna in Warsaw, Marta Roszkopfová joined the state theatres in Ostrava as a resident designer, and Ostrava theatres have remained her home base ever since, even though she has also worked in a number of theatres in other parts of the Czech and Slovak lands. Ostrava is a large city of heavy industry and coal mining in the north-east part of what is now the Czech Republic. Roszkopfová characteristically referred to it as a city,

> where all the men remained smothered under a layer of coal dust and alcohol, where interest in Thalia is minimal. Ostrava is a hard environment and anything but a pleasant cradle for the spirit, creativity, art. Life in this black, noisy city . . . this industrialized surrounding – all this strongly influenced my theatrical handwriting.[4]

Jana Zbořilová's freelance career, on the other hand, has been interrupted by only one moderately long, stable residency (1984–88) with the theatre in Cheb, the westernmost city in the Czech Republic. During her time there she also became chief of technical operations, which familiarized her with workshop routines and demands. It proved to be a welcome total experience. 'It was good to do more elaborate productions, have my own workshops, and get used to their personnel, and to work systematically with the same people – not only technicians but also directors and actors.' Nevertheless, Zbořilová was again attracted to freelance work, which she has done since 1988, not only in Prague, Brno, Pilsen, and other Czech cities, but also in Greece, Poland, Hungary, Germany, and Finland. Since the early 1980s in these many theatres, she has worked with over thirty directors. Her base since 1990 has become Prague, specifically as part of the faculty at the theatre academy where she herself studied; it is a position which still allows her ample opportunity for freelance assignments, most of which have recently been in Brno.

Marta Roszkopfová, on the other hand, has worked with a much narrower range of theatres and directors. In a letter to me she cited only four directors as truly satisfying collaborators, in particular Josef Janík, with whom she has worked since the early 1980s, on some fifty productions. Part of the explanation lies in her own words:

> Only with a similarly oriented director is it possible to search side by side for the expressive resources for each new production. Then it makes no difference if it's in Ostrava, Brno, or Prague. . . . I'm [even] willing to work for an unpopular theatre if there is hope that a deep mutual understanding with the director will be the foundation for honest work on a production.[5]

It is with Janík that she has done some of her most striking work with panels. Two examples are *Hamlet* and Sartre's *Trojan Women*. In *Hamlet* (Ostrava, 1983), individual movable panels of varied size are seen standing on either their long or short sides, loosely distributed but filling up much of an otherwise empty stage to create the impression of a random, sinister labyrinth that provides hiding places from which to spy or eavesdrop (Plate 40). The panels suggest stage flats, a consciously theatricalistic touch typical of both Roszkopfová and Zbořilová. The theatrical effect is heightened by the exposed stage platforming that forms the base on which the panels stand. In *Trojan Women* (Olomouc, 1994), panels are hung in a row that stretches across the full width of the stage just behind the curtain line to form a snaggle-toothed wall with irregularly placed openings to provide entries onto a shallow relief stage. The front edge of the stage borders an orchestra pit, which is piled high with the wreckage and domestic detritus of war extending back to the rear wall of the stage in some scenes. What seems to be the

Plate 40   Marta Roszkopfová's *Hamlet* (1983) in Ostrova. Photo: J. Burian.

permanent fire curtain is seen at various menacing heights, occasionally revealing behind it a bleak sky with an ominous cloud also composed of the human refuse of war. For Roszkopfová,

> Multiple panels or structural boards standing next to each other or behind each other, arranged to form angles, . . . hung horizontally or vertically, become for me a boundary beyond which lies a secret. . . . I'm drawn to suggesting the invisible behind the boundary, or to hint at it by the surface treatment of the panels.[6]

A more complex setting appeared in O'Neill's post-civil war tragedy, *Mourning Becomes Electra*, the April 1988 premiere of which I attended in Brno. It was directed by Zdeněk Kaloč, one of Roszkopfová's other favored directors. Within completely anachronistic metal-sheeted walls with sliding panels, Marta Roszkopfová created an indoor–outdoor simultaneous setting that had the virtue of making possible a Shakespeare-like flow from scene to scene on a curtainless stage. A larger than life-sized monumental statue of the seated patriarch Abe Mannon was situated at stage right (its pose an echo of Lincoln's statue in the Lincoln Memorial); its pedestal contained a roll-out double bed (the elder Mannons'). An equally oversized standing statue of Abe's brother, David Mannon, was at stage left. Both statues were illuminated by spotlights down center aimed upward from just below stage level and openly controlled by the actors, as were other special lighting effects. The third permanent on stage object was a rolling metal scaffolding unit used primarily as a stairway to the upper-rear gallery level, which housed, behind sliding panels, Christine's private chambers. Below this up stage upper level was a chamber containing a series of busts of the other illustrious Mannon dead.

As presented in this production, nothing that I have mentioned had any source in O'Neill's stage directions, but such novelties are typical of the ways in which director and scenographer felt free to adapt O'Neill's given text. It was an example, perhaps, of action scenography for a revival of a large-scale classic. Instead of a stage composition of varied elements designed to create a recognizable, logical, and aesthetically pleasing image of reality, Roszkopfová brought together a deliberately illogical cluster of realistic but deconstructed elements (i.e., torn from their familiar contexts) to form an almost surreal assemblage of objects that would not coexist in any space other than on a stage.

A particularly interesting example of Roszkopfová's later work was seen in a dramatization of a classic early-twentieth-century Czech novel, *A Year in the Country*, by the Mrštík brothers (Plate 41). I saw it in Prague's National

Plate 41 Roszkopfová's original design for a dramatization of the Mrštík brothers' *A Year in the Country* (1993), National Theatre. Photo: J. Burian.

Theatre in November 1993, when it was well into its repertory run. The dramatization and direction were by Miroslav Krobot, a third, more recent director in Marta Roszkopfová's favored circle. The play, which had its premiere in the spring of 1993, won the prize for the best Czech production of the year. To create the most useful and yet expressive spatial, visual context for the large cast, multi-scene flow of village life at the turn of the century, with its crisscrossed lives and seasonal rituals, Roszkopfová once again set up a 'container,' this time of roughly textured, whitewashed, undecorated walls with regularly spaced, plain doorways. Dominating this neutral space was to be a massive tree trunk situated slightly stage left of stage center and meant to be present throughout the play. In one of her early notes to the director, Roszkopfová wrote 'I see a tree growing through this room, its walls, floor, even ceiling – time-time – a tree is eternity. It's a piece of nature – the outdoors.'[7] As seen in her rendering, the jagged top of the broken, phallic-like trunk was to rupture and penetrate through an abstractly stylized ceiling (or cloud?) of tightly stretched, red-stained white canvas, held taut by lines extending beyond the confines of the universal chamber that became the place of action for all the interior and exterior scenes, depending on whether it remained empty or had some minimal furniture within it.

Like other instances of Roszkopfová's scenography, this verged on the expressionistic or even surreal, yet still was based on tangible, authentic, elemental reality. But the special 'rub' in this instance was that the director made a decision at dress rehearsal to eliminate the tree trunk, allegedly because it hampered the blocking and sight lines. But the ceiling or 'cloud' remained, no longer with red streaks but all white. A critic commented on the missing tree trunk in relation to Roszkopfová's overall profile: 'A director in the first phase accepts her intense dramatic-design feel for the space of a play and doesn't suspect how dangerous a partner for him is a scenographer whom he doesn't want to or isn't able to follow.'[8] On the other hand, what remained was still very effective. When I saw the play I was not aware that any tree was ever to have been there, and I must say that I did not feel that anything was missing. I took the ruptured ceiling/cloud to be a poetically expressive symbol of the various traumas generated by the human element and its often erotic passions within the grand cyclic flow of time and nature.

What is also striking in this production, which was still in the repertoire in the 1998–99 season, is that it seems to have nothing to do with action scenography, with which Roszkopfová has sometimes been identified. Rather, it exemplifies her observation that 'even before the actors begin performing and the text begins to reveal a particular event, it's possible – acoustically or visually – to determine the aim and even the focal point of a production,' a remark which could be taken as a commandment of most twentieth-century stage design prior to the advent of action scenography, and which seems inconsistent with another of Roszkopfová's observations: 'I'm in favor of scenography that becomes justified only in the context of the activity of the actor.'[9] A larger point to be made here is that Roszkopfová seems likely to commit to a basic scenographic concept or image fairly early in the total production process rather than to let one evolve during the course of rehearsals.

The latter approach or method seems more characteristic of the work of Jana Zbořilová. As she has written, 'A production does not emerge at the writing table, but on stage during rehearsals.'[10] Unlike Roszkopfová's scenography, which relies heavily on hard-surfaced enclosures or 'borders' of hard-edged (at times metallic) panels and boards, with mostly hard, unyielding objects inside them, Zbořilová's scenography seems largely dependent on cloths and drapes to form walls, ceilings, floors, tents, and a variety of specific items like sails, wings, or, quite simply, bed sheets. What is of interest are the various forms and functions of the cloths, as well as their mode of support and their treatment with colors or graphics.

A key principle for Zbořilová, which may help account for her repeated use of fabrics, is a certain minimalism in the search for imaginative theatre: 'I prefer striving for magic but with the simplest means.' It is a remark close to but not synonymous with Roszkopfová's 'I try by minimal means to create a "slice from life".'[11] Beyond Zbořilová's selective use of authentic objects in conjunction with drapes is a pull toward fantasy; beyond Roszkopfová's often metaphoric, near-expressionistic grouping of deconstructed, material elements is a pull toward realism and relevance.

A relatively complex environment of structurally draped, painted cloths occurred in *Princess T*, by the contemporary Czech Daniela Fischerová (Cheb, 1988), a darkly satiric version of Gozzi's *commedia* play, *Turandot*. The colorfully painted cloth walls were extensions of the floor. Bamboo poles formed the vertical supports for walls and for a large but delicate baldachin, which could function as sky, ceiling, or high mountains, largely depending on how it was lit. Similarly the bamboo poles could be used as weapons. Bright red cloths punctuated the basic gray–white scale of the abstract patterns painted on the large sections of cloth. The red cloths were sometimes used as banners, or to cover the pillows hanging from the bamboo poles, or even as parts of Turandot's costume. Multifunctionality has been a hallmark of Zbořilová's scenography. As she has put it:

> I've always emphasized scenography that is functional, 'actional,' that serves the text, action, and actors. It's not a matter of 'design,' but of making sense of the given circumstances and action, but concurrently being concerned with the visual, aesthetic aspect; the two go hand in hand. I prefer more austere elements than decorative ones because the former force viewers to use their imagination. I also prefer elements that alter their form and function in the course of a play.

'Elements that alter their form and function' were evident in a two-level skeletal construction placed on a turntable as the key scenic element for Shakespeare's *Taming of the Shrew* (Brno, 1994). At first bare and providing a space for Sly and the mistress of the inn, it was covered by the arriving troupe of actors with strategically placed cloths with window openings and thereby became transformed into a town square; and when reversed via the turntable, it became Petruccio's unkempt household. According to Zbořilová, 'It was all very playful, actional, non-literal, and lent itself to the actors' actions and business.'

Two productions made use of an interesting combination of cloth and kinetic objects. A huge cloth with many graphic elements formed both the rear wall and the floor for a dramatization of *Alice in Wonderland* (Cheb, 1984). The rear wall was pierced by two mysterious holes through which passed a circular railroad track and its whimsically shaped car. This 'mechanical' component along with the paintings on the cloth, especially the bare tree curving around one of the holes, caught something close to the spirit of the fantasy.

Considerably more complicated was a flamboyant 1994 production of Václav Havel's adaptation of *The Beggar's Opera* on one of the largest Czech stages, in a theatre built in the 1980s in Most. Here, too, objects came through holes in a canvas wall, but the principle and its embodiment were significantly different (Plate 42). A variety of furniture and props were strategically placed on a large turntable, intersected from above by a large, suspended bi-fold canvas wall with four doorways. As the turntable rotated, the various three-dimensional pieces rode off stage or on stage *through* the existing doorways in the canvas wall. At the end, the canvas wall lifted up and back, thereby revealing all the props and furniture plus whirling colored lights and a fancy convertible with Macheath and his girls. Especially interesting here was Zbořilová's expansion of her distinctive scenography to include larger, *technically* more complex elements. In fact, but for the cloth and the playfulness inherent in the total scenographic concept, this could have been a Svoboda production.[12]

One play provides a final example of the work of these two leading contemporary scenographers. In the spring of 1995, each one worked on a production of Eugene O'Neill's *Long Day's Journey into Night*, Roszkopfová in Ostrava with director Janík, Zbořilová in Brno with director Zdeněk Kaloč (Plate 43). Both production teams had to deal with a large proscenium stage and both decided to heighten the intimacy of the performance by seating the audience on the stage itself. The Roszkopfová production had the entire audience seated at the rear of the stage, facing toward the proscenium opening, beyond which was the empty auditorium. The Zbořilová team placed the acting area above the orchestra pit, with the audience on two sides: part up stage and part in the auditorium, thus presenting the actors with the challenge of playing to some spectators very close to them at one side, and others

Plate 42 Jana Zbořilová's scenography for a production of Václav Havel's *Beggar's Opera* (1994). Photo: J. Burian.

quite further removed on the other side. Zbořilová's signature was obvious in the relatively empty stage and, especially, the huge cloth drapery suspended from the upper proscenium boxes and swooping down to form the side walls (with doorways) and to cover the floor, including the significant table around which the family often gathers. The plain, unadorned cloth was intended to evoke the motif of sails as well as the neutral fog that encompasses much of the action; moreover, of course, it suggests the alienating effect the house has on Mary Tyrone, for whom it was never a home but only a temporary dwelling. Adding to the metaphoric theatricality of this approach were the small spotlights that formed the chandelier above the table, as well as the proscenium lighting bridge, where Mary could be seen pacing. Probably the only elements to suggest the setting as described in O'Neill's stage directions were a number of wicker chairs.

Contrasting with the relative spareness of the Zbořilová set was what one critic described as the 'warehouse' feel of the Roszkopfová set: in addition to a large central dining table and several chairs, at stage right were two grand pianos with open lids, plus an upright piano, while a writing table and a large wardrobe were at stage left. Of particular interest is that Roszkopfová, like Zbořilová, made use of the lighting bridge as a place associated with Mary's quarters on the second floor. In the absence of any visual evidence of the

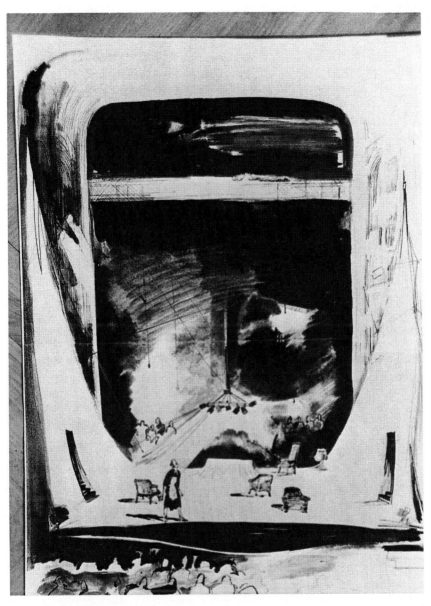

Plate 43 Zbořilová's drawing for a production of *Long Day's Journey into Night* (1995), directed by Zdeněk Kaloč in Brno. Photo: J. Burian.

Roszkopfová set, I find it difficult to be more precise about its quality or effect, beyond noting the recurrence of her tendency to have a stage relatively fuller of material than is true of Zbořilová's sets.[13]

In retrospect, a few final observations might be made. Both women are experienced professionals who have developed distinctive styles and techniques which are similar in their rejection of traditional and realistic stage design and in their inclination toward many aspects of action design, but which differ in their relative tone, scope, and 'weight.' Each in her own way seems in recent productions to be stretching her talents in productions of a larger scale, without sacrificing her individually evolved style. What remains is a primary impression of Marta Roszkopfová's darker, heavier, more aggressive scenography, and her total, subjective involvement in her projects. And not to be forgotten is the early influence on her of Josef Szajna, to whom she probably owes much of her strong, harsh imagery as well as her inclination to make directorial-like choices with her scenography.

Jana Zbořilová's scenography, on the other hand, seems not only lighter, softer, and more fanciful and playful, but also less rooted in deeply felt personal attitudes. She seems more detached (and thereby wittier), but also more focused on creating scenography that is less a personal statement than an instrument to be used by the director and actors and perhaps help shape their style in performance. Rather than being intimately bound up with her own life and convictions, scenography for her is an ongoing professional challenge to her skills and ingenuity in combining form and function with a special touch of theatricality. Needless to say, when I suggest that scenography to Roszkopfová seems more fused to a subjectively evolved life-view than does scenography to Zbořilová, I am simply trying to account for some of the characteristics of each one's artistry rather than passing any value judgment on the theatrical or aesthetic qualities of either's work.

* * *

Indeed, the best work of all four of these late-twentieth-century designers seems to possess a special balance between a respect for form, structure, and materials, and a fresh perception of the very identity and role of scenography. Much of recent Czech scenography started as a mainly functional element in a teamwork project, subordinating its distinctive identity in order to facilitate the work of directors and actors. What has saved this recent Czech scenography from being merely an organizer of props or an anonymous instrument of directors and actors is perhaps its consciousness of the historically significant scenographic tradition in Czech theatre, as well as the rigorous training that its designers receive. And these two factors – in addition to a basic reaction against the literalism of television – may lie behind the recent tendency of these designers to move toward asserting a stronger, more expressive role for scenography in the theatre production process. In the broadest sense, this recent tendency is perhaps also related to a natural instinct in artists to seek a fuller, personal outlet for their visions. At all events, scenography in Czech theatre has been the richer for the work of designers like Malina, Dušek, Roszkopfová, and Zbořilová.[14]

10

CZECH *HAMLETS* OF THE
TWENTIETH CENTURY

Every production of *Hamlet* assays the talents of its creators and the temper of its times. It may also reveal its creators' relative preoccupation with artistic forms or with social issues, or even the creators' specific philosophic or ideological outlook on the immediate world they inhabit. The following exploration of representative Czech productions of *Hamlet* from the turn of the century until the 1990s provides, moreover, a special view of the collaborative work among many of the actors, directors, and designers previously encountered in the separate chapters of this book.[1]

At times presenting a showcase of Czech cultural maturity, at other times venting the frustration and distress arising from harsh social and political conditions prevailing during their respective eras, and always revealing the distinctive artistry of their creators, Czech productions of *Hamlet* have served as a microcosm of the Czech theatre and its relation to the forces that have dominated the life of this nation in the heart of Europe. In a broader sense they also provide further testimony of the ongoing debate over ways of staging Shakespeare, between those who strive for maximal expressive fidelity to Shakespeare's presumed intentions as derived from his text and those who champion maximum freedom in manipulating the text in order to release the creative fantasy and vision of the director most fully.

Although the emphasis in this survey will be on several *Hamlet* productions since the 1950s, some consideration of general background and certain prewar productions provides a useful historical perspective. To begin with, one must recognize the great significance that Shakespeare has held for Czech culture and Czech theatre. Lacking a sense of national identity since their defeat by the forces of the Habsburg Empire at the Battle of White Mountain in 1620, the Czechs began a slow revival of their culture and their political aspirations in the last decades of the eighteenth century. Czech theatre had no building of its own, no tradition in acting, and no stock of native drama. During the next hundred years, Shakespeare became a model and an inspiration for generations of theatre artists and audiences, especially in their efforts to free themselves from the hegemony of German culture and theatre. As Jan Mukařovský noted,

Czech theatre put on Shakespeare's plays not only in order to interpret to the full their philosophical and artistic message, but in order
to place the Czech theatre itself on a high level of acting, direction,
and staging . . . [and] . . . the growth of Czech theatre would be
unthinkable without [Shakespeare].[2]

Following the earliest production of *Hamlet* in Czech, in Prague in the
early 1790s, nineteenth-century productions were primarily notable for the
increasing number of translations and the stage effectiveness of leading performers rather than for special interpretations or production concepts. More
importantly, Shakespeare became progressively identified with the nationalist
aspirations of the Czech people, who saw in his plays, especially in the
tragedies and histories, many parallels to their own complex situation. On a
more fundamental level, to translate and perform Shakespeare was a sign of
cultural maturity. Nowhere was the connection between homage to Shakespeare and national pride more evident than in a Shakespeare cycle of four
productions presented in 1864 to mark the tricentennial of Shakespeare's
birth. The festivities also included 230 costumed Shakespearian characters in
a gala public procession to the accompaniment of a march by Bedřich
Smetana.

Early-twentieth-century productions of *Hamlet* epitomized the increasing
artistry and sophistication of interpretation evident in Czech theatre. At the
same time, they placed less emphasis on the social relevance and the educa-
tive potential of the drama. The landmark production of *Hamlet* in 1905 in
the National Theatre was hailed as the first great creative achievement of the
Czech dramatic (i.e., nonmusical) theatre. The production was dominated by
the towering presence of Eduard Vojan (1853–1920), who combined the bra-
vura technique of the romantic theatre with a complex psychological analysis that led to a deep exploration of a character's intellectual and emotional
life. The result was a Hamlet of deep thought and biting irony, isolated from
others by the nobility of his soul and the intensity of his suppressed grief.
Concentrating on Hamlet's subjective, personal concerns, this turn of the
century *Hamlet* was essentially an apolitical production, evidence of which
included the elimination of Fortinbras from the end of the play. Director
Jaroslav Kvapil's blending of psychologically realistic acting with a sensitive
orchestration of atmospheric lighting and selective, symbolist-influenced
scenery created unified, carefully shaded productions in which considerable
room existed for the creativity of individual actors.

Kvapil's and the Czech theatre's devotion to Shakespeare was most strikingly demonstrated in a 1916 cycle during which fifteen of Shakespeare's
plays were presented in a six-week period in honor of the three-hundredth
anniversary of Shakespeare's death. Vojan's sovereignty among actors was
reaffirmed by his playing of the roles of Macbeth, Hamlet, Lear, Othello,
Shylock, Richard III, Benedict, and Petruchio during the festival. Although

none of the productions was notable for its political slant, the sheer cycle as a whole made a provocative political statement in itself, occurring as it did in the midst of World War I, when Shakespeare's England was locked in bloody conflict with the Austro-Hungarian empire, of which the Czechs were still unwilling members.

The next notable Hamlet was that of Eduard Kohout (1889–1976), in a production directed by the next great (some would say the greatest) Czech director, Karel Hugo Hilar, in 1926 at the National Theatre in Prague. Hilar is chiefly identified with the expressionist movement, but in 1926 he subordinated this tendency to what he called civilism, by which he meant a shift to concerns of everyday life after the devastation and hysteria of the great war. Kohout represented a pale, sensitive youth, a 'melancholy lyricist,'[3] at a loss and impotent within the hostile, often grotesque world of the Danish court. In striking contrast to the manly, mature, philosophic Hamlet of Vojan, Kohout presented an inexperienced boy, alternately confused and vehement, tearful and explosive: a reflection of the young, postwar generation and its resentment toward the alienating world it inherited. Not focused as exclusively on Hamlet as was the Kvapil–Vojan production, Hilar's *Hamlet* thereby also allowed the other characters to make a greater impact.

Hilar's direction involved what critics called a revue format, a series of rapidly changing scenes that deliberately accentuated contrasts in tone between the comic and the serious. The residue of Hilar's penchant for expressionist staging was more evident in the scenography provided by Vlastislav Hofman, the first great Czech designer, whose own bent was toward heightened, bold expressiveness (Plate 44). Here, Hofman modified his often baroque effects and created a series of stark, austere settings based on a variety of silvery-gray screens, tall, thin prisms, wall units, and pieces of massive furniture mounted on easily movable platforms in the midst of black space, accentuated by harsh, sharply focused lighting that avoided almost all color. The settings were deliberately designed to facilitate the rapid, abrupt entrances of actors from behind the various units, but they also conveyed the sense of alienation Hilar was obviously seeking. Like the furniture, the costumes were a blend of period and modern in style. Hamlet's costumes included a short black jacket, vest, sweater, and basque cap; Gertrude wore a modern evening gown with train for the 'mousetrap' scene. Although Hilar consistently eschewed a theatre of political, much less ideological, orientation, he was responsive to the social currents of his day. In this *Hamlet*, Hilar wanted a largely young, postwar audience to identify with the world of the play on a personal level.

The last significant *Hamlet* before the German occupation and World War II was in fact not simply Shakespeare's *Hamlet* (however much edited) but a radical adaptation that combined elements of Shakespeare's text with one of Jules Laforgue's *Moralités légendaires*, a prose retelling of Hamlet's story

Plate 44 One of Vlastislav Hofman's many renderings for Hilar's *Hamlet* (1926), National Theatre. Photo: J. Burian.

with a modern psychological slant. The author of this hybrid, titled *Hamlet III*, was the celebrated avant-garde director E. F. Burian, a committed Communist. As discussed in previous chapters, Burian's ideological commitment underwent crises arising from the clash of his artistic will toward free creation with the shifting demands of the Communist program.

Reacting against the ostracizing by the Soviet authorities of his idol, Meyerhold, who severely attacked the official Communist policy of Socialist Realism in the arts, Burian created *Hamlet III* in 1937 not only as a forceful attack against Fascism but also as a defiant statement in support of free artistic creation against any restrictions. Far from an introspective or sensitive figure, Burian's Hamlet, Václav Vaňátko (1904–49), dressed in white satin and with a dagger in one hand and a pen in the other, became not only a disillusioned, embittered intellectual, but virtually a terrorist, whose aim was to destroy a senseless world. The King and Queen were presented as crude murderers, members of a ruling class destined for extinction. A sole ray of hope in the world of this production lay in the gravediggers, representatives of the people, whose children might one day overthrow the castle, instead of standing impotent before it. Attacked by Marxist critics, Burian eventually relented in his rejection of contemporary Communist policy for the arts, and ultimately spoke of the production as something of an aberration.

Nevertheless, the production was perhaps even more notable because of the inventiveness and imagination of its highly stylized staging. The action took place on two turntables, sometimes silent, sometimes screeching in their movement. The acting frequently conveyed the impression of a waxworks of monstrous, dehumanized puppets, and Burian's own score for the production included sirens and other *musique concrète* sound-effects. Operating on a very small proscenium stage, Burian pioneered in what we have come to know as multimedia theatre. His distinctive use of stage space, lighting, and especially projections in combination with the play of actors created highly metaphoric, theatrically synthesized performances that truly warrant the frequently abused term, 'theatre poetry.' One example in this *Hamlet* may stand for many others: on a relatively bare stage with black background and no curtain, the drowning of Ophelia was presented by an actress miming drowning behind bent wires and a scrim-like, lightly rippling white drape onto which was projected a specially made film of the enlarged details of an aquarium, in soft focus (see Plate 6, p. 56). Burian's theatrically creative imagination seemed to have an inescapable corollary: one rarely remembers any of Burian's actors. In his theatre, Burian was the dominating artist.

In wartime, occupied Prague, a 1941 production of *Hamlet* in the Vinohrady Theatre was chiefly notable for its scenography by František Tröster, the significant designer and teacher whose career spanned the 1930s to the 1960s (Plate 45). Most critics found the production uneven, an unsuccessful mixture of a rationally focused intellectual drama with overly expressive staging. Miloš Nedbal (1906–82) played an aristocratic, embittered intellectual attempting to endure in a ruthless environment. It was an interpretation reflecting the perilous state of the Czechs at a time when the Axis forces were riding the crest of military successes.[4] Most of the acting occurred within an oval shaped area on the stage floor, the closed end of the oval pointing up stage, the open end downstage. Mirroring this form was a configuration of draperies hung just beyond the up stage end of the stage oval. Varied colored lighting in conjunction with selective scenic elements placed behind the draped oval created striking visual effects, such as the scene on the battlements, Hamlet's encounter with Fortinbras on the plain, and the graveyard.

The first major *Hamlet* of the postwar, Communist era was a response to the change from the hard Stalinist years of the 1950s to a gradual softening of oppression and a corresponding loosening of tight controls on the arts, which had been most painfully apparent in the forced policy of Socialist

Plate 45 The Vinohrady Theatre *Hamlet* (1941), directed by B. Stejskal with scenery by František Tröster. Photo: J. Burian.

Realism that weighed like a heavy blanket on all creative activity. The late 1950s saw the emergence of the studio theatre movement and its implicit rejection of traditional forms. It also saw the creation of a striking evolution in scenography, which was perhaps nowhere more evident than in the work of Josef Svoboda, a trail-blazer of great subsequent influence in international stage design.

Building on the visions and innovations of men like Adolph Appia and Gordon Craig, as well as on the Soviet avant-garde of the 1920s, and the work of his own countrymen, E. F. Burian and František Tröster, Svoboda developed an approach to staging which incorporated extensive use of contemporary technology. Scenography was to have a dynamic role in production, at times equivalent to the acting. Like the play of actors, scenography should also be capable of being modified and varied in response to the ongoing action. It is a new variation of 'synthetic theatre,' the premise of which is that theatre is an art of interacting, constantly variable components and relationships – an evolving *Gestalt* in which the text may be the core or spine but by no means is the sole or even necessarily the main element. This concept or vision is certainly not uniquely Svoboda's; it owes much to the strong structuralist tradition in modern Czech aesthetics and to the influence of outstanding Czech stage directors like Otomar Krejča and Alfred Radok, with whom Svoboda worked on many productions.

The National Theatre's production of *Hamlet* in 1959 was directed by a contemporary of Svoboda, Jaromír Pleskot (b. 1922), designed by Svoboda, and had Radovan Lukavský (b. 1919) as a sober, older, very disciplined Hamlet, who acted practically and decisively against a corrupt order only after careful analysis and reflection (Plate 46). Lukavský's journal of the production reveals the director's concept of Hamlet as a knight and Claudius as a politician. Hamlet the humanist discovers his dependence on and his responsibility to society. Hamlet becomes a 'positive hero' in the best sense of the word: 'Not mystic fate, but a clear mission.'[5] The production had great appeal to its audiences, perhaps primarily because Lukavský's portrayal of Hamlet embodied many of the qualities most Czechs admire: a practicality based on thorough, sober reasoning; an independent intellect not subject to emotional indulgence; determined action at the right moment. Emerging from the dark Stalinist era, the production seemed to echo the need for cautious, responsible action leading to a careful, rational liberalization of society. The production remained in the repertoire until 1965, by which time it had 171 performances, a record for Czech *Hamlets*.

Svoboda's contribution reinforced the motif of an alienating though elegant and monumental environment. A total of twenty tall panels covered with a black plastic material and measuring approximately 10×30 feet each were situated in five planes parallel to and behind the proscenium opening. The twenty-four scene changes of the production were effected by laterally sliding the panels in differing configurations for each scene. Supplementing this architectonic, labyrinthine shaping of space was the reflective surface of the panels, which made them function as semi-glossy black mirrors, a striking vision in itself, but also highly conducive to certain lighting effects. For example, two spotlights reflected from the surface of a panel formed an abstract impression of two glaring eyes. This became the visual accompaniment to the Ghost's speeches, which were simply the recorded voice of Lukavský himself. Another example occurred during the 'To be or not to be' sequence: Lukavský was essentially in silhouette, illuminated from behind by light *reflected* from one of the panels.

A provocative variation of the 1959–65 Prague *Hamlet* as well as of Svoboda's ideal of scenography as an instrument to be placed at the disposition of the director was the *Hamlet* created by the Czech team of Svoboda and Otomar Krejča in Brussels in 1965. The impression of a hostile environment was strengthened and made more overt by the use of an oppressive wall

Plate 46 The Jaromír Pleskot–Svoboda *Hamlet* (1959), with Radovan Lukavský as Hamlet, in the National Theatre. Photo: Dr. Jaromír Svoboda.

constructed of rectangular, geometric masses that were individually movable along a downstage–up stage axis. Suspended at a 45-degree angle above this kinetic construction was a mirror that extended the full width and depth of the wall; in effect, the mirror reflected the groundplan view of the set to the audience. Thus, when the various pieces of the wall moved forward or backward as much as 6 feet either way, the spectator saw a double, now also vertical, movement of menacing, monolithic objects vividly conveying the sense of a crushing, dehumanized world with which Hamlet must cope. The wall itself was highly practicable; not only could action occur on top of the wall, but also individual pieces formed staircases, and the various positions of the others could provide openings or hiding places. Of particular interest is that the mirror originated as a way of embodying Krejča's directorial concept of the Ghost being an alter ego of Hamlet; in the Ghost scenes, Hamlet was talking to himself, as the audience could witness by means of the mirror.

The great breakthrough of the Prague Spring of 1968, toward which the country had been painfully evolving for some ten years, was aborted before any Shakespeare productions could celebrate or respond to it. For most of the following twenty years, theatre was once again forced to speak in cryptic, indirect terms; imagination, much less any hint of criticism of the status quo, was regarded with suspicion or simply censored. The leading directors were prevented from working, as were many actors; it goes without saying that playwrights who had in any way taken a critical view of the twenty-year socialist regime were banned from the stage. Václav Havel was only the best known among many others. The goad for most Czech productions of Shakespeare was likely to be the neo-oppression of the Moscow-dominated Husák regime and the depressing state of Czech culture and society.

In this context, the 1978 production of *Hamlet* by the Balustrade theatre in Prague became a landmark. The theatre for which Havel had been dramaturge and resident playwright was the site of a bitter, grotesque caricature of traditional *Hamlets* with their stress on the eventual victory of humanistic ideals. Directed by Evald Schorm, this *Hamlet* created a world dominated by idiocy as much as evil. Going beyond the frustrated, impassioned bitterness of E. F. Burian's prewar *Hamlet III*, it was a tragi-farcical *Hamlet*, a cruel vision in the spirit of Jarry or Beckett. The characters, including Hamlet, seemed to be not individualized characters with passion and conviction, but shards of humanity operating in a fatalistic, absurdist universe in which the struggle against evil was at best quixotic. Most appropriately, Schorm chose the first quarto *Hamlet* for his text. The unpoetic, unphilosophic near-melodrama of that version, as well as its condensed and swift moving action, lent itself well to Schorm's neo-expressionistic vision.

On the very small Balustrade stage, designer Jan Dušek created a setting of white vertical panels made of buckram, an inexpensive, expendable material that became spattered with 'blood' and torn down during each performance. The panels made for a variety of easy entrances and enabled actors to hide and yet be seen. To create an Elsinore resembling a military fortress poised for war, all furniture was constructed of varying configurations of boxes painted in military camouflage patterns, and a sack of similar camouflage netting was suspended above the stage.

A basic parodistic tone was established at the start by presenting the Ghost loudly lamenting in full clanging armor. Costuming and makeup also signaled a deliberately eccentric approach: Hamlet (Oldřich Vlach) had blackened eye sockets, black jeans, and a sweater; Claudius also had blackened eyes, a vest without a shirt, a blanket-like cape, and a very small crown; Horatio wore a safari outfit. Only the Players appeared in Elizabethan costumes. Hamlet himself was played as cool, reserved, matter of fact, and reasonable as he progressed without any particular hesitation or emotional stress toward what appeared to be a pre-programmed death.

Symptomatic of the production as a whole was the graveyard scene. The gravediggers were presented as circus clowns, in whiteface, with red balls for noses, making infantile nonverbal sounds, half whistling, half humming. They wore shorts, no shirts, and had gloves and long rubberized aprons curiously appropriate to their duties as exhumers. In jarring contrast to the stylized quality of the properties, costumes, and abstract white panels, Yorick's skull was ultra-naturalistic, muddy and with stringy, matted hair. During the subsequent encounter between Hamlet and Osric, the gravediggers rearranged the components of the setting for the duel.

The duel itself was marked by a directorially imposed irony: both Laertes and Hamlet put on soft headcoverings that obviously blocked their vision: we witnessed a duel of two blinded opponents. At the culmination of the ensuing bloodbath, the gravediggers, who had been observing the duel, pushed Claudius back and forth between them before presenting him to Hamlet, who stabbed him. One of the gravediggers then dragged on the bodies of Ophelia and Polonius and added them to the corpses of the duelling scene, while the other gravedigger, still making infantile sounds, pulled down the camouflage net to cover all the bodies. Fortinbras, portrayed by the most oafish and drunken of the touring actors to the court, entered in traditional armor, put on Claudius's crown and presented the final speech in a memorized, mechanistic way, thereby suggesting that all the turmoil really had not made much difference and that a criminal had been replaced by a dolt, but militant power was maintained.

The Balustrade *Hamlet* illustrates the special complication that was attendant on most Czech productions for the previous fifty years (that is, since the Munich dismemberment of the country): a need to communicate on more than one level, and in hidden, indirect, often cryptic terms because of severely oppressive conditions. A production, especially a revival of a classic, was expected to offer some comment or special perspective on the play in relation to the sociopolitical conditions prevailing at the time. By the same token, a Czech audience saw productions in at least two ways: it saw the inherent set of circumstances and characters in action as provided by the playwright, but it was also conditioned to perceive and appreciate the work of the director in setting up special parallels or resonances between the world of the playwright and the world in which they were living. The Balustrade *Hamlet* seen by an American audience would probably have been taken as a jaundiced takeoff or burlesque of Hamlet as play and/or character, not as a despairing, grotesque comment on the current regime. To put it another way, the Balustrade *Hamlet* to American eyes might have seemed a somewhat labored though ingenious parody with an enigmatic or questionable purpose; but to the Czechs it was an intensely bitter, grotesque reflection of their world and their predicament within it.

In striking contrast to the Balustrade *Hamlet* was the 1982 National Theatre revival, which remained in the repertoire until December 1988. Not only was the text drawn from the more traditional Second Quarto and Folio sources, and the staging mounted in the much grander space of the Smetana Theatre building, but also the entire aim of the production was more traditional in presenting Hamlet as a sympathetic, positive figure locked in a desperate, principled struggle to outwit evil forces, and succeeding. His and other lives are lost, but the clear point was that it was worthwhile. In his approach to *Hamlet*, director Miroslav Macháček seemed to challenge the premise that one must find a 'new' way to interpret classic material in order to make it 'relevant.' He did not adopt any striking view or concept or style, other than to emphasize the humanity of the story and its characters as they were shaped by Shakespeare and to relate the result as directly as possible to the audience, on a traditional proscenium stage.

František Němec (b. 1943), an actor in his early forties, played Hamlet as a masculine, often brooding figure, occasionally explosive, given to darting and sprinting about the stage. He was frank, direct, intelligent and quick-witted, but neither a poet nor an intellectual. Warm and responsive with friends and those he trusts, he was not neurotic, indecisive, or isolated, but very much part of the court's life. The implicit point is that Macháček viewed the play as a group, social phenomenon, rather than a study of an unusual individual. Reinforcing this approach was Macháček's characteristic stress on the tangible humanity of the agents rather than some abstract concept or special key to each figure. Outstanding examples were Hamlet's two scenes with the Players. The bantering, exhorting, and incidental by-play were those of old and tried friends. The scenes glowed with an almost Dickensian life of their own; they were not simply functional plot units with a few touches of humor. The First Player's account of Hecuba was an impassioned, totally convincing testimony that became reality to the First Player; his fellow actors had to snap him out of his despair. When I saw the production a second time, in 1988, Macháček himself was playing this role, memorably. The overall result of such performances had the immediacy, color, and texturing of a genre painting but without its excessive, naturalistic detail.

From one point of view, this *Hamlet* might be considered as undistinguished in so far as it lacked a dominating metaphor, style, or image, but the sheer involvement and intensity of the performers in their moment by moment life on the stage prevented any such negative judgments. One other theatrical technique contributed to this effect and was crucial in this production: direct address to the audience. Every soliloquy was overtly shared with the audience, even Claudius's private confession of his rank offense. Hamlet did not speak to himself or verbalize his inner thoughts in some sort of limbo; he simply and impulsively took the audience into his confidence. Macháček extended this technique to several other moments in the play, presumably to increase the involvement of the audience. For instance, at the end of Act 3, Scene 1, Ophelia, left alone on stage after the exit of Polonius and Claudius, turned and stared in despair at the audience. Horatio was included in Act 4, Scene 4, as Hamlet was dispatched to England; left on stage as the others leave, he turned to register dismay to the audience. And at the end of the play, left alone and spotlighted on stage, Horatio appealed despairingly to the audience in mime.

It is impossible to arrive at a neat interpretation of these various directorial touches, but it may be that Macháček, who was frequently in difficulties with authorities, deliberately avoided any sharp or overtly critical slant in the production, and instead chose to establish an implicit bond with the audience, almost a complicity of allies against a common foe. Even though Fortinbras was presented as a noble, commanding figure rather than a Nordic fascist, the waste of humanity in the central action is what Macháček seemed to underline by his business with Horatio at the end, as if to say, 'Must it come to this before a land is rid of its evil?'

To emphasize the human action of the play most forcibly, Josef Svoboda created an austere, virtually bare stage setting consisting solely of plain black drapes to enclose the action, and several shallow stairs running the full width of the stage (Plate 47). Minimal furniture and occasional touches of color (such as a rose-colored valance for the Players scene) were introduced into this space, which was illuminated with relatively high intensity lighting throughout. Moreover, the acting area was extended forward over the orchestra pit, so that much of the action took place between the frontal side boxes of the auditorium at stage level. The resulting added exposure of the characters obviously reinforced the direct communion with the audience. Having abstained from many of his signature devices (projections, mirrors, kinetic scenery), Svoboda saved one striking effect for the very end. In his death throes, Claudius grabbed the black drape at the rear of the stage, pulling it down to reveal a massive staircase wreathed in smoke to heighten Hamlet's last moments, the entrance of the ruler-to-be, Fortinbras, and the mournful but grand movement of the soldiers bearing Hamlet's body up the topless stairs.

Plate 47 The last major *Hamlet* (1982–88) in Prague, directed by Miroslav Macháček, with minimal scenography by Josef Svoboda. Photo: Dr. Jaromír Svoboda.

Considering the universal tradition of adaptations, even burlesques, of Shakespeare, and recalling E. F. Burian's *Hamlet III*, it is fitting to complete this survey with a glance at yet another approach to *Hamlet*, this one presented without costumes or scenery by three performers on a bare platform with a table and two chairs. It was the creation of Ivan Vyskočil (b. 1929), something of a maverick, gadfly Renaissance man who has been operating on the fringes of Prague theatre since the late 1950s. A graduate of the theatre academy, and an initiator of the small theatre movement of the 1960s, he prefers paratheatrical activities involving psychology and sociology to traditional dramatic and theatrical forms. A variant of what he calls his 'text appeals,' *Haprdans* (an acronym of *Hamlet Princ Dánský*) was a unique adaptation of *Hamlet* that was part lecture, part demonstration, and part editorial, which Vyskočil began performing in 1986. Assuming the central function of narrator-actor-critic, Vyskočil wittily reviewed some classic critical interpretations of the play before offering his own version of a *Hamlet* appropriate for our time: no longer a tragedy but, in line with today's standards, a normalized action in which much occurs but nothing of significance actually happens. First, he and his two co-performers (at present, both women) presented a very funny, sardonic, twenty-minute condensation of the main action that consisted of some dialogue and considerable narrative bridging, and during which each character was represented by a kitchen utensil: e.g., a rather worn-out egg beater for Hamlet, a wooden ladle for Claudius, a colander for Polonius, a whisk for Ophelia, and so on.

The *pièce de résistance* which followed was Vyskočil's revisionist *Hamlet*, a view behind the scenes during which we were shown moments of what really lay under Shakespeare's camouflaged version of events. Interspersed with running critical comment or quick asides implying contemporary parallels were Vyskočil's neo-*Hamlet* scenes between the main characters that revealed Hamlet with an Oedipal complex and an alter ego, and Claudius as a power-hungry, effective manager, who was manipulated by both Gertrude and Polonius, the powers behind the throne. In Vyskočil's version, Polonius was never killed; Hamlet received psychotherapy in England, returned normalized and completely adaptable (embodied as a brand new, shining egg beater), and married Ophelia. A final scene revealed that Claudius, who remained as king, was really Hamlet's father, and that Polonius was looking forward to being a grandfather.

Haprdans was far more than an ingenious charade; it represented but one more agile employment of *Hamlet* for purposes extending beyond the theatre. With wit and acumen, Vyskočil stressed often grotesque but also hilarious psychological and political tactics among the characters that made the play resonate, albeit indirectly, with the realities of Czech society before November 1989. His version has been running since 1986 and is but one of Vyskočil's presentations of a similarly idiosyncratic type.

* * *

Setting Vyskočil's eccentric adaptation aside, several concluding observations may be made with regard to this glance at Czech productions of *Hamlet*. First, the productions since World War II did not introduce approaches or tendencies that were not fundamentally present in one or more prewar productions; only the degree of sophistication in production techniques and the reference points or targets varied. On a more general level, because they were not really able to deal with the verbal beauties of image, metaphor, and sound patterns of Shakespeare in the original tongue, the Czech productions, perhaps like many foreign language productions, tended to place greater emphasis on character interplay, theme, and overt stage action. Moreover, Czech theatre and its audiences, because of their historical and cultural background, were inclined to be especially sensitive to the social and political relevance of Shakespeare's works, particularly in a play like *Hamlet*, which is as rich in political implications as it is in psychological complexities. This tendency was particularly noticeable in periods of social and national stress, such as the era from 1948 through 1989, which was dominated by an oppressive regime. As early as 1966, Zdeněk Stříbrný noted, 'the tragedies of Shakespeare . . . are . . . courageous in their attack on the knotted complexity of life and history, and we ourselves are trying to grapple with this, too.'[6]

Concurrently, however, there was a distinct tendency to place almost equal emphasis on the sheer production values of striking mise en scène, often with particular concern for the functional role of scenography. It is as if the Czech theatre artists were always conscious of a dual if not a triple responsibility: as interpreters of the dramatic values inherent in the text, as veiled commentators on forces influencing if not determining contemporary life in their land, and as artists who are ultimately as concerned with the aesthetic values of their efforts as they are with their sociopolitical relevance.

A final consideration suggests that unlike many other recent foreign productions of Shakespeare, which have often departed radically if not grotesquely from the original conventions and configurations of the plays, Czech productions have been notable for their relatively conservative, traditional (some might say 'outdatedly conventional') orientation toward the plays. Even those productions that introduced striking shifts of tone and emphasis (e.g., the Balustrade *Hamlet*) still maintained an essential fidelity to the basic structure and action of the play. They did not presume to use Shakespeare as a mere initial vehicle for their own radically subjective, often radically politicized, visions. Even Vyskočil's *Haprdans*, which was not, strictly speaking, a production of *Hamlet*, implicitly retained the crucial elements and structural flow of Shakespeare's original in order to make its own points. This is essentially different from relegating Shakespeare's text to the role of a bare armature for surrealistic accretions, such as those evident in the productions of Peter Zadek, Andrzej Wajda, or Ingmar Bergman, which suggest a reluctance to acknowledge the special artistic challenge of revitalizing this difficult, often cryptic play on its own terms, but instead used the text as an occasion for the director's own (more important?) statement.

The Czech productions, on the other hand, seemed to rise to the challenge of staging *Hamlet* while still remaining close to its form and substance. They still seemed to respect the text, in a double sense: not only what Shakespeare wrote but also the way that he wrote it. These productions drew on the Czech theatre's tradition of imaginative direction and expressive scenography to present in visual terms of line, mass, movement, color, and lighting – in concert with acting that was centered in psychological realism – a dynamic, often metaphoric embodiment of the respective concepts underlying the *Hamlet* productions noted here. In this sense, the Czech stagings of *Hamlet* may also be perceived as the aesthetic response of theatre artists to a universal masterwork of dramatic literature as much as they have been responses to external social and political pressures and their echoes within the play. The fact that they have shown relatively more fidelity to their source than have other postwar productions in Europe may owe something to the after-effects of an imposed policy of socialist realism, to a long affinity with a Stanislavskian acting tradition, and to a cultural tradition that values reason and moderation above impulse, passion, or subjectivity. To these contributing causes must be added one other: with few exceptions (1968–69 and the very late 1980s), the Czech theatre after 1948 was not in communication with the iconoclastic postmodern movements that characterized so much of western theatre since the late 1960s or so. Now that the country is nearly wide-open, it will be extremely interesting to see the extent to which this new freedom will be reflected in theatre, and in its new productions of *Hamlet*.

* * *

Postscript: subsequent to the publication of the original version of this study on Czech *Hamlet*s, I had the opportunity to see a post-liberation *Hamlet* in Prague, the work of Jan Nebeský (b. 1953), with David Prachař (b. 1959) in the leading role. First produced in a fringe theatre in 1994, it is currently performed in Prague's Komedie Theatre. Nebeský has a reputation for radically adapting texts to convey what seem to be his private Freudio-surrealistic perceptions, much in the vein of what has frequently been the practice in western Europe for many years. Operating on the premise that classic works can no longer be done as they were written, his version of *Hamlet* has Polonius and the First Gravedigger played by a single *actress*. His Hamlet draws insight and inspiration from reading Sophocles' *Electra* with Horatio, and cross-dresses in a strapless black sheath during his antic phase. In one of their scenes, Hamlet and Ophelia hang upside down by their legs while conversing. More generally, it is as if hardly a speech or even line can go by without the interpolation of a presumably metaphoric physicalization or other visual effect that is more cryptic (if not opaque) than revelatory. Lacking any stimulus or frame of reference from its sociopolitical context comparable to those of many of its predecessors (Schorm's production at the Balustrade theatre comes to mind), Nebeský's interpretation registers as an example of little more than a thoroughly liberated imagination solipsistically indulging itself.

11

VÁCLAV HAVEL

Although this book has dwelt on those primarily responsible for the creation of modern Czech theatre as an art of production and performance – its directors, actors, and designers – it would perhaps seem perverse not to include at least one playwright, particularly when he is better known to the world at large than are his production-oriented colleagues. I mean, of course, Václav Havel. As Karel Čapek was the best known Czech associated with theatre in the first half of the twentieth century, so Havel has been in the second half, although his direct, sustained engagement with theatre activity lasted less than ten years.[1]

Internationally known as a playwright by 1968, Havel became even better known in the 1970s and 1980s as a philosophical, articulate, and often imprisoned dissident who still managed to write well-regarded plays. Ironically, they were plays he did not see produced for years because his work was banned in his own country and he was not able to travel abroad. Then, in circumstances that would strain credibility if seen on a stage, he led the movement culminating in the dismantling of the Communist regime in Czechoslovakia in late 1989, and took office as its President in 1990. He has continued in that demanding position, now as President of the Czech Republic, to the present day, having survived political as well as personal crises (e.g., the breakup of Czechoslovakia into the Czech and Slovak Republics, the death of his wife, and his own serious medical problems). He has maintained his role as conscience of his nation and gained further international respect and honors for his principled and reasoned positions on issues of political morality and social ethics. But he has written no plays since 1987. It was almost as if he had a premonition of this radical turn of events in 1986 when, in the course of an extended interview, he said:

> I'm not at all certain that theatre is my very own, unique and indispensable mission. I can easily imagine that, if an irresistible opportunity were to come my way, I could just as easily devote the same amount of energy to another discipline. I certainly don't feel

184

like a professional theatre person, one inevitably drawn to theatre, whose destiny is forever linked with the theatre.[2]

Given the limitations of this one chapter, I should like to offer three perspectives on this remarkable public figure with whom I have had various brief encounters over the years: an overview of his life up to the crucial events of late 1989, a closer look at his direct, practical involvement with theatre before his fame as a playwright, and a consideration of his plays.[3]

* * *

The installation of Václav Havel as President of Czechoslovakia on January 1, 1990, culminated a scenario of real-life events that would have seemed fantastical even in his early absurdist works, as full of improbabilities as those plays were.

Less than a year earlier, in January 1989, he was imprisoned for several months for his involvement with demonstrations commemorating the twentieth anniversary of the self-immolation of the student Jan Palach in protest of the Soviet occupation. Imprisoned or detained at least a half-dozen times for a total of some five years after 1969, not allowed to live in his home, Prague, for several other years, and prevented from having any of his writings published or performed in his own country for over twenty years, he now found himself in a position of political leadership and responsibility at odds with what was known of his temperament, instincts, and ambitions. And yet, as Czechoslovakia's best known and most articulate dissident, he had indirectly been building a broad, deep foundation for the esteem of his fellow citizens.

To put Havel and his career into some perspective at the decisive juncture of 1990, it is worth reviewing some of the chief 'moments' in his life. He was born in 1936 into a wealthy Prague family of engineers and real estate entrepreneurs, who were rudely swept from their privileged position after 1948, the year the Communists took power and nationalized all private enterprises in Czechoslovakia. As a sheltered offspring of the upper bourgeoisie, attended by a governess, Havel had already felt estranged from his schoolmates during the war years. Now, in 1948, his family's resources were commandeered by the new regime, and he was repeatedly denied admission to the higher education of his choice. In the Stalinist-tainted 1950s, his applications were rejected at the Philosophic Faculty of Charles University, at the Film Academy, and at the Drama Academy. Instead, during those alternating years of repression and thaw, Havel began to write and publish literary articles, became a technician in a chemical lab, a technical school student of the economics of motor transport, and a two-year conscript in the Czech army. Reflecting on those years, Havel found them not without value: 'I saw life from the very bottom. . . . I was forced to learn about life.'[4]

In 1960, Havel began his illustrious affiliation with Prague's Theatre on the Balustrade. Havel himself perceived the Balustrade years as a fortuitous conjuncture of his own youthful creativity and a new cultural period during which non-ideological thinking and artistic expression began to flourish even within the restrictive climate of the Communist regime. The Balustrade theatre was in the forefront of the new wave, reflecting it and contributing to it, and Havel became an active co-creator, involved day in and day out in all aspects of the theatre's operation, not simply contributing his internationally esteemed plays. (On the side, having finally been accepted to the Theatre Academy as a part-time 'external' student, he also satisfactorily completed studies in dramaturgy in 1967.)

I first met Havel in the lobby of the Balustrade theatre in the early fall of 1965. I had already seen both of his early satiric hits, *The Garden Party* (Zahradní slavnost) and *The Memorandum* (Vyrozumění). I carried away from our relatively brief chat the impression of a blond, youthful, almost collegiate type, short but inclined to be chunky, who could have played guard on a 150-pound football team. Blue-eyed and heavy jawed, he had a relatively deep, throaty voice, a slight hesitancy if not stammer in his speech, and a certain shyness or reticence that coexisted with his obvious willingness to comment on or explain the work of his theatre. After another brief meeting in the summer of 1966 during a Prague theatre conference, we corresponded about plans for my SUNY Albany production of *The Memorandum*. With his friendly consent, we produced the play in December 1966, the first performance of that work in English.

Those were heady days, full of promise, when Havel, the Balustrade theatre, and Czech society at large were moving toward the Prague Spring of 1968, the reform movement that ironically could have been a model for Soviet *glasnost* and *perestroika* in the 1980s. Referring to the earlier period, Havel said,

> With each new work, the possibilities of the repressive system were weakened; the more we were able to do, the more we did, and the more we did, the more we were able to do. It was a state of accelerated metabolism between art and its time . . . always inspiring and productive for phenomena as social as theatre.[5]

The third of Havel's full-length plays, his last to be written for the Balustrade, *The Increasing Difficulty of Concentration* (Stížená možnost soustředení) opened during that spring of 1968. A few months later, in August, the tanks of the Soviet Union and its Warsaw Pact allies rolled in to abort the feared liberalization.

Our next meeting occurred in darker days, after the 1968 invasion. Havel had temporarily written himself out, and had decided to sever his connection with the Balustrade theatre even before the invasion. He had begun to play a prominent part in the activities of writers' organizations, especially in their efforts at progressive reforms during the Prague Spring. The forward thrust or inertia of that pre-invasion period had not yet been brought to a halt in the spring of 1969 when I visited him in his spacious but rather plain apartment on the Vltava embankment, with a fine view of Hradčany Castle. Havel had recently published his basic credo concerning theatre in a time of crisis:

> What should a theatre do, actually? In my opinion, it should awaken in man his authentic self; it should help him to become aware of himself in the full span of his problems, to understand the situation in which he lives, to provoke him to think about himself. . . . I at most can only help the spectator to formulate problems, which he must solve himself.[6]

A bizarre, prophetic incident during that meeting was his showing me a recently discovered listening device or 'bug' awkwardly sticking out of his ceiling near a lighting fixture. The regime had begun its surveillance of Havel, whose works even then represented a threat to what was to be euphemistically called the process of Normalization after the invasion.

Six years later, when we met again in Prague, his plays as well as his other writings had been banned, and he had been detained or charged on more than one occasion for conspiracy against the state in relation to his activities protesting against abuses to civil liberties (Plate 48). Because he was banned

Plate 48 Václav Havel in the spring of 1975. Photo: J. Burian.

from residency in Prague, he spent a year or more at his summer dwelling, some 80 miles northeast of Prague, where he worked as a laborer in a local brewery. It was an activity on which he seemed to thrive in so far as his physical condition was concerned, for he seemed genuinely fit and in reasonably good spirits when we met, somewhat surreptitiously, in the Prague apartment of a mutual friend in the spring of 1975, to compare views of the low state to which Czech theatre had fallen.

The 1970s – the era of official Normalization – were a time of tacit repression and utter conformity. Theatre productions were almost universally routine and banal, imagination and genuine creativity were immediately suspect, and a profound hypocrisy governed most of life and all the arts. Exhibitions and performances went on, but without the slightest acknowledgement of the reality dominating the country as a whole, namely that it was occupied by nearly a hundred thousand Soviet troops and that Czechoslovakia was autonomous in name only. Later in the spring of 1975, in his first major, overt challenge to the regime, a lengthy open letter to President and First Secretary Gustav Husák (widely printed in the West), Havel asserted that, 'Order has been established. At the price of a paralysis of the spirit, a deadening of the heart, and devastation of life, and went on to refer to 'the total emasculation of culture as an instrument of human and therefore social self-awareness.'[7]

By 1980, Havel was serving the early years of his lengthiest imprisonment (October 1979 to April 1983), on a charge of subversion, a charge clearly related to his central role in the organization of Charter 77, a movement initiated by Havel and several others in 1977 to challenge in a sustained, public manner the many ways in which the regime continued to violate its own pledges to the Helsinki accords on human rights. Havel was by now the best known of a growing number of intellectuals and artists who were willing to sacrifice their careers and even put their lives at risk in calling the regime to account.

Havel somehow managed to continue writing plays during most of the 1970s, when his day-to-day life was dominated by his commitment to civil liberties. Some of these later plays, though of real interest to Havel students, have not subsequently had much public success, nor – to my knowledge – have they been translated into English. *The Conspirators* (Spiklenci, 1970), *The Beggar's Opera* (Žebrácká opera, 1974) and *Mountain Hotel* (Horský hotel, 1976) all seem extensions of his work in the 1960s. It was not until he drew more directly on his personal experiences in the 'normalized' 1970s that dramatic effectiveness and sheer stage vitality returned to his work in the form of several one-acters: *Audience* (1975), *Private Viewing* (Vernisáž, 1975) and *Protest* (1979). These plays, usually in combination, were produced almost everywhere in the West but not in Czechoslovakia.

Havel's extended incarceration from 1979 to 1983 produced in him acute psychological stresses, which had an effect on his next two plays. He has referred to a near nervous breakdown and fits of depression that lasted long after his release. Earlier, he had experienced feelings of guilt relating to his feelings of responsibility for the difficulties of others who had followed his lead. Such mental and emotional states are most clearly reflected in *Largo Desolato*, his most autobiographical work, which he composed very quickly, in four days in 1984. *Temptation* (Pokoušení), his variation on the Faust motif, was written almost as quickly, in ten days, in 1985. He has said that the writing of these plays represented 'an act of self-preservation, an escape from despair. ... I wrote both plays with increasing impatience, in feverish haste, in a bit of a trance.'[8] Havel's choice of words was unexpected for an author who has been seen so consistently to be analytical, exact, and rational, but at the same time the words and images were a reminder that his favorite authors were Kafka and Dostoyevsky.

Havel's next and most recent work, *Urban Rehabilitation* (Asanace), was written in 1987 and departed in several ways from his familiar patterns without abandoning them completely. It provides a chilling recapitulation in parable form of the Czech experience of 1968–69 and its demoralizing aftermath.

My last meeting with Havel occurred in the spring of 1988. I had had no direct communication with him since 1975. By 1988 he had become a legend. He had of course aged and weathered; the frame was heavier, the face a bit thickened, but his manner was as courteous and focused as ever. (It was, incidentally, the first time I had seen him dressed in suit and tie, as distinct from his favored sweater attire.) One of the ironies of Havel's situation was not only that he maintained a West German publisher and agent, to whom he managed to send his manuscripts, but also that he was allowed to receive his royalties, although these were heavily taxed, as was all income derived from hard-currency countries. Although the conservative, hard-line regime was still intact, Gorbachev's reforms in the USSR had clearly begun to have an effect in Czechoslovakia, and Havel's prominence had given him a degree of hitherto unknown freedom of communication with others; ironically, it also kept him further away from his playwrighting. I did not have much opportunity for conversation other than to get some information relating to the availability of his latest work, *Urban Rehabilitation*, before he had to meet with his next visitor, from Italy.

The events of 1989 included increasingly overt public demonstrations on key anniversary dates throughout the year. They culminated on November 17 in the decisive overreaction of the police to the student demonstration on the fiftieth anniversary of a Czech student's killing by the Nazis. The police action led to massive confrontations of the populace with the authorities and the almost inevitable elevation of Havel to a position of not only moral and ethical but also practical leadership of the newly improvised Civic Forum, an embryonic political party. Even more impressive was the central role he played in the tough, marathon, head-to-head negotiations that dismantled the entrenched regime and installed the new personnel that gave promise of genuine parliamentary democracy and a redressing of accumulated wrongs. Some six weeks after the November 17 confrontation, Havel was voted by parliament to the Presidency of Czechoslovakia. A new career began. Havel as playwright and Havel as dissident were succeeded by Havel as statesman-politician.

That Havel did not seek, much less covet, his new position seems clear. His remarks in 1983, reported in *Le Monde*, reveal feelings that are not likely to have changed since then:

> I am not, never have been, nor do I want to become a politician, a revolutionary or a professional dissident. I am a writer. I write what I want and not what others want from me. If I get involved in anything other than my literary work, I do this simply because I see there a natural human obligation and civic duty which, when all is said and done, flows directly from my position as a writer – that is, of a man who is in the public eye and is thus duty bound to speak up on certain subjects in a louder voice than one who is not.[9]

Havel is a complex figure who evolved from an extremely clever and funny satiric critic of repressive bureaucracies run rampant to an almost elder statesman with an appreciation of realities both seen and unseen. Among his many assessments of the particular plight of contemporary humanity, one observation especially suggests that he approached his present responsibilities not with a pragmatism restricted to immediate sociopolitical circumstances, but with a philosophy that acknowledges the need for values beyond the material and secular:

> We live in the first atheist civilization in human history. People have ceased to respect any so-called higher metaphysical values. I am not talking about a personal god, necessarily. I'm referring to whatever is absolute, transcendental, suprahuman. These fundamental considerations once represented a support, a horizon for people, but now they have been lost. The paradox is that in losing them we are losing our grip on civilization, which is running out of control. As soon as humanity declared itself to be the supreme ruler of the universe – at that moment, the world began to lose its human dimension.[10]

* * *

An often neglected aspect of many playwrights' careers is their production experience, their direct involvement with the age-old but still unpredictable process that transmutes dialogue on a page to animated corporeal existence in time and place on a stage. Havel's experience encompassed both passive and active participation, and it acquainted him directly with the personalities and practices of several major Czech theatre artists, such as Jan Werich, Alfred Radok, Otomar Krejča, and Josef Svoboda.

Havel, usually thought of as springing to artistic birth in the Theatre on the Balustrade in the 1960s with the aid of Jan Grossman, actually had published theoretical and critical studies of theatre and also had several crucial theatre experiences with others both before and during his early years at the Balustrade. By the time his own first full-length play was produced there (*The Garden Party*, December 1963), he had already had years of practical theatre work, and not only in that theatre. Moreover, even *Garden Party* was not really a pure Balustrade production but a work of decidedly more mixed creative parentage.

Havel began his work at the Balustrade in the fall of 1960 on a rather informal basis, as a stagehand and general factotum, although he had already been writing and publishing articles, some relating to drama, since 1955. He had his first hands-on theatre experiences as an army conscript in 1957–59, when in addition to his regular duties he became involved – as general stagehand, actor, and writer – in two productions dealing with army life, Pavel Kohout's *September Nights* and a collaborative work by Havel and some fellow army recruits, *The Life Ahead*.

At loose ends in Prague at the beginning of the 1959–60 season after his two-year army service was finished, and still keenly interested in theatre, he got a job as scene shifter-stagehand in the ABC Theatre, headed at the time by one of the legendary figures of Czech theatre, Jan Werich, one half of the the fabled team of Voskovec and Werich (V + W) and their prewar Liberated Theatre. In the late 1950s, Werich was still reviving some of their hits, and thus keeping a notable tradition of prewar cabarets and small theatres alive. Just what the full-season experience at the ABC as a backstage worker meant to Havel is evident in his own remarks:

> I came to understand ... that theatre doesn't have to be just a factory for the production of plays ... it must be something more: a living spiritual and intellectual focus, a place for social self-awareness, a vanishing point where all the lines of force of the age meet, a seismograph of the times, a space, an area of freedom, an instrument of human liberation. ... The electrifying atmosphere of an intellectual and emotional understanding between the audience and the stage, that special magnetic field that comes into existence around the theatre – these were things I had not known until then, and they fascinated me.[11]

It was also during his season with Werich that Havel wrote an original one-act play in the vein of Ionesco, *An Evening with the Family* (not produced until February 2000), and the first version of what became, years later, *The Memorandum*.

The Balustrade had been operating since 1958 under the leadership of Ivan Vyskočil and Jiří Suchý in a freewheeling manner, producing essentially revue-type entertainments of poetry, music, and sketches with high spirits and imagination, but without a stable drama ensemble until the fall of 1960, when Havel joined the theatre.

For Havel, the 1960–61 season was marked by his becoming Vyskočil's collaborator as playwright and dramaturge. The chief product of their efforts was the jointly authored *Autostop* (March 1961), a loosely organized, very entertaining satire of contemporary fads, which solidified the Balustrade's status as the most popular of the country's growing number of avant-garde studio theatres.

In 1961–62, however, Havel curtailed his work at the Balustrade and instead worked as assistant director to Alfred Radok on two productions at the Municipal Theatres, where he had the rare opportunity to learn from a man who even then was recognized as a great theatre artist by his peers, if not by the authorities. I have included some of Havel's accounts of Radok's work with actors in Chapter 4 on Radok. Havel also felt that Radok's work was a model of what he hoped his Balustrade theatre could be:

> a form of theatre . . . that is essentially living and existential. It can emerge only from a live, intellectual tension that makes its presence felt; only by means of living, concrete, dynamic acting, supported by a genuinely open human personality, can it be achieved – otherwise it's a fiction or a mistake. . . . This is the completely personal signifi-cance brought to me by becoming familiar with Radok's work.[12]

By early summer 1962, Radok was planning on Havel literally being his dramaturge for his next production at the Municipal Theatres, Gogol's *Marriage*, but by that time Havel had become fully engaged back at the Balustrade. The direct collaboration of Radok and Havel had come to an end, although they remained close and corresponded regularly.

In the fall of 1962, Jan Grossman became the new artistic head of the Balustrade. During the next six years, until 1968, together with Havel, Grossman brought the Balustrade to international prominence, but it is the beginnings of their collaboration that concern us here. Realizing that the Balustrade ensemble needed to become more fully professional and to experience work with an established, strong director, Grossman managed to bring Otomar Krejča in for two guest directing appearances, and sceno-grapher Svoboda came with him. As indicated in Chapter 5 on Krejča, the premises, methods, and aims of Grossman–Havel and the Krejča team were not entirely compatible, but the important point is that they shared funda-mental convictions about the role of theatre as an indirect critic of its society, and about the necessity of a thoroughly prepared, demanding production process.

Krejča's production of a contemporary West German play based on Sophocles, Claus Hubalek's *Antigone's Hour*, in November 1962 became prototypical of the emphasis on productions in fully developed dramatic form (rather than witty assemblages of varied genres) that would characterize virtually all of the work at the Balustrade during the subsequent Grossman–Havel era. One year later, in December 1963, Krejča staged his second production at the Balustrade, Václav Havel's *The Garden Party*, which Havel had written earlier that year with the assistance of Grossman's informal critical feedback. It was Havel's first full-length play to be professionally staged, and the work that brought him to the attention of most of Europe. It also established the essential 'signature' of most of the Balustrade plays to follow: absurdist-slanted works with distinct though indirect social relevance.

As noted in an earlier chapter, it is clear that Krejča felt he had to abandon his more universal thematic concept of the play in favor of what he considered Havel and Grossman's more pointed, contemporarily focused satiric vision, which Krejča believed sacrificed the potential philosophic levels of the play. Brief and indirect anecdotal testimony in a Czech biography of Havel presents the other side of the coin: Grossman's and Havel's uneasiness with what seemed to them to be Krejča's 'heavy-handed' direction during rehearsals, their hesitant suggestion to him to ease up somewhat, and the resultant success of the production.[13]

The production of *Garden Party* culminated the various instances of notable, often forgotten collaborations among these theatre artists at a significant historical 'moment' in postwar Czech theatre, and at critical times in their respective careers. To speak of specific influences is difficult. What seems indisputable, however, is that Havel's observations of these major artists in action provided him with invaluable insights and perspectives on the realities and the possibilities of stage creation. Although Havel's responses to the production process seemed genuinely positive, even enthusiastic in the early years, later, after noting many more productions of his and others' plays, Havel developed a jaundiced view of the relation between the playwright's script and irresponsible treatments of it. In essence, he would have playwrights' texts produced with an absolute minimum of 'creative interpretation' by ego-driven directors who feel they must express *themselves* at the expense of playwrights. As he said during a roundtable discussion in 1987:

> It always upset me when I used to read . . . that someone was doing *Macbeth* as a play about this or that, or that someone conceived of Hamlet as such and such a character. Why not play *Hamlet* as *Hamlet*, the way it's written? Why the constant need to keep on playing something as something else, or interpreting something

according to a personal vision? If they have their own ideas, why don't they write their own play? I've had countless personal, bitter experiences with it, and I know that the best way to spoil a play is to think up some sort of personal interpretation of it.[14]

* * *

Even a partial consideration of Havel's plays might well begin by reviewing some of his own astute observations about his playwrighting, particularly those made in the course of interviews in 1986, when Havel had written all but his last play, *Urban Rehabilitation*. He began by referring to his sustained concentration on the sheer structure and composition of his plays, including construction of dialogue with consciously wrought variations, repetitions, and counterpoints. Havel summed up this aspect of his work by saying, 'My plays are consciously, deliberately, and obviously constructed, schematic, almost machinelike.' They are this way, he added, not because of some calculated decision, but due to his inclination, his 'nature.' He acknowledged that this focus on the structural and machinelike nature of the plays could be interpreted as

> an attempt to demonstrate clearly the inner mechanism of certain social and psychological processes, and the mechanical nature of how man is manipulated in the modern world, which is in turn related to the scientific and ultimately the technological origin of this manipulation.[15]

The importance Havel places on sheer pattern and structure is conveyed even more strongly in one of his letters: 'The composition and development of motifs, the way they are arranged, repeated, reinvoked, combined ... whether they are more the result of conscious effort or "merely" of a sensitivity to the matter – are what make a play a play.'[16]

Moreover, Havel sees in his 'composition and development of motifs' more than neutral, even aesthetic, patterns. The very patterns and forms and their permutations may contain within them a certain sense of mystery and even transcendence:

> I think that every genuine work of art has some mystery in it, though this may only be in its structure, in the secret of its composition, the touch, the clash, or lack of clash, among the forms, in the mystery of those structural events. Every work of art points beyond itself; it transcends itself and its author, it creates a special force field around itself that moves the human mind and the human nervous system in a way that its author could scarcely have planned ahead of time.[17]

At this point, one might think that Havel's works are primarily abstract, mysterious constructs, but he sees in them a central, recurrent motif. Concerning thematic issues, or what his plays are ultimately about, Havel puts it in a nutshell: 'the theme of human identity . . . identity in crisis . . . decaying, collapsing, dissipating, vanishing.'[18]

As to the ultimate effect of his plays on an audience, Havel is blunt; the ultimate effect is to be more ethical than aesthetic:

> My ambition is not to soothe the viewer . . . I'm trying to . . . propel him, in the most drastic possible way, into the depths of a question he should not, and cannot, avoid asking; to stick his nose into his own misery, into my misery, into our common misery, by way of reminding him that the time has come to do something about it. The only ways out . . . the only hopes that are worth anything are the ones we discover ourselves, within ourselves, and for ourselves.[19]

What is this 'common misery'? Has it to do with the erosion or absence of 'identity'? But what does *that* mean, or imply? Havel's comments in a previous interview (1975) provide at least one answer, one that echoes a generic lament of the modern era. Expanding on his idea of the crisis in human identity in a still earlier interview, he said:

> I believe that with the loss of God, man has lost a kind of absolute and universal system of coordinates, to which he could always relate anything, chiefly himself. His world and his personality gradually began to break up into separate, incoherent fragments corresponding to different, relative coordinates. And when this happened, man began to lose his identity, that is, his identity with himself. Along with . . . a sense of his own continuity, a hierarchy of experience and values, and so on.[20]

It is a classic statement of alienation, of the absurd, which puts Havel in the company of not only Kafka, Camus, Ionesco, Beckett, and Pinter, but other playwrights from Euripides to Eugene O'Neill.[21]

Offsetting such somber analyses by Havel are the plays themselves. They accentuate the comic rather than the tragic absurdity of humanity adrift without moorings or polar star. While in his non-dramatic writings he explicitly and earnestly laments the loss of God, identity, continuity, and other value systems, his plays do not focus on the angst, grief, or tragedy of the loss, but on its bizarre, painfully ludicrous behavioral, social, and institutional symptoms.[22] For example, as Havel observed, 'An inseparable aspect of the crisis of identity is a conflict between words and deeds . . . the most coherent ethical speeches [in my plays] are usually delivered by the weakest characters and the greatest villains.'[23]

Perhaps the most concentrated illustration of Havel's remarks on his playwrighting may be found in one of his least known plays, *Mountain Hotel*. It presents an extreme example of his purely formal, mechanistic construction as well as the most sustained depiction of vanished identity. Moreover, it is this play that Havel cites when commenting on the effect he wishes his plays may have on an audience. In five acts, a cross-section of lightly sketched social types are seen on a hotel veranda in relationships and speeches that start out in a superficially realistic manner, but progressively, as in a fugue, enter into countless permutations before the non-action culminates in a hectic waltz, after which the characters stand in a line, exhausted, staring at the audience as the curtain falls. It is the play that Havel discusses most often in his *Letters to Olga*, an indication of its significance to him. He refers to it as an 'attempt to be a "play about itself," in the sense that the subject of the play is . . . its mathematical construction and all its structural tricks.' The play was to have the effect of an

> unsettling poem about a world with no center, no fixed identity, no past and no future, with no coherence or order, a world where all certainties are disintegrating and where . . . there hangs a memory of a different world, where things were themselves. . . . The play's unnerving impact should derive from the contrast between the endless merry-go-round represented by the swapping of roles, situations, and banal speeches on the one hand, and living people – living humanity [the actors] – on the other.[24]

In another letter, he added,

> this play . . . aspires to be 'about nothing,' yes, but at the same time, 'about everything.' In other words, its most important elements are its rhythm, its structure, its spatiotemporal architecture. At the same time, however, these elements must not obtrude in any banal way . . . they must be concealed behind completely straightforward, realistic acting.[25]

In yet a later letter, he expressed his hope that an audience should

> feel that [the play] has something compelling to do with the most serious questions of their own existence; they should even experience it as a strange and provocative 'probe' into their own existence.[26]

In other words, it seems that, as cited above, the performance should stick the viewer's nose into 'our common misery.'

Havel's dramaturgic self-diagnoses might be restated briefly: in a world no longer unified by a vital belief in a transcendent power that gives meaning to life, humans become subject to various crises, maladies, and urges, such as an abuse and degeneration of language, a corresponding evaporation of self-identity, and a resultant tendency toward either gaining power (essentially illusory) or seeking a security by giving in to arbitrary mechanisms of thought and behavior, which are especially rampant in a technological era. And the optimal way of projecting this in a play is to manipulate the plot, action, and dialogue, as well as the presentation of time and place, so as to create stage metaphors – rather than explicit discussions – of all that is dislocated, askew, and missing in our sense of things.

* * *

The plays lend themselves to several groupings. Chronologically, they can be viewed as three groups of three full-length works and one group of three one-acters. The first trio (*Garden Party*, *Memorandum*, and *Increasing Difficulty of Concentration*) were written in the 1960s, a time of increasing liberalization culminating in the Prague Spring of 1968. In *Garden Party*, the sterile banality of a bourgeois household is paralleled by absurdly bureaucratic procedures in a nameless institution; symptomatic of both worlds are endless clichés and depersonalized characters. The temporary victor in the world of this play is he who most ingeniously manipulates mindless rhetorical patterns while deliberately minimizing if not eliminating his own remnants of identity. The identity theme is explicitly expressed by Hugo Pludek's final summary: in a world where all is relative and randomly alterable it is better not to be oneself than not to be at all.

Much the same applies in *Memorandum*, which takes place entirely within an institutional mechanism dominated by power ploys involving an artificial language (Ptydepe). Allegedly designed for greater efficiency, it is actually incomprehensible and useless as anything except a device for gaining power, and when the initial tactics fail, another synthetic language is announced. *Memorandum* is a richer play than *Garden Party* because of its more complex, cyclic pattern of plotting as well its greater range of character types and their interactions (Plate 49). It also introduces a definitive Havelian character in Gross, a self-proclaimed concerned humanist who seems programmed with an ability to rationalize diametrically opposite positions while sacrificing anyone who might threaten his security.

A similar character, Huml, is the protagonist of *The Increasing Difficulty of Concentration*, which is perhaps the most intricately structured of Havel's plays, dealing with characters and time in a cubistic, surreal manner. In fact, this play served as part of Havel's dissertation in the theatre academy. More domestic in its orientation, it takes place entirely in Huml's home. He is a philosophically inclined sociologist who is concurrently dictating a new book and carrying on – almost as if on automatic pilot – a relationship with three women (his wife, his mistress, and his secretary) in a series of scenes with repetitive dialogue, which slide forwards and backwards in time.

A highly comic plot device is introduced into this ménage à quatre in the

Plate 49 The original production of Václav Havel's *The Memorandum* (1965) in the Theatre on the Balustrade, directed by Jan Grossman. Photo: Lubomír Rohan.

form of a research group with an electronic instrument (Puzuk), capable of simulated speech and designed to measure personality but, like Ptydepe, totally useless in practice. Infantile and effeminate, needing constant coddling, it finally breaks down emotionally and has to be carried away, but not before Huml begins a fourth relationship, with the female scientist who has headed the investigative team. The play is also notable for introducing another recurrent Havelian device, a nightmarishly farcical scene in which the central characters run in and out of doors repeating variations of their own and others' previous speeches before settling down – à la Ionesco's *Bald Prima Donna* – into a cyclic repetition of the opening scene of the play (the difference being that it is now supper time rather than breakfast).

The second trio of full-length works (*Conspirators, Beggar's Opera*, and *Mountain Hotel*) and the three one-acters (*Audience, Private Viewing*, and *Protest*) are products of the 1970s, the period of Havel's increasing difficulties with the Normalization regime. The three full-length works (as suggested earlier) do not introduce any new component. Rather, they are variations on the themes and situations of the first three plays. *Conspirators*, his first play as a proscribed author, follows a cyclic form in showing behind-the-scenes machinations of four characters to gain power in a new regime that recently overthrew a dictator. Havel himself referred to the play as 'a chicken that had been left in the oven too long and completely dried out.'[27]

More successful in Havel's eyes was his next work, *Beggar's Opera*, based on John Gay's eighteenth-century prototype, not Brecht's *Threepenny Opera*. Havel's only adaptation of previously existing material, it is much less mechanically structured than Havel's previous plays, and has relatively more developed characters. Like *Memorandum* and *Conspirators*, it focuses on the tactics of a power struggle, here among three very articulate, infinitely adaptable, and totally cynical masters of the underworld, Macheath, Peachum, and Lockit. The play seems to have been one of Havel's favorites; he referred to it as 'this seldom performed play, about which I have . . . fewer reservations than any other play.'[28]

In *Mountain Hotel* (as noted above) Havel's penchant for intricately structured composition of stage action and dialogue became an end in itself. As ingenious as the play might be, however, it seems unlikely that audiences received the total message that Havel wanted to send. Rather, the play's lack of success may suggest that, beyond a certain point, any play courts failure when its structural and verbal patterns significantly overshadow its depiction of characters in an action (in the Aristotelian sense).

The three autobiographical one-act plays of the 1970s remedy that deficiency. They each present two or three fundamentally realistic, psychologically motivated characters in a recognizable, dramatic situation with a minimum of Havel's schematic, machine-like construction. The Havel figure, who has come to be referred to generically as Vaněk, is presented as a reticent, almost shy dissident. In each play he confronts one or two other figures who embody variations of those who have sold out to the forces and temptations of Normalization for reasons of power or privilege. In *Audience* it is a buffoonish but vulnerable brew master; in *Private Viewing* an upwardly mobile young couple; in *Protest* a successful, establishment writer. Vaněk is their tacit conscience; despite themselves they reveal their frustrations and guilts in the face of his quiet resistance. In terms of Havel's total output, these plays present a striking diversion in form and substance. What remains constant is Havel's masterful use of dialogue to reveal subtle shadings of motivation and manipulation in social intercourse.

The final three plays, all full-length, written following Havel's release after years of confinement, represent Havel's matured artistry. They are not as striking in their distinctive shaping and patterning, but also not as depersonalized and abstract. They retain his need for structured forms, as well as his signature theme of identity, but with more realistically developed, human oriented, emotive situations and characters.

The earliest, *Largo Desolato*, is perhaps Havel's most impressive dramatic achievement. Its delayed opening night in Prague in April 1990 in the Balustrade theatre marked the production reunion of Havel with director Grossman after twenty-five years. The script itself is a very effective blend of Havel's patterned, cyclic plotting, a restricted cast of characters in a single domestic setting, and an almost naturalistic insight into the neuroses if not paranoia of a writer reluctant to maintain the identity of a heroic dissident (almost as if the Vaněk character of the one-act plays had evolved to a further stage). It is Havel's most openly autobiographical, complex study of identity in crisis. Balancing the play's potentially Dostoyevskian given circumstances with comic, expressionistic stylization, scene after scene reveals Kopřiva's inner queasiness and angst as well as the sometimes farcical absurdity of his predicament, as if the play were a collaboration of Kafka and Feydeau. Kopřiva is threatened by imprisonment unless he renounces some of his writings, the very writings that are the basis of his identity and his supporters' adulation. Beleaguered by friends, mistresses, representatives of the people, and police agents, Kopřiva finally begs to be taken away by the police to escape his present tortured stresses, only to be informed by them that it is no longer important. In essence, they believe he is no longer the man he was, although they will still keep an eye on him.

Temptation, Havel's version of the Faust theme, has prompted a variety of interpretations, partly due to Havel's writing being less precise in its handling of the action and its issues. In several respects, Havel reverts to his earliest plays. Once again, as in *Garden Party* and *Memorandum*, a nameless 'scientific' institution becomes a setting for a contest of tactics. Again, as in *Garden Party*, the action is linear and cumulative, and pits an individual against an institution. However, while Hugo winds up as victor in *Garden Party*, Foustka is destroyed, which may reflect something of the contrast of attitudes in Czechoslovakia regarding the individual and the state in 1965 and in

1985. Foustka, tempted to explore matters of the occult as a relief from the utterly secular, scientific work of his institute, accepts the assistance of a worldweary, sardonic, self-deprecating Mephistopheles figure named Fistula. At first, Foustka's wishes are gratified (seducing Maggie, an institute secretary, at a garden party), but he is soon charged by the institute staff with trafficking in the occult. Foustka seemingly throws them off the scent, but is ultimately exposed at a second garden party – a masquerade with a Witches' Sabbath motif – when Fistula is revealed to have been an agent of the institute all along. The play ends rather abruptly and inconclusively with spectacle: the celebrants dance to pulsating music while an accidentally started fire ignites Foustka's clothing. Smoke fills stage and auditorium, and the curtain falls.

The confusing ending is characteristic of several other problematic elements of the play. Foustka, the central character, lacks adequate definition; what he stands for is not clear, beyond his superficial dabbling in the occult. As a challenger of the institute, he is almost trivial, certainly not motivated by any strength of will or desire. The institute staff is equally trivialized, distracted by erotic affairs, as is Foustka in several scenes with his mistress, scenes which seem inadequately integrated with the main action. Perhaps Havel meant to say that, in 1985, the regime was simply an all-powerful, perhaps moribund force, but opposed only by second-rate challengers with no vision and little wit. In any case, the outcome pessimistically suggests that any attempt to outsmart the institute (or regime) is doomed to failure, which seems the opposite of the conclusion in *Garden Party*, however ironic that conclusion may have been. The contrast is related to the two eras. An ironic optimism was possible in the 1960s, but not even glasnost and perestroika seemed able to shake the entrenched power of the Communist regime in the 1980s.

The main point that emerges from the scenes between Fistula and the outmatched Foustka – that temptation and sin are essentially self-generated, not the product of the devil's snare but one's own ego – finally seems trite and not clearly related to the rest of the play. It is another symptom of what seemed to be Havel's inability to integrate the elements of the play or adequately develop a central theme with the precision evident in most of his earlier work.

Urban Rehabilitation, Havel's most recent play, composed in 1987, deals with a team of state architects assigned the project of rehabilitating an ancient, decayed urban residential quarter (Plate 50). By far the most realistic of Havel's plays and the most explicit in its allusions to recent history, it presents a varied, individualized group of characters coping with their conflicting attitudes regarding the project (should the state plan or the preferences of the inhabitants receive priority?), their own personal relationships (several characters' emotional problems are presented without irony), and arbitrarily shifting mandates from vaguely defined but still omnipotent

Plate 50 Havel's last play, *Urban Rehabilitation*, had its first Prague production at the Realistic Theatre in 1990, directed by Karel Kříž, scenography by Jaroslav Malina. Photo: Vladimír Svoboda, Courtesy Realistic Theatre.

governmental levels. It is a parable depicting the fate of Czechoslovakia twenty years earlier, for the parallels between the oscillating mandates given the architectural team and the drastic swings of fortune from unexpected liberation to harsh clampdown to ambiguous Normalization occurring in Czechoslovakia in 1968–70 are inescapable. Alternatively, one might view the play as an inadvertent foreshadowing of the great liberation of 1989 that was unforeseen when Havel wrote the play. The final impression of the play is that of a questioning, unresolved critique of a people's ability and will to respond positively to freedom and responsibility, rather than settle for a champagne party celebrating a sudden lifting of restraints.

What is striking in the context of Havel's other plays is the degree to which this play, even more than *Largo Desolato* and *Temptation*, shifts away from the highly patterned, absurdist satire of the early works. Repetition of action and stage effects (six doors are in almost constant use) is still present, but the ironic and farcical effects are offset by the humanized individual and social complications of the work, as well as by the serious emotional overtones of some characters. Moreover, it is the only Havel play in which a character dies; the most mature, thoughtful character (who is not satirized at all) actually commits suicide. What prevents the play from becoming a sentimental melodrama is the elements of mechanization in some of the action as well as the satiric distance that Havel maintains at least intermittently in portraying some of the characters. Overall, however, Havel was evolving in the direction initiated in the Vaněk plays and carried forward in *Largo Desolato* and *Temptation*: less abstract patterning in plotting, characterization, and dialogue; increased depiction of psychological, emotive states; and a more direct, less camouflaged, confrontation of ethical, moral issues inherent in contemporary society. On reflection, all three plays leave a more depressing, if not grim, impression of the human condition as it approached the millennium than did Havel's earlier works. The alienation between individuals and the institutionalized machines they themselves have witlessly created seems greater than ever, and more sad because the individuals seem genuinely sensitive to their pains and losses.

Although *Urban Rehabilitation* was Havel's last published play, it is likely that he has probably made outlines or sketches of others. The question is whether he will ever have the time and freedom from distraction to complete one. He was evolving away from the type of play that made him famous. What might the next one be like? Or has Havel finished with his playwriting? Perhaps we should recall his remark in 1986: 'I certainly don't feel like a professional theatre person, one inevitably drawn to theatre, whose destiny is forever linked with the theatre.'

CODA

Václav Havel was born one year after Karel Hugo Hilar's death and two years before Karel Čapek's death. Little more than fifty years later, Havel became President of Czechoslovakia. In those astonishing decades the world experienced repeated stresses: a world war with genocidal concentration camps, atomic bombs, and the collapse of colonial empires; a cold war, missile crises, moon landings, and probings of outer space; television, computers, rock and roll, op art, pop art, happenings, deconstruction, and postmodernism; epic theatre, theatre of the absurd, theatre of cruelty, poor theatre, and performance art. The Czech specifics included liberation from the swastika followed by subjugation to the hammer and sickle, a false spring of liberation followed by invasion and cultural stultification, and a period of gradual easement before being caught up in the tide of still another, broader liberation that ultimately swept a playwright to presidency.

As different as their respective eras may have been, and as varied as their careers and their responses to their eras may have been, each of the artists presented here shared in a quest that has always defined the creative process as it transcends the attractions and threats of ideologies and political systems. The American critic Stark Young articulated what is at the heart of any artistic effort, whether by playwright, director, designer, or actor:

> Life, the energy, the living essence . . . goes on, finding itself bodies or forms to contain and express it. Behind whatever is dramatic lies the movement of the soul outward toward forms of action, the movement from perception toward patterns of desire, and the passionate struggle to and from the deed or the event in which it can manifest its nature. Behind any work of art is a living idea, a soul that moves toward its right body, a content that must achieve the form that will be inseparable from it. A perfect example in any art arrives not through standards but when the essential or informing idea has been completely expressed in terms of this art, and comes into existence entirely through the medium of it. . . . The supreme

thing in the theatre is a work of art in which we perceive that an idea
has found a theatrical body to bring it into existence.

(Stark Young, *The Theatre*, 1927)

Being a Czech theatre artist in the twentieth century undoubtedly affected
the kinds of ideas he or she conceived, but the ultimate test of the importance of these artists is how fully each one created a theatrical form to
embody the artist's controlling idea or vision on stage before an audience. I
believe that the record of these artists' work testifies to their sustained
concern with this *artistic* process – even in the hardest times – and to the
frequency of their success in achieving its goal.

NOTES

1 K. H. HILAR

1 Emil František Burian, *O nové divadlo* [The New Theatre] (Prague: Ústav pro učebné pomůcky, 1946), p. 156. Originally written in 1940.
2 This chapter is based on my article 'K. H. Hilar and the Early Twentieth Century Czech Theatre,' *Theatre Journal* 34(1) (March 1982), pp. 55–76. Hilar's family name was Bakule, but as early as 1902 he used the name Hilar and by 1911 had made the change legal. I have not been able to determine the reason for the change but find the etymology of 'Hilar' appropriate to his sense of irony: from the Greek 'hilaros' (cheerful, gay, merry) or 'hilum' (a trifle, a little thing).
3 In K. H. Hilar, *Boje proti včerejšku* [Battles against Yesterday] (Prague: Fr. Borový, 1925), p. 57.
4 Hilar, *Boje*, p. 68.
5 Hilar, *Boje*, p. 54.
6 Hilar, *Boje*, p. 71.
7 Quoted in František Černý, *Měnivá tvář divadla* [The Changing Face of Theatre] (Prague: Mladá fronta, 1978), p. 149.
8 Miroslav Rutte, 'Člověk a dílo' [The Man and his Work], in *K. H. Hilar*, ed. Miroslav Rutte (Prague: Československý dramatický svaz a družstevní práce, 1936), pp. 9 f.
9 Ladislav Pešek, *Tvá bez masky* [The Unmasked Face] (Prague: Odeon, 1977), p. 21.
10 Jiří Frejka, 'Hilar v práci' [Hilar at Work], in *K. H. Hilar*, ed. Rutte, p. 295.
11 Rutte, p. 144.
12 Hilar, *Boje*, pp. 280 f.
13 Josef Träger, 'Hilarova osobnost ve vývoji novodobého českého divadla [Hilar's Personality in the Evolution of Modern Czech Theatre], in *K. H. Hilar*, ed. Jiří Hilmera (Prague: Narodní Muzeum, 1968), p. 9.
14 Träger, *O Hilarovi* [About Hilar] (Prague: Umělecká beseda, 1945), p. 12.
15 Eduard Kohout, *Divadlo aneb snář* [Theatre, or The Dream Book] (Prague: Odeon, 1975), pp. 88 f.
16 Hilar, *Boje*, pp. 251–53.
17 Hilar, *Boje*, p. 116.
18 Romain Rolland, quoted in František Götz, 'K. H. Hilar in the National Theatre' [K. H. Hilar v Narodnim divadle], in *K. H. Hilar*, ed. Rutte, p. 234.
19 František Götz, 'K. H. Hilar in the National Theatre,' pp. 235 f.
20 Götz, p. 237.
21 K. H. Hilar, *Pražská dramaturgie* [Prague Dramaturgy] (Prague: Sfinx Janda, 1930), p. 36.

22 Rutte, p. 120.
23 Frejka, 'Předbojník K. H. Hilar' [K. H. Hilar the Pioneer], *Divadelní zápisník* [Theatre Notebook] 1 (3–4) (January 1946), p. 87.
24 Hilar, *Boje*, p. 228.
25 Hilar, *Boje*, p. 56.
26 Hilar, *Boje*, p. 69.
27 Hilar, *Boje*, p. 262.
28 Frejka, 'Hilar v práci,' p. 299.
29 Hilar, *Boje*, p. 29.
30 Hilar, *Boje*, pp. 26 f.
31 Pešek, p. 26.
32 Josef Hurt, cited in *Divadlo* 2 (March 14, 1922), p. 1.
33 Hilar, *Boje*, p. 227.
34 Hilar, *Boje*, p. 66.
35 Hilar, 'Bilance moderní režie a co dále' [An Accounting of Modern Stage Direction and What Follows], in *Nové české divadlo 1927* (Prague: Aventinum, 1928), p. 38.
36 Frejka, 'Hilar v práci,' p. 297.
37 Pešek, p. 37.
38 Götz, p. 250.
39 Hilar, 'Bilance moderní režie . . . ,' p. 37.
40 Vlastislav Hofman, 'O Hilarovi [On Hilar],' in *K. H. Hilar*, ed. Rutte, pp. 99, 279–81.
41 Hilar, *Pražská dramaturgie*, p. 20.
42 E. F. Burian, 'K. H. Hilar,' *Tvorba* [Creation] 10 (1935), p. 175.
43 Jindřich Honzl, quoted in Milan Obst, 'K. H. Hilar a česká avant-garda' [K. H. Hilar and the Czech Avant-Garde], in *K. H. Hilar*, ed. Jiří Hilmera (Prague: Narodní muzeum, 1968), pp. 22–23.
44 *K. H. Hilar*, ed. Hilmera, as in note 43.
45 Pešek, p. 37.

2 THE LIBERATED THEATRE OF VOSKOVEC AND WERICH

1 This chapter is adapted from my article, 'The Liberated Theatre of Voskovec and Werich,' *Educational Theatre Journal* 29(2) (May 1977), pp. 153–75.
2 Voskovec and Werich made four feature-length films during off-season summers: *Greasepaint and Gasoline* (Pudr a benzín, 1931); *Your Money or your Life* (Peníze anebo život, 1932); *Heave Ho* (Hej rup, 1934); and *The World Belongs to Us* (Život patří nám, 1937).
3 Josef Träger, 'Přišel Videl Zvítězil' [He Came, He Saw, He Conquered], in *Jan Werich . . . tiletý* (Prague: Orbis, 1965), p. 35.
4 Quoted in *Deset let Osvobozeného divadla* [Ten Years of the Liberated Theatre] (Prague: Fr. Borový, 1937), p. 105.
5 Vitězslav Nezval, quoted in Karel Honzík, *Ze života avantgardy* [From the Life of the Avant-Garde] (Prague: Československý spisovatel, 1963), p. 71.
6 Jiří Voskovec, *Klobouk ve křoví* [A Hat in the Shrubs] (Prague: Československý spisovatel, 1966), pp. 28 f. On p. 254 of the same book, Voskovec also noted their specific debt to Chaplin: 'As far as those poor fellows V + W are concerned, if it weren't for Chaplin they would never have even begun, much less scrambled as far as they did.' Werich observed, during one of our interviews, that at first neither he nor Voskovec believed in theatre. 'We thought the future was in films.'

7 Voskovec, Preface to *Heaven on Earth*, in *Hry Osvobozeného divadla*. [Plays of the Liberated Theatre], vol. 4 (Prague: Československý spisovatel, 1957), p. 32.
8 A speech from *A Fist in the Eye*, in *Hry Osvobozeného divadla*, vol. 3, p. 450.
9 *A Hat in the Shrubs*, p. 141.
10 *Hry Osvobozeného divadla*, vol. 1 (Prague: Československý spisovatel, 1954), p. 520.
11 *Fata Morgana a jiné hry*. [Fata Morgana and Other Plays] (Prague: Československý spisovatel, 1967), p. 149.
12 Quoted in Josef Träger, 'Od poetismu k politické satire' [From Poetism to Political Satire], in *Hry Osvobozeného divadla*, vol. 2 (Prague: Československý spisovatel, 1955), p. 414.
13 Voskovec's attitude toward Brecht's humor in relation to their own is worth noting:

> He often went in the same direction as we, but he toiled at it, like a real Bavarian – and so his attempts at laughter finally resulted only in a socially conscious grimace. We didn't belabor matters, and so [in our theatre] the same themes produced side-splitting laughter and 'socially' it was all the more effective.

These and other unattributed citations are from extensive interviews I had with Voskovec and Werich in the mid-1970s in New York and Prague, respectively.
14 *Hry Osvobozeného divadla*, vol. 1, pp. 132 f.
15 Jan Werich, 'Slovo na závěr' [A Concluding Word], in *Hry*, vol. 1, p. 526.
16 Quoted in Franta Kocourek, 'V + W a D34,' *Rozprávy Aventina*, 9(15) (May 1934), p. 129.
17 Preface to *Rag Ballad*, in *Hry*, vol. 1, p. 147. Symptomatic of the times was the participation of dancer and choreographer Lotte Goslar. Like many other German performers who fled the new order in Nazi Germany, she at first sought work in democratic Czechoslovakia. *Rag Ballad* was her sole work with V + W, although their paths crossed again later when all three were briefly exiles in France.
18 *Heads or Tails* was turned into their last film, *The World Belongs to Us*, the following year.
19 Preface to *Big Bertha*, in *Hry*, vol. 1, p. 389.
20 *Hry*, vol. 3, p. 535.
21 Václav Holzknecht, *Jaroslav Ježek a Osvobozené divadlo* [Jaroslav Ježek and the Liberated Theatre] (Prague: Státní nakladatelství krásné literatury, 1957), p. 143.

3 E. F. BURIAN

1 The material in this chapter is drawn primarily from my 'E. F. Burian: D34–D41,' *The Drama Review* 20(4) (December 1976), pp. 95–116.
2 In E. F. Burian, *O nové divadlo 1930–1940* [About the New Theatre] (Prague: Ústav pro učebné pomůcky průmyslových a odborných škol v Praze, 1946), pp. 7 f.
3 Burian, in *Kronika armádního uměleckého divadla* [Chronicle of the Army Art Theatre] (Prague: Naše vojsko, 1955), p. 40.
4 *Kronika*, pp. 29 f.
5 *O nové divadlo*, p. 48.
6 Radok and I conducted an extended interview in 1974–75 by means of tape-recorded cassettes that we exchanged by post between Sweden and Germany.
7 *O nové divadlo*, pp. 221 f.
8 *O nové divadlo*, p. 227.

9 Bořivoj Srba, *E. F. Burian a jeho program poetického divadla* [Burian and his Program for a Poetic Theatre] (Prague: Divadelní ústav, 1981), pp. 185–89.

10 Jan Grossman, '25 let Světelneho Divadla' [25 Years of Theatre Keyed on Lighting], *Acta Scaenographica* 8 (1961), p. 143.

11 Voskovec and Werich, *Fata Morgana a Jiné Hry* (Prague: Orbis, 1967), pp. 210 f.

12 *Kronika*, pp. 128 f.

13 Jan Mukařovský, *Kapitoly z české poetiky* [Chapters from Czech Poetics], vol. 1 (Prague, 1948), p. 154.

14 Lola Skrbková, 'Herec o scéně a D34' [An Actress Talks of the Stage and D34], *Acta scaenographica* 2(4) (September 1963), p. 36.

15 *O nové divadlo*, p. 52.

16 E. F. Burian, *Pražská dramaturgie* (Prague: Csl. Kompas, 1938), pp. 64–65.

17 *Pražská dramaturgie*, p. 20.

18 *Pražská dramaturgie*, p. 16.

19 *Pražská dramaturgie*, p. 86.

20 For example, Mordecai Gorelik's classic text on modern theatre, *New Theatres for Old*, cites Burian (as well as V + W) in the context of internationally significant, socially committed theatre people.

21 An account of Burian's postwar experiences may be found in my earlier study, 'The Dark Era in Modern Czech Theatre: 1948–1958,' *Theatre History Studies* 15 (1995), pp. 42–65, and also in my *Modern Czech Theatre*, Chapter 4.

4 ALFRED RADOK

1 Václav Havel, *O lidskou identitu* [About Human Identity] (Prague: Rozmluvy, 1990), p. 142. Some of the following material first appeared in Jarka Burian, 'Alfred Radok's Contribution to Postwar Czech Theatre,' *Theatre Survey* 22(2) (November 1981), pp. 213–28.

2 From Radok's unpublished, tape-recorded remarks mailed to me in 1975, in response to my questions mailed to him. Unless otherwise noted, other quotations are from the same source.

3 Radok, quoted by Antonín Liehm in 'Alfred Radok,' *International Journal of Politics* 3(1–2) (Spring–Summer 1973), p. 39.

4 Alfred Radok, 'Divadelní novověk' [Theatre's Modern Age], *Divadlo* (November 1962), p. 33.

5 Radok often expressed his fondness for the early years of the twentieth century, viewing it as a period with an unusual tolerance for individuality, if not eccentricity – an era when nineteenth-century naiveté first fully confronted the wonders of technology and was charmed by them.

6 The whole affair around the production is described in Zdeněk Hedbávný, 'Alfred Radok: Chodská nevěsta' [Alfred Radok: *The Bride from Chod*], *Divadelní revue* 3 (1992), pp. 29–38.

7 Jan Grossman, 'Síla věcnosti' [The Strength of Věcnost], *Divadlo* (October 1961), p. 586.

8 Radok, 'Divadelní novověk,' p. 31. A fuller description of Laterna Magika may be found in my article, 'Laterna Magika as a Synthesis of Theatre and Film,' *Theatre History Studies* 17 (1997), pp. 33–62.

9 Suzanne Langer, *Problems in Art* (New York: Charles Scribner's Sons, 1957), p. 86.

10 Radok, 'Zrod Laterny Magiky a její inscenační principy' [The Birth of Laterna Magika and its Principles of Staging], in *Laterna Magika* (Prague: Filmový ústav, 1968), p. 9.

11 Jan Grossman quoted in Zdeněk Hedbávný, *Alfred Radok* (Prague: Narodní Divadlo-Divadelní Ústav, 1994), p. 280. Hedbávný's book is now the definitive single source for information and commentary on Radok.

12 Radok had his own staff and a number of assistants, including the future Academy Award winner Miloš Forman and future playwright and director Ladislav Smoček.

13 See Jarka Burian, 'The Scenography of Ladislav Vychodil,' *Theatre Design and Technology* 15(2) (Summer 1979), p. 14.

14 Václav Havel, 'Několik poznámek z Švédské zápalky' [Several Notes from *The Swedish Match*], in *O divadle* (Prague: Lidové noviny, 1990), pp. 376f.

15 Havel, quoted in Hedbávný, pp. 291f.

16 Havel, in *O divadle*, p. 394.

17 Havel, 'Radok dnes' [Radok Today], in *Do různých stran* [In Various Directions] (Prague: Lidové noviny, 1989), pp. 318f. Originally written 1986.

18 Leos Suchářípa, 'Film v Jevištnim Obrazu' [Film in the Stage Picture], *Divadlo* (March 1967), p. 19.

19 It is important to note that throughout his career, Radok and his wife, Marie Radok, were the primary if not exclusive dramaturges for his productions.

20 In Zdeněk Hedbávný, 'A. Radok: Poznání je cesta k odstranění zla' [Recognition is a Way to Ward Off Evil] *Zítřek* (n.d.), p. 3 (an undated newspaper clipping). In my first and only personal meeting with Radok in 1971 in Göteborg, I was struck by one of Radok's remarks on culture. He said it was not to be judged solely by the quality of art or theatre in a given society, but also by that society's penal system and provisions for the aged. I believe that Radok's observation reflected the harsh realities he had confronted in practising his art as well as the underlying humanism of his art. The esteem in which Radok was held by the Czech theatre world became fully evident after the overthrow of Communism. Annual theatre awards bearing his name were established in the early 1990s; the chief award is given to the director of the production voted best of the year by critics and other theatre people.

5 OTOMAR KREJČA

1 This and some other documents I shall be citing are located in Krejča's folder in the National Theatre archives.

2 Krejča, quoted in Jindřich Černý, *Otomar Krejča* (Prague: Orbis, 1964), p. 10.

3 From a dated but otherwise undesignated transcript in the National Theatre archives.

4 Cited in Barbara Mazáčová, 'Dramaturg,' *Literarní noviny* (March 23, 1995), pp. 10f.

5 Krejča quoted in 'Divadla je pro politiku škoda' [Theatre is Wasted on Politics], an interview with Krejča by Ladislava Petišková in the National Theatre program for Goethe's *Faust* (1997), p. 116.

6 Krejča acted for Radok in the latter's film *Distant Journey* and in the following plays: Stehlik's *The High Summer Sky* (Vysoké letní nebe, 1955), Zinner's *The Devil's Circle* (1955), and Heyduk's *The Return* (Návrat, 1959). Krejča obviously saw all of Radok's other productions in the National Theatre in the 1950s.

7 When Radok left the National Theatre to work on the Laterna Magika in 1959, Krejča brought in another talented young director-actor, Miroslav Macháček, to help restore the directorial strength lost with Radok's departure.

8 Černý, p. 111.

9 From a letter from Krejča to me, dated August 27, 1996.

10 From an interview in an undocumented clipping from the weekly *Scéna* (1988).
11 From a letter from Krejča to me, dated August 27, 1996.
12 'I can't go on . . . Let's Go!' An interview with Krejča by Émile Copfermann on July 6, 1992, for the program for Krejča's production of Sophocles' *Antigone* (1992) in the Comédie Française, Paris.
13 Krejča, 'Co je režisérismus' [What is Režisérismus?], *Divadelní zápisník* 1 (1945–46), p. 146.
14 In 'Divadlo malé a velké' [Theatre Small and Large], *Svět a divadlo* 1 (1990), p. 50.
15 In Miroslav Petříček, '*Faust*: Riskantní svoboda vůle' [A Risky Freedom of Will], *Svět a Divadlo* 1 (1998), p. 7.
16 Jana Patočková, 'Svět Na Divadle Ukázat, A Celý' [To Show the World on the Stage, All of It], *Svět a Divadlo* 1 (1998), pp. 13 f.
17 Havel, quoted in Copfermann, see note 12.

6 GROSSMAN, MACHÁČEK, SCHORM

1 What follows is an expanded version of what I wrote about them in 1993, 'Grossman, Macháček, Schorm: The Loss of Three Major Czech Directors of the Late Twentieth Century,' *Slavic and East European Performance* 13(3) (Fall 1993), pp. 27–30.
2 News of Lébl's sudden death in December 1999, at the age of 34, struck a particularly somber note at the end of the twentieth century. Lébl was perhaps the brightest new directorial presence of Czech theatre in the 1990s. His work as well as that of others of his generation is described in my *Modern Czech Theatre*, Chapter 11.
3 For details of the vital involvement of Czech theatre in the Velvet Revolution see my *Modern Czech Theatre*, Chapter 9; also, Petr Oslzlý, 'On Stage with the Velvet Revolution,' *The Drama Review* 34(3) (Fall 1990), pp. 97–108.
4 See the chapters in this book on scenography since 1968, and on *Hamlet*s of the twentieth century.
5 Other twentieth-century directors whose work would warrant attention if space allowed include: Jan Bor, *Hana Burešová, Karel Dostal, *Lída Engelová, Miloš Hynšt, *Jan Kačer, *Zdeněk Kaloč, *Karel Kříž, *Ivo Krobot, *Miroslav Krobot, *Vladimír Morávek, *Jan Nebeský, Ota Ornest, Karel Palouš, Luboš Pistorius, *Jan Antonín Pitínský, *Jaromír Pleskot, Aleš Podhorský, *Ivan Rajmont, Peter Scherhaufer, *Jan Schmid, Jan Škoda, *Ladislav Smoček, Oldřich Stibor, Viktor Šulc, *Eva Tálská. * = still active.

7 JOSEF SVOBODA

1 Material in this chapter has been drawn from the following: J. Burian, *The Scenography of Josef Svoboda* (Middletown, CT: Wesleyan University Press, 1971); Josef Svoboda, *The Secret of Theatrical Space* (New York: Applause Books, 1993); J. Burian, 'Josef Svoboda,' *Theatre Design and Technology* 30(5) (Fall 1994), pp. 37–45; and J. Burian, 'Laterna Magika as a Synthesis of Theatre and Film,' *Theatre History Studies* 17 (1997), pp. 33–62. Undocumented quotations are from my personal interviews with Svoboda.
2 Craig, 'The Artist of the Theatre,' in *Directors on Directing*, eds T. Cole and H. K. Chinoy (New York: Bobbs-Merrill, 1963), pp. 161 ff.
3 Erwin Piscator, 'The Theatre Can Belong to our Century,' in *The Theory of the Modern Stage*, ed. Eric Bentley (Baltimore, MD: Penguin, 1968), p. 473.
4 Svoboda, *The Secret of Theatrical Space*, p. 121.
5 Burian, *The Scenography of Josef Svoboda*, p. 143.

6 Svoboda employed the same silhouette principle for the cyclorama in two later productions in Prague's Vinohrady Theatre: Friedrich Dürrenmatt's *The Visit* (1996) and John Ford's *'Tis Pity She's a Whore* (1998).

7 *Récit d'une Liberté* (1991), Cedre Productions, directed by Marco Motta. Svoboda's pursuit of still further challenges in stage space and form was evident in his latest Laterna production, in the fall of 1999. The production, *The Trap* (Past), involves the problematic social and psychological aspects of virtual reality in our culture.

8 TWENTIETH-CENTURY CZECH SCENOGRAPHERS IN THE INTERWAR ERA

1 The material in this chapter draws on my two-part article, 'Scenography in Czech Theatre, 1920–1939,' *Theatre Design and Technology* 41 (Summer 1975), pp. 14–23, 35; 42 (Fall 1975), pp. 23–32.

2 František Tröster, 'Měřeno dneškem' [Measured by Today], *Divadlo* (1964), p. 62.

3 Kysela was a graduate of the Academy of Design Arts and subsequently a Professor of Fine and Applied Arts from 1913 until his death. He designed over forty productions, mostly opera for the National Theatre. His work evolved toward cubism and a certain monumentality but was not as innovative or striking as that of his contemporaries.

4 Vlastislav Hofman, from an article originally appearing in *Jeviště* 1(1) (1920), reprinted in *Vlastislav Hofman*, ed. F. Musil (Prague: Osvěta, 1951), p. 19.

5 Hofman, 'O konstruktivní realismus' [About Constructive Realism], *Nové české divadlo* (Prague: Aventinum, 1927), p. 49.

6 Hofman, 'O konstruktivní realismus,' p. 49.

7 In relation to this production it is hardly possible not to recall Gordon Craig's prototypal staging of *Hamlet* (1911) in Moscow. An equally striking analogue is Svoboda's *Hamlet* (1959) in Prague. Of course each production approach had distinctive features, and screens or panels on stage are hardly unique. Nevertheless, the echoes are fascinating.

8 Hofman, in *Vlastislav Hofman*, p. 25.

9 Antonín Heythum, quoted in Jaroslav Svehla, 'Heythumova Výprava Lenormandovy hry, At' žije divadlo!' [Heythum's Setting for Lenormand's Play, *Long Live the Theatre!*], *Interscena* 71 (3–1) (May 1971), p. 55.

10 Heythum, 'O jevištní konstrukci' [About Stage Construction], *Pásmo* 1(5–6) (1928), p. 2.

11 Tröster, 'Poznámky o scéně' [Remarks about the Setting], *Život* 15(3–4) (1937), p. 84.

12 Jiří Frejka, 'O novém jevištnim realismu' [About New Stage Realism], *Život* 15(3–4) (1937), p. 84.

13 Tröster, 'Měřeno dneškem,' p. 68.

14 Tröster, 'Měřeno dneškem,' p. 67.

15 Tröster, 'Měřeno dneškem,' p. 64.

16 Tröster, 'Měřeno dneškem,' p. 64.

17 Tröster, 'Měřeno dneškem,' p. 65.

18 Tröster, 'Poznámky o scéně,' p. 87.

19 Miroslav Kouřil, 'Dramatický prostor' [Dramatic Space], *Život* 15(3–4) (1937), p. 88. A detailed account of Burian's and Kouřil's work with projections can be found in František Černý, 'Lighting that Creates the Scene and Lighting as an Actor,' *Innovations in Stage and Theatre Design*, ed. Francis Hodge (New York:

American Society for Theatre Research and Theatre Library Association, 1972), pp. 126–45.

20 Jan Kučera, 'Film na českem jevišti' [Film on the Czech Stage], *Život* 15(3–4) (1937), p. 101.

21 Kouřil, 'Procitnutí jara' [The Awakening of Spring], *Acta Scaenografica* 6(8) (1968), p. 164.

22 A basic source of information and comment on Czech designers is found in Věra Ptáčková, *Česká scenografie XX. století* [Czech Scenography of the Twentieth Century] (Prague: Odeon, 1982). Other designers of note in the first half of the century include the following: Josef Čapek, Jan Sládek, Josef Wenig, František Zelenka, Jan Zrzavý.

9 CZECH SCENOGRAPHY SINCE 1968

1 The material in this chapter is drawn in part from the following articles I published in 1989 and 1996: 'Designing for the 90s,' *Cue International* 62 (November– December 1989), pp. 32–37; 'Two Women and their Contribution to Contemporary Czech Scenography,' *Theatre Design and Technology* 32(5) (Fall 1996), pp. 19–29.

2 This quote and all other unattributed quotes are from my tape-recorded interviews with the artists from 1988 to 1994.

3 The full name is Theatre Goose on a String. The background of the theatre, including its odd name, may be found in my article, 'Czech Theatre, 1988: Neo-Glasnost and Perestroika,' *Theatre Journal* 41(3) (October 1989), pp. 381–95. See also my *Modern Czech Theatre*, Chapter 8.

4 Roszkopfová letter to J. Burian, July 25, 1994.

5 Roszkopfová letter.

6 Roszkopfová letter.

7 Quoted in the official program for the National Theatre production (Prague: National Theatre, 1993), p. 19.

8 From a text by Helena Albertová for a touring exhibit of Czech scenography, 1994.

9 Both quotes are from Roszkopfová's letter.

10 Zbořilová, *Vztah režie a scénografie v inscenacich Evy Tálské v divadle Husa na provázku* [The Relation of Direction and Scenography in the Productions of Eva Tálská in the Goose on a String Theatre], unpublished dissertation (DAMU 1993), p. 12.

11 Roszkopfová letter.

12 Not that Svoboda has never been playful. For example, consider *Insect Comedy* (1946); *Wastrels in Paradise* (1946); *Eleventh Commandment* (1950). See J. Burian, *The Scenography of Josef Svoboda* (Middletown, CT: Wesleyan University Press, 1971).

13 My sources for the *Long Day's Journey into Night* productions were, in addition to interview comments from Zbořilová and her rendering prior to the productions, two reviews that covered both productions: Karola Štepanová, 'O'Neill on Moravian Stages,' *Lidové Noviny* [People's Newspaper] (May 17, 1995), n.p.; Barbara Mazáčová, 'A Drama – and What To Do With It?' *Divadelní Noviny* [Theatre Newspaper] (May 2, 1995), pp. 1, 4.

14 Other stage designers who did interesting work in the second half of the twentieth century include the following: Květoslav Bubeník, Libor Fára, Karel Glogr, Luboš Hrůza, Zbyněk Kolář, Miroslav Melena, Vladimír Nývlt, Albert Pražák, Tomaš Rusín, Otakar Schindler, Oldřich Šimáček, Jan Vančura, Ivo Žídek.

10 CZECH *HAMLETS* OF THE TWENTIETH CENTURY

1 This chapter is drawn from my '*Hamlet* in Postwar Czech theatre,' in *Foreign Shakespeare: Contemporary Performance*, ed. D. Kennedy (Cambridge: Cambridge University Press, 1993), pp. 195–210.

2 Jan Mukařovský, 'Shakespeare and Czech Theatrical Criticism,' in *Charles University on Shakespeare*, ed. Zdeněk Stříbrný (Prague: Universita Karlova, 1966), pp. 14, 21.

3 František Černý, *Měnivá tvář divadla* [The Changing Face of Theatre] (Prague: Mladá Fronta, 1978), p. 155.

4 Černý, p. 254.

5 Radovan Lukavský, *Hamlet: pracovní deník* [A Working Diary] (Prague: Divadelní Ústav, 1965), p. 105.

6 Zdeněk Stříbrný, 'Shakespeare Today,' in *Charles University on Shakespeare*, ed. Stříbrný, p. 35.

11 VÁCLAV HAVEL

1 I am including Havel rather than Čapek in this study not only because a considerable body of criticism in English already exists for Čapek's plays, but also because I have written about Čapek in my more inclusive *Modern Czech Theatre*. Havel's plays also seem to me to be closer to the sensibility of today's readers and audiences. Nevertheless, I should like to note a few points of interest that relate these two Czech playwrights of different eras, different life experiences, and different dramatic styles.

They are virtually the only two Czech playwrights to have gained worldwide acclaim, yet playwrighting is only one of the forms of literature they practiced: Čapek's novels and Havel's critical prose are often regarded as highly as their plays. Moreover, their relationship with theatre was not limited to their playwrighting: both functioned as dramaturges, and Čapek also directed, while Havel worked as a stagehand and as an assistant director. Furthermore, after departing from received patterns of realistic dramaturgy in their early plays, both authors evolved toward a greater degree of realism and psychological characterization in their later work.

Both were politically sophisticated and engaged, Čapek as part of two presidents' informal inner circle, Havel as a dissident and then unexpected president himself. Most interesting of all, both were preoccupied with the impact and effects of technocracy and social engineering on humanity, and both worked such issues into some of their best known plays. Their many differences are probably inseparable from their respective eras. Čapek's 1920s and 1930s still bore remnants of nineteenth-century romanticism and idealism, supplemented by vigorous patriotism. Such values and attitudes are almost wholly absent in Havel's post–1950 decades, in which scepticism, irony, and the absurd are pervasive and increasingly hard to resist.

Finally, by their varied, serious engagements with such issues, however different their concepts, styles, and techniques, Čapek and Havel earned the distinction of being the two leading Czech playwrights whose works are both philosophic and theatrically effective.

2 Václav Havel, *Disturbing the Peace*, ed. Karel Hvížďala, transl. and introd. Paul Wilson (New York: Alfred A. Knopf, 1990; London: Faber & Faber, 1990), p. 202.

3 Some of the material in this chapter draws on my previously published studies: 'Václav Havel: From Playwright to President,' *Soviet and East European Perform-*

ance 9 (2–3) (Fall 1989), pp. 12–19; 'Havel and the Velvet Revolution,' *American Theatre* 6(12) (March 1990), pp. 38–40; 'Václav Havel's Notable Encounters in his Early Theatrical Career,' *Slavic and East European Performance* 16(2) (Spring 1996), pp. 13–29.

4   Antonín J. Liehm, *The Politics of Culture* (New York: Grove Press, 1968), p. 379.
5   Havel, 'Second Wind,' *Open Letters*, ed. Paul Wilson (London: Faber & Faber, 1991), p. 6.
6   Havel, 'Ještě jednou obrození?' [Yet Another [National] Revival?], *Divadlo* (January 1969), p. 32.
7   Havel, 'Dear Dr. Husák,' *Open Letters*, pp. 62, 64.
8   Havel, *Disturbing the Peace*, pp. 63 f.
9   Havel, 'I Take the Side of Truth,' *Open Letters*, p. 247.
10 Havel, untitled clipping from *Times Literary Supplement* (London: January 23, 1989), n.p.
11 Havel, *Disturbing the Peace*, p. 40.
12 Havel, 'Několik poznámek ze Švédské zápalky' [Some Notes from *The Swedish Match*], *O divadle 1*, ed. Karel Kraus (Prague: Lidové noviny, 1990), p. 394.
13 Eda Kriseová, *Václav Havel*, transl. Caleb Crain (New York: St. Martin's Press, 1993), pp. 52 f.
14 In 'Dramatists on Drama I' [Dramatici o dramatu I], *O divadle 1*, p. 58.
15 Havel, *Disturbing the Peace*, p. 193.
16 Havel, *Letters to Olga*, transl. Paul Wilson (New York: Alfred A. Knopf, 1988; London: Faber & Faber, 1988), p. 286.
17 Havel, *Disturbing the Peace*, p. 198.
18 Havel, *Disturbing the Peace*, pp. 195 f.
19 Havel, *Disturbing the Peace*, p. 199.
20 Havel, 'It Always Makes Sense to Tell the Truth,' in *Open Letters*, pp. 94 f.
21 For example, some fifty years before Havel's statement, O'Neill wrote of 'the death of the old God and the failure of science and materialism to give any satisfying new one for the surviving primitive religious instinct to find a meaning for life in, and to comfort its fears of death with.' Quoted in the introduction to *Nine Plays by Eugene O'Neill* (New York: Random House Modern Library, n.d.), p. xvii.
22 Although Havel's diagnosis of the absurd does not explicitly identify any real-life, i.e., worldly, cause or model of this psychic malady, he had one available in the Marxist-Leninist Communist society within which he came to maturity. Not only in its denial of God in favor of the state, but in the existential absurdities of that society, above all in its bureaucratic manifestations, from the Central Committee of the Czechoslovak Communist Party to the most petty aparatchik seeking his bit of security. In other words, Havel's sense of the absurd did not come to him from his reading about it or by an epiphany, but most forcefully from his intelligent observations of day-to-day life in Prague after February 1948.
23 Havel, *Letters to Olga*, p. 305.
24 Havel, *Letters to Olga*, p. 85.
25 Havel, *Letters to Olga*, p. 108.
26 Havel, *Letters to Olga*, pp. 171 f.
27 Havel, *Disturbing the Peace*, p. 120.
28 Havel, *Letters to Olga*, pp. 303 f.

SELECTED BIBLIOGRAPHY

The following publications provide useful additional information on the key figures discussed in this book.

Burian, Jarka, *The Scenography of Josef Svoboda* (Middletown, CT: Wesleyan University Press, 1971).

—— *Svoboda, Wagner* (Middletown, CT: Wesleyan University Press, 1983).

—— *Modern Czech Theatre: Reflector and Conscience of a Nation* (Iowa City, IA: University of Iowa Press, 2000).

Černý, František, *Měnivá tvář divadla* [The Changing Face of Theatre] (Prague: Mladá fronta, 1978). Essays on Czech actors and directors.

Černý, Jindřich, *Otomar Krejča* (Prague: Orbis, 1964).

Dejiny českého divadla [History of the Czech Theatre], ed. František Černý (Prague: Československá akademie věd, 1969–88), Vol. III, 1848–1918; Vol. IV, 1918–45. Thoroughly documented historical essays, very well illustrated; Marxist perspective.

Goetz-Stankiewicz, Marketa, *The Silenced Theatre: Czech Playwrights without a Stage* (Toronto: University of Toronto Press, 1979).

Havel, Václav, *Letters to Olga* (New York: Knopf, 1988; London: Faber & Faber, 1988).

—— *Disturbing the Peace* (New York: Knopf, 1990; London: Faber & Faber, 1990).

Hedbávný, Zdeněk, *Alfred Radok* (Prague: Národní divadlo, Divadelní ústav, 1994). An excellent biographical and critical study.

Hilar, K. H., *Boje proti včerejšku* [Battles against the Past] (Prague: Fr. Borový, 1925). Hilar's perceptive, subjective view of his work and that of others during his era.

Holzknecht, Václav, *Jaroslav Ježek a Osvobozené divadlo* [J. J. and the Liberated Theatre] (Prague: Statni nákladatelství krásné literatury, 1957). Focus on V + W's theatre.

K. H. Hilar, ed. Miroslav Rutte (Prague: Československý dramatický svaz a družstevní práce, 1936).

Kronika armádního uměleckého divadla [Chronicle of the Army Art Theatre] (Prague: Naše vojsko, 1955). Solid documentation on E. F. Burian's theatre from its pre-origin to his death.

Liehm, Antonín, 'Alfred Radok,' *International Journal of Politics* 3(1–2) (Spring–Summer 1973), pp. 23–39.

Nové české divadlo 1918–1926 [The New Czech Theatre], eds Miroslav Rutte and Josef Kodiček (Prague: Aventinum, 1927). Informative, well-illustrated series of four irregularly issued volumes devoted to contemporary Czech theatre between 1918 and 1932. The series ended with *Nové české divadlo 1930–32*, eds Miroslav Rutte and František Götz (Prague: Aventinum, 1932).

Ptáčková, Věra, *Česká scenografie XX. století* [Czech Scenography of the Twentieth Century] (Prague: Odeon, 1982). Definitive study of modern Czech stage design, exceptionally well illustrated.

Srba, Bořivoj, *E. F. Burian a jeho program poetického divadla* [E. F. B. and his Program for a Poetic Theatre] (Prague: Divadelní ústav, 1981). A collection of Burian's writings and an extended essay by Srba.

Svoboda, Josef, *The Secret of Theatrical Space* (New York: Applause Theatre Books, 1993). The master scenographer's career autobiography.

Trensky, Paul I., *Czech Drama since World War II* (White Plains, NY: M. E. Sharpe, 1978).

—— 'Václav Havel's "Temptation Cycle",' *Czechoslovak and Central European Journal* 10(2) (Winter 1991), pp. 84–95.

Unruh, Delbert, 'Action Design,' *Theatre Design and Technology* (*TD&T*) 23(1) (Spring 1987), pp. 6–13; 'Practical Problems of Space,' *TD&T* 26(2) (Summer 1990), pp. 33–40; 'Philosophical Problems of Space,' *TD&T* 26(4) (Fall 1990), pp. 25–32; 'The Problem of Costumes,' *TD&T* 27(1) (Winter 1991), pp. 27–34; 'The Problem of Acting Style,' *TD&T* 27(2) (Spring 1991), pp. 29–34; 'The Problem of Production Style,' *TD&T* 27(3) (Summer 1991), pp. 21–29. Observations chiefly on Czech stage designers from 1970s onward.

INDEX

Page numbers in *italics* refer to illustrations in the text.

219